a guide to the
DRAKENSBERG

August Sycholt

I dedicate this book to the men and women who have worked so hard – and continue to work – to keep the Drakensberg as near as possible to its pristine condition when the San first painted their images in smoke-filled shelters. This book is dedicated to those early occupants whose spirit infuses modern-day efforts to protect nature, and to those who have so painstakingly collected the information that comprises our knowledge of 'the Berg' today. Their ultimate reward is there for all to see: the Drakensberg in its glory.

Struik Publishers

(a division of New Holland Publishing (South Africa) (Pty) Ltd)

Cornelis Struik House, 80 McKenzie Street, Cape Town, 8001

New Holland Publishing is a member of the Johnnic Publishing Group.

www.struik.co.za

Log on to our photographic website **www.imagesofafrica.co.za**

for an African experience.

First published in 2002

1 3 5 7 9 10 8 6 4 2

Publishing manager: Pippa Parker

Managing editor: Helen de Villiers

Editor: Roxanne Reid

Design director: Janice Evans

Designer: Lyndall du Toit

Cover design: Robin Cox

Cartographer: James Whitelaw

Project manager: Jeanne Hromnik

Reproduction by Hirt and Carter Cape (Pty) Ltd

Printed and bound by APP Printers, Singapore

ISBN 1 86872 593 6

contents

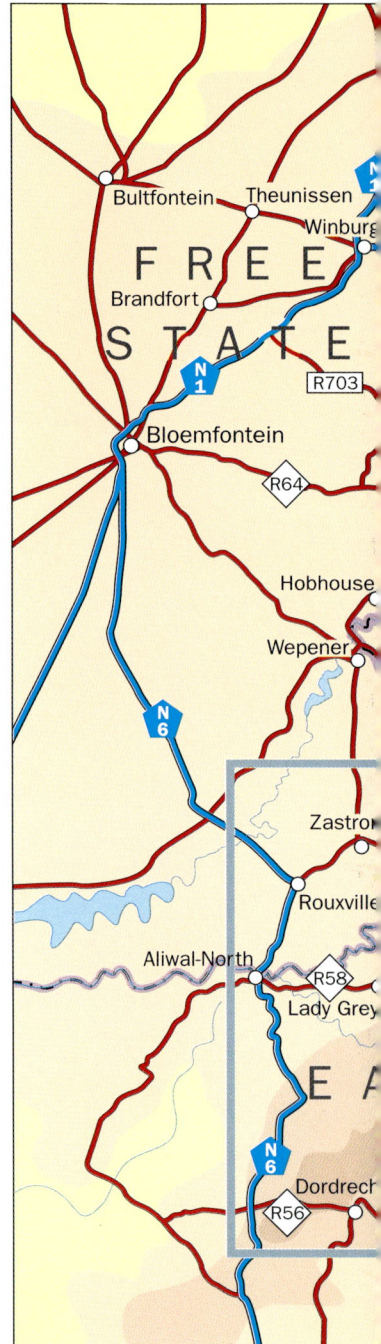

The region covered in this book belongs to the eastern part of the 'Great Escarpment'. It stretches from the north-eastern Free State (including the Golden Gate Highlands National Park) to the KwaZulu-Natal uKhahlamba Drakensberg Park – and south-west, past Lesotho's Sehlaba-Thebe National Park, to the northern part of the Eastern Cape.

Its borders are formed by the Drakensberg in the north-eastern Free State, the Lesotho Highlands, Maloti Mountains, and the so-called Cape Drakensberg in the north-eastern corner of the Eastern Cape.

The extensive (2 400 km^2) uKhahlamba Drakensberg Park extends across northern, central and southern divisions of the KwaZulu-Natal Drakensberg (the 'Berg'). Accessible via major highways and by way of many towns and villages with a rich and interesting past, it lies at the heart of the Drakensberg region, and, in November 2000, was declared a cultural and natural World Heritage Site.

KEY TO SYMBOLS ON ALL MAPS

National parks & reserves	
3165m	Peak in metres
	Mountain pass
○ ■	Towns & cities
▲	Place of interest
	National & provincial boundaries
	Walking trail
	River
	Cave
	Waterfall
	Marsh

FACILITIES

🏠	Hutted camp
	Caravan site
⚊	Camping site
i	Petrol
✈	Airfield
◀	Border post
🅗	Hotel
	Fishing

	above 2 400 m
	2 100–2 400 m
	1 800–2 100 m
	1 500–1 800 m
	1 200–1 500 m
	900–1 200 m
	600–900 m

ROADS

	Freeway
Tarred Untarred	Principal road
Tarred Untarred	Secondary road
N5 R56 R617	Route numbers

FREE STATE

Bultfontein   Theunissen

Winburg

Brandfort

R703

Bloemfontein

R64

Hobhouse

Wepener

Zastron

Rouxville

Aliwal-North

R58

Lady Grey

E A

Dordrecht

R56

4

Lindley

Reitz

Ventersburg

N3

Bethlehem

Harrismith

N11

Senekal

N5

Qwa Qwa
National Park

Sterkfontein Dam
Nature Reserve

Golden Gate
National Park

Ladysmith

Marquard

Phuthaditjhaba

Bergville

Royal Natal-
National Park

Ficksburg

Winterton

R74

Clocolan

Hlotse

Cathedral Peak
Reserve

Estcourt

MALOTI MOUNTAINS

Monk's Cowl
Reserve

R622

Ladybrand

Injisuthi Reserve

Giant's Castle
Reserve

Mooi River

Katse
Dam

Highmoor
Reserve

Kamberg
Reserve

Maseru

Lotheni
Reserve

Mkhomazi
Nature Reserve

N3

Howick

Vergelegen
Reserve

DRAKENSBERG

Sani Pass

Cobham
Reserve

Pietermaritzburg

Garden Castle
Nature Reserve

Underberg

R56

Mafeteng

Bushman's Nek

Coleford
Nature Reserve

Sehlaba-Thebe
National Park

K W A Z U L U

Qacha's Nek

R617

Ixopo

L E S O T H O

- N A T A L

Mount
Moorosi

Matatiele

Cedarville

Franklin

R56

Quithing
(Moyeni)

R56

Mount Currie
Nature Reserve

Sterkspruit

Kokstad

N2

Port
Shepstone

Rhodes

Mount
Fletcher

N

R58

R56

W

E

S T E R N

S

C A P E

Barkly East

Maclear

R61

Elliot

N2

0

100 km

INDIAN

OCEAN

5

introduction

the great escarpment

Early morning on the escarpment above the Amphitheatre, northern KwaZulu-Natal Berg.

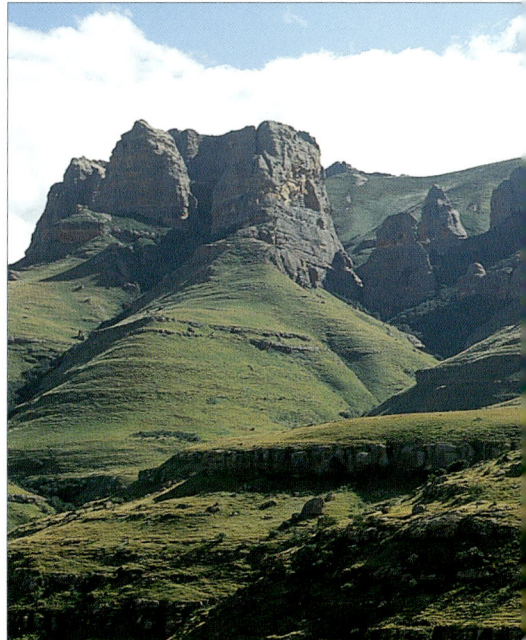

The imposing peaks of the KwaZulu-Natal Midlands gleam like the upright blades of assegais over a blanket of cloud in the light of the morning sun. In Zulu they are called 'uKhahlamba', meaning 'barrier of spears'. They are the highest mountains of the 'Great Escarpment' in southern Africa, rising to 3 000 m or more in places. The highest peak in the region is Thabana Ntlenyana in neighbouring Lesotho. At 3 482 m, it is four metres higher than the Matterhorn in the Swiss Alps.

The eastern part of southern Africa's 'Great Escarpment', which extends all the way into Zimbabwe, Namibia and Angola, is known to most people as the Drakensberg – so named by early Dutch settlers for the resemblance to the ridges of a dragon's back. The steep ridges of its dragon-like back are formed by the headwater erosion of rivers that separate southern Africa's highveld plateau from the coastal lowlands.

The escarpment lies parallel to the south-eastern coast of South Africa all the way from the Northern Province to the Eastern Cape. Near Giant's Castle, the name of a rock formation in the central KwaZulu-Natal Berg, the escarpment swings to the south-west and enters the Eastern Cape, where it is transformed into a chain of mountains: Stormberg, Bamboes, Suurberg, Nieuveld and Komsberg. Among them is an insignificant peak called Drakensberg, but it is doubtful whether the name of the range originates here.

Further to the west lie the Cape mountain ranges, which are much older than the KwaZulu-Natal Berg. From the Western Cape onwards, the escarpment runs almost due north through the Roggeveld Mountains, via Hantamsberg/Calvinia and Namaqualand to Maltahöhe in Namibia and even further north.

Identified as a hotspot of biodiversity, the KwaZulu-Natal Drakensberg (more specifically the uKhahlamba Drakensberg Park) was declared a World Heritage Site in November 2000, providing protection for its pristine or near-pristine landscapes, its exceptional natural beauty and the priceless San rock art of its sandstone shelters. It is nevertheless under threat from forestation, overgrazing, plant invasion, indigenous plant harvesting, agriculture and tourism development.

Peace Park

Discussions and negotiations between Lesotho and South Africa are underway in an effort to establish a trans-border conservation area or 'Peace Park'. The aim is to merge a part of the Lesotho plateau, stretching along the escarpment, with South Africa's uKhahlamba Drakensberg Park. This would almost double the size of the present Drakensberg Park and bring a greater part of its alpine environment under the conservation blanket.

Giant's Castle (on the left), not the famous central Berg basalt giant but a bizarre rock formation at Barkly Pass.

Layers of rock

Southern Africa is shaped like a shield, most of it consisting of a vast plateau edged by an escarpment that separates the highlands from the narrow coastal strip. The most majestic part of the escarpment is the section comprising the KwaZulu-Natal Drakensberg and Lesotho, where sandstone and shale are overlaid with basaltic lava.

The KwaZulu-Natal Drakensberg – or the 'Berg' as it is generally known – consists of a huge, uniform layer of lava that is continuously being eroded to expose the underlying sand and shale strata of the Karoo system. The minor mountains in front of the Main Berg, consisting primarily of sandstone and shale, are known in KwaZulu-Natal as the 'Little Berg'.

It is not easy to determine the geological origins of the Drakensberg, the early South African geological record being somewhat fragmentary. Geologists assume, however, that lava poured out over large sections of the sub-continent during the Precambrian era, forming the primitive, 8–40 km deep, crust of the earth. During the earth's middle life (the Mesozoic era, about 200–180 million years ago), wind and water deposited thick layers of shale, mudstone and sandstone, now known as the Karoo Supergroup, over the ancient primary rock.

Gondwana, the ancient landmass

Lichen-covered Clarens sandstone in the foothills near Maclear (north-eastern Cape).

Locked into lava

Many agates, including moss agates, pale lilac amethysts, chalcedony and jasper zeolites, are locked in the Drakensberg basalt, but are rarely found in great quantities. A heavily mineralized layer of lava near Barkly East, about 40 by 15 km in extent, is an exception. Basalts containing crystallized minerals (amygdaloidal basalts) also occur near Rhodes, Carlisle's Hoek and Naude's Nek. Sought-after collectors' items, they were created when hot gasses and mineralized solutions in the lava-flow were trapped as bubbles once the lava began to cool and solidify on the earth's surface. The bubbles (called amygdales or, when bigger, geodes) are often associated with dolerite dykes and sills, which intrude into the lavas.

once covering the southern hemisphere from the south pole to the equator, began to break up approximately 200 million years ago and enormous extrusions of red-hot magma, known as Drakensberg lava, poured out through fissures and cracks onto the earth's surface. In the Drakensberg region it capped the sedimentary rock formations with layers of solid basalt up to 1 400 m thick. The outflows lasted for about 50 million years, from the early Jurassic period to the Cretaceous period.

It took millions of years before the desolate lava landscapes became hospitable. Debris from the rapidly weathering basalt was swept away by wind and water, to be deposited elsewhere on the land or into the Indian Ocean. The process was aided by the seaward tilt of the landmass. Rivers formed and merged. The high plateau receded – as it still does at a rate of about a metre every 350 years – leaving behind fertile coastal plains and midlands furrowed by streams and rivers. Erosion is still at work, slowly reshaping the gigantic escarpment. Torrential floods still hurl debris and millions of tons of topsoil towards the oceans.

Continuing erosion has exposed some of the underlying ancient sediments. Upper Beaufort layers are the oldest rock outcrops, followed by the Stormberg group, which includes the gritty-white sandstone known as the Molteno formation. This, in turn, is overlaid by the Red Beds known for their fossilized wood and dinosaur remains. On top of the Red Beds or Elliot formation, lies fine-grained Clarens sandstone seen in the cliffs and overhangs of the 'Little Berg'. It is capped, finally, with basalt.

The weather

South Africa lies within the subtropical belt of high pressure. This accounts for its dry climate and abundance of sunshine. Altitude and surrounding oceans exert a moderating influence on the general climate, but there are strong regional variations. For instance, the rainfall of the Drakensberg varies greatly from South Africa's annual average of 464 mm. It rises from about 800 mm in the area of the Little Berg to over 2 000 mm in the vicinity of the escarpment. Heavy frosts occur during the winter months between April and September, when snow is also most likely to fall, although snow is possible at any time of the year on the KwaZulu-Natal escarpment and in Lesotho.

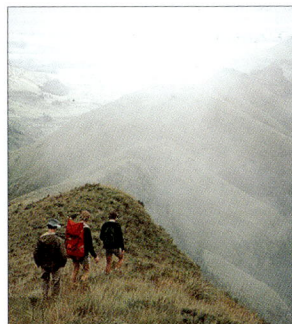

Mist over sandstone and shale mountains of the Little Berg.

Blesbok (*Damaliscus dorcas phillipsi*) find walking heavy-going in snow in Himeville Nature Reserve.

Cradle of rivers

The Berg is known as a cradle of rivers and initiator of rain, snow and sunshine, which give life to a parched land. South Africa's major rivers rise in the region.

The Lesotho highlands are drained mainly by the Orange River (the Gariep) and its tributaries, while the Eastern Cape watershed divides the flow of its headwaters, either to feed the Orange or to flow into the Umzimvubu River that enters the Indian Ocean at Port St Johns. Numerous rivers and streams drain into the catchment areas of KwaZulu-Natal's largest rivers, the Thukela, Mkhomazi and Mzimkhulu. As people do not live in the upper catchment areas, Drakensberg streams are normally free from pollution and disease, and the water is safe to drink.

The KwaZulu-Natal and Free State Drakensberg, along with the Maloti Mountains, form southern Africa's most important and vital watershed. Stream catchment areas high up in the mountains yield high-quality water for the benefit of large parts of the country.

Conserving these water reserves may well prove to be even more important than conservation of the Drakensberg's ecosystems, its landscapes and its wilderness character.

KwaZulu-Natal's largest river, the Thukela (the Amphitheatre in the background).

Pristine montane grassland at Jacobs Ladder Waterfall, Lotheni Reserve, in the southern Berg.

Vegetation types

The vegetation of the Drakensberg is divided into an Afro-montane and an Afro-alpine floral region. The Afro-alpine belt is the only one in southern Africa, and is shared by the KwaZulu-Natal Drakensberg, Lesotho and the Eastern Cape. This belt contains extensive pristine or near-pristine wetlands.

Both floral regions are dominated by various species of sweet and unpalatable sour grasses. Rainfall and grazing animals influence the quantity and quality of the grasses, which are embellished by an abundance of geophytic plants, including beautiful ground orchids. Most plants survive the harsh winter by having underground buds, bulbs, corms or rhizomes. To avoid competition from the tall grasses, they start to flower even before the rains come.

Berg wetlands

Marshy areas in the Berg are responsible for a wonderful diversity of species. Small but numerous, the Berg's wetlands are important in controlling water flow, especially in the rainless period. They range from springs, seeps, mires and bogs to the alpine wetlands on the summit. Here, sodden soil and water lie under many short grasses and colourful alpine plants. Together with those on the Rift Valley mountains in Kenya, the wetlands of the Drakensberg form the only true mires in Africa.

Wetlands store water throughout the year and feed rivers, such as the Thukela and Orange, that rise on the high plateau of the escarpment. Unfortunately, though vital for life on earth, wetlands are being destroyed at an alarming rate. Over the past 100 years or so, more than half the wetlands in KwaZulu-Natal alone may have been destroyed or virtually eliminated in some catchment areas.

Fed by grassveld wetland, the Ngwangwane River meanders from its source in the moutains towards the Mzimkhulu.

Harvesting Common Thatch Grass in the Royal Natal area in the northern KwaZulu-Natal Drakensberg.

Montane grassland

Ecologically, the Drakensberg region is classified mostly as grassland biome, a classification that extends to most of the high central plateau of South Africa, including KwaZulu-Natal, the Free State and the Eastern Cape.

Grassland existed long before the break–up of the ancient supercontinent of Gondwana. Older and more complex than indigenous forest, it covered more than half of Africa's land surface about three million years ago, before 'global warming' caused the encroachment of plants and trees and converted great parts of the grassland into savannah.

To this day, most of Africa's herbivorous mammals remain grazers rather than browsers, although Africa's pure grassland has shrunk to about 200 000 km^2 – all of it in South Africa, where it has created different environments. The South African 'veld' is one of the world's great grasslands, on a par with the North American prairie, the South American pampas and the Eurasian steppe. As annual rainfall is quite low, most of the soluble nutrients remain in the ground to develop a relatively rich, fertile topsoil.

The grassveld biome covers the sediments of the Karoo system, out of which rise the mighty basalt cliffs of the Drakensberg escarpment. Apart from about 12,5 per cent of alpine mountain grassland, very little of this precious biome is conserved, although it is home to a rich diversity of protected plants and animals. Grasses are the primary source of food for grazing animals.

Parts of the grassland region have reached pollution levels as bad as any in the world, but less than two per cent of African grassland is protected. What is protected is mainly the high altitude alpine grassland of the Drakensberg summit, 2 500–3 480 m above sea level, and the montane grassland reaching down to the 1 400 m. Moist upland grassland at altitudes of 600–400 m covers parts of the rolling Drakensberg foothills of KwaZulu-Natal and the Eastern Cape, but it is very poorly conserved and heavily used for grazing, crop farming and forestry.

At grass-roots: a short-horned member of the order Orthoptera.

The fire–breathing dragon

Veld fires were a natural and essential process in the ecology of the Drakensberg, but they did, at times, cause confusion. In 1877, for instance, the Bloemfontein Express reported that 'a 120 m-long fire-breathing Dragon' had threatened a father and his son!

In former times, only lightning set fire to the growing thicket of dead winter grass, removing a threat to water conservation and biodiversity. Lightning struck at intervals, irregularly but often enough to stimulate the emergence of fire-resistant plant species and keep forests tucked away in gorges and along rivers and streams – to the benefit of grassland.

More recently, man has decided he can do better than nature by managing fires – a complex issue because different plant communities require different types of burn.

The unpredictability of natural fires was replaced about 50 years ago by controlled burning 'to aid the conservation of a healthy biodiversity and avoid damage to soil structure'.

The KwaZulu-Natal Berg has been divided into 'management compartments' that are burnt regularly at specific times. Every year, about a third of the total area, including the untouchable wilderness areas, goes up in flames. This is intended partly to encourage new growth. After a controlled, planned fire the grass grows vigorously, which is good for grazing and water conservation, and provides additional cover for animals.

Controlled fires also help to prevent devastation of huge areas as a result of fires caused by poachers, herders seeking winter grazing, or frustrated illegal immigrants from Lesotho seeking revenge for discovery and deportation by hurling rocks wrapped in burning grass down the escarpment. To counter this, huge firebreaks are created at strategic places, such as some of the mighty spurs, which usually prevents fires from sweeping through the whole region.

In summer, the grasslands are assaulted by rain during short but vehement thunderstorms. Fortunately, erosion is checked since most of the water is stored as groundwater in vleis and pans, and released slowly throughout the year. However, much of these precious water reserves are now drawn off by monocultures of pine, bluegum and wattle. Where these alien trees have been planted, such as in the foothills of the central and southern KwaZulu-Natal Berg and the north-eastern Cape, grassland diversity has been destroyed and rivers have ceased flowing in winter. This has reduced the ability of the grassland to combat soil erosion.

Man-made veld fire, with Kamberg Mountain visible in the distance.

Indigenous forest (an example of which appears here in Rainbow Gorge) covers a minute part of South Africa's land area, but is of great ecological importance, diversity and beauty.

In the Berg, stabilizing and protecting the soil is a crucial concern since intact montane grassland minimizes the dangers of erosion by preventing fast run-off of rainwater.

In spite of the negative influence of forestation, the grasslands of the Berg still maintain a rich diversity of species, among them many beautiful flowers for which the region is famous. Many other living organisms, such as mammals, especially rodents, and birds and insects (including 'big users' like the brown locust *Locustans pardalin*), also depend on grassland. Harvester termites consume the grass, seeds and roots, while baboons make use of the wealth of bulbous plants.

Grasses such as Red Grass, Common Thatch Grass or Giant Turpentine Grass are the dominant plants, sheltering more than 100 plant species that are endemic (that is, they occur only in the grassland of the Berg region). Some 30 butterfly species also need the grassland to survive, as do birds like the Drakensberg Siskin, Sentinel Rock Thrush, Eastern Longbilled Lark and Drakensberg Prinia, which are endemic to the grassland biome.

Forest

South Africa is by no means a tree–rich country, with indigenous forests covering less than 0,5 per cent of the land area. Of this, roughly a third is in KwaZulu-Natal, a substantial portion of which falls under problematic private ownership. The remaining protected patches of cool, moist indigenous montane forest, which change at lower altitudes to mist-belt forest, are thus of particular value.

Although some 90 million exotic gum, wattle and pine trees are planted every year, the plantations cover just 1,2 per cent of South Africa's land. However, each alien tree uses an average of 25 litres of water per day, and some 80 per cent of such trees occur along the length of the Drakensberg from the Northern Province to the Eastern Cape.

Drakensberg Cycad (*Encephalartos Ghellinckii*) in sub-alpine fynbos.

By comparison, the areas of indigenous forest look extremely small on maps of South Africa's eco-regions, but they play a vital role in storing and regulating the country's water resources. With a biodiversity as impressive as that of the grasslands, their beauty also makes them an invaluable tourist attraction.

About 650 woody plants, mostly evergreen trees, grow in South Africa's forests. Some, especially the Yellowwood and Black Stinkwood, reach heights of more than 40 m and provide a dense canopy, often reached by Monkey Ropes and other climbing plants. The canopy gives shelter to birds and a colourful array of butterflies. In the middle layer, nectar, fruit and insect-eating birds survive. The shrubs and herbs of the under-storey support bushbuck, a few red duiker and some birds, while the leaf carpet of the forest floor feeds small life forms, which convert plant mate-rial to humus to supplement the rich-ness of the soil. Here, too, mammals and birds are essential as seed dis-persers and pollinators.

South African rainforests?

Owing to the sharp rise in altitude, the Drakensberg's forest system has evolved plant communities not encountered in other parts of South Africa. Patches of indigenous forest that remain are often called 'rain-forests', although this is not quite correct.

Real rainforests create their own climate and even influence faraway regions as they create rain clouds through evaporation. Precipitation easily reaches 10 000 mm annually. Temperatures throughout the year hover around 28–30° C. Real rainforests there-fore know no seasons. By contrast, change of season is an influential feature of the whole South African Drakensberg, with many rainless months.

South Africa's remaining patches of montane forest could thus, at best, be classified as seasonal rainforest, even though their structure is similar to that of the ever-shrinking rainforests of the world. The Amazon rainforest alone covers an area of about 6 million km². South Africa's forests are midgets by comparison, though no less precious.

Red-hot Pokers (*Kniphofia ichopensiscaulescens*) at Sani Pass.

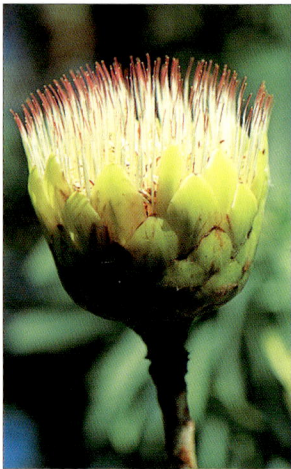

Waterlily Sugarbush or Lip-flower Protea (*Protea subvestita*).

Diversity of species

Although it took millions of years to establish the Drakensberg's great ecological diversity, its rich variety of plant life is regarded by many today as its greatest attraction.

Ancient species such as algae, lichens and mosses were probably the first to arrive, followed by ferns, cycads and other gymnosperms – the first primitive group of plants, which produce seeds but not flowers. Some ancient species have survived, among them the indomitable Yellowwood, still thriving in sheltered valleys along the whole range. Plants with true leaves and flowers (angiosperms) also developed and gradually took over the floral kingdom.

Apart from the dominant grasses, 2 153 plant species occur in the Berg's many different habitats, ranging from wetlands to alpine tundra on top of the escarpment. Among the 50 families of flowering plants are species known and admired the world over. Some such as the beautiful Fire Lily (one of the more than 1 700 flowering plants that occur in these mountains) are very rare and lie hidden in remote, inaccessible places. Equally important are five gymnosperms, 300 mosses, and 75 ferns. Lichens are not too well known except for Old Man's Beard and a few species growing on boulders. The Drakensberg's only cycad species also survives in the grasslands.

Bell Agapanthus (*Agapanthus Campanulatus*) along a hiking path to Thukela Gorge.

The widespread Krantz Aloe (*Aloe arborescens*).

Some 200 plant species occur only in the Drakensberg, among them the famous *Protea nubigena*, which survives in snow, icy winds and thunderstorms only in the Little Berg area of the Royal Natal National Park.

• See lists of flora at the back of this book.

'South Africa is noted for its tremendous richness of flowering plants – like nowhere else on the planet. Although the country occupies less than one per cent of the world's landmass, it contains 10 per cent of all the earth's species of plants. All important segments have been protected by an extensive national park system and progressive conservation practices.'

(Thomas S Elias, director of the US National Arboretum, October 1997.)

A large population of eland (the main motif in San rock art) inhabits the Drakensberg grasslands.

Wildlife – a 'living ocean'

James Chapman, one of the first travellers to skirt the 'lofty range of the Drakensberg', wrote in 1849: 'The plains for miles around had somewhat the appearance of a living ocean, the tumultuous waves being formed by various herds criss-crossing each other in every direction.'

Big game hunters, the exterminators of the 19th century, many killing indiscriminately, soon put an end to such abundance. In 1863, lions were still found in the Cathkin area, but the last Drakensberg lion was shot in 1872. In the Thukela valley, elephants survived until at least 1876, but by 1880 all the larger mammals had gone, including zebra, oribi, wildebeest and the carnivores.

Although leopards still occur in the Berg, they are seldom seen or heard. Today most of the Drakensberg, from the foothills to the summit, is a protected area and has been restocked with many of the larger species that once roamed there. The numbers of the smaller species have increased to acceptable levels, and rare species have found a place of safety.

Ice rats (*Otomys sloggetti*), tough inhabitants of the High Berg.

Mammals

As many as 64 mammal species – from aardvark to zorilla (polecat) – are found in the region. Many are not easy to find, as population densities in mountain areas are generally lower than in lowveld game reserves. Giant's Castle Game Reserve, Kamberg Mountain Reserve and Golden Gate Highlands National Park are among the best sites.

Although the populations of eland and clawless and spotted-necked otter are probably the largest in South Africa, it pays to look out for the more elusive species like aardwolf, caracal, genet, serval, large and small grey mongoose, water mongoose and white-tailed mongoose.

Some species regularly venture into higher regions in search of food, particularly herds of eland and the omnivorous baboons. A few defy the harsh climate of the High Berg permanently, like the sure-footed klipspringer, which can negotiate steep slopes easily. Higher up still, the tough ice rat suns itself between snow and ice. Generally, however, mammal species tend to remain below the alpine belt.

• See lists of mammals at the back of this book.

Reptiles

Of the 48 reptiles found in the KwaZulu-Natal Berg, 25 are snakes and 23 lizard species. The Nile monitor leguaan (*Varanus niloticus*), listed as vulnerable in the Red Data Book, depends on the Berg's wetlands for its future survival. All lizards, many of them endemic, are harmless.

Only three snakes in the Berg are dangerously venomous: puff adder, berg adder and rinkhals. The Berg is the hub linking the Cape mountains to the subtropical regions of Mpumalanga and the Northern Province. By permitting gene flow between species, this has allowed the Berg to develop into one of southern Africa's major centres of herpetofauna diversity.

• See lists of reptiles at the back of this book.

Rock monitor (*Varanus albigularis*), a relative of Africa's largest lizard, the Nile monitor (*V. niloticus*).

Amphibians (especially frogs)

Drakensberg nature reserves are increasingly important sanctuaries for frogs, which are exceptionally vulnerable to human influence and therefore valuable indicators of the status of the environment. Many species around the world have suffered heavy losses through pollution or have been decimated by traffic. Frogs can be found everywhere in the Berg, but patience and care is required to track down a few of the 26 species and subspecies.

Giant bullfrog (*Pyxicephalus adspersus*), part of a rich frog fauna.

Of the four living orders of amphibians, two are represented by a substantial number of species in South Africa: the order Anura, comprising frogs and toads; and the order Caecilia, comprising worm-like subterranean amphibians. Examples of five of the 17 Anura families present in South Africa occur at all altitudes and in all parts of the Drakensberg. They include true frogs, true toads, tree frogs, narrow-mouthed frogs, terrestrial, arboreal and aquatic frogs, and tongueless frogs. A few are adapted to very high altitudes and harsh conditions and are found nowhere else. All display the general characteristic of the order: the tail is absent and the hind legs are enlarged for jumping.

• See list of amphibians at the back of this book.

An endangered resident, the Wattled Crane (*Bugeranus carunculatus*).

Birds

More than 300 bird species have been recorded in the Drakensberg. Of these, 41 are considered to be endemic to southern Africa, with at least eight endemic to the montane grassland. In addition, 36 are listed in the international Red Data Book as critically endangered, threatened or vulnerable.

Birds inhabit many different habitats, from the low altitude evergreen montane forests up through the montane grasslands and sandstone cliffs to the alpine belt at 3 000 m or more. The immense diversity ensures the Berg's position as one of the most rewarding birding destinations in South Africa. A few species, such as the Black Stork, Striped Flufftail and Wattled Crane, depend strongly on the region's wetlands for their survival.

The Bearded Vulture (Lammergeier), Cape Vulture and Black Eagle may be seen soaring in the thermal updrafts, whereas Jackal Buzzard and Lanner Falcon prefer the cliffs of the Little Berg. The Grass Owl and all three South African crane species live in safety at the lower levels where they are joined in summer by flocks of White Storks from Europe and Asia. Among the smaller birds are species such as the Natal Sugarbird, Orangebreasted Rockjumper, Buffstreaked Chat, Bush Blackcap, Fairy Flycatcher, Forest Canary, Greater Doublecollared Sunbird, Ground Woodpecker, and Yellowbreasted Pipit.

At least 50–60 bird species survive and breed in the alpine belt, some at the highest altitude but extending their range lower down in winter time, while others spend only the short summer at the lofty heights. The most common species in the alpine belt is the Rock Pigeon, followed by the Drakensberg Siskin and Sicklewinged Chat, which are uncommon below the escarpment. The Whitenecked Raven, Greywing Francolin, Sentinel Rock Thrush, Thickbilled Lark, Malachite Sunbird and others also live in or visit the alpine belt, as do palaearctic migrants such as the European Swift, Eastern Redfooted Kestrel and Steppe Buzzard. The Bearded Vulture and Bald Ibis breed in

Malachite Sunbird (*Nectarinia famosa*) in alpine grassland.

Cape Eagle Owl (*Bubo capensis*).

Jackal Buzzard (*Buteo rufofuscus*).

Rock Pigeon (*Columba guinea*), the most common alpine-belt bird.

Grasshoppers (*Phymateus* nymphs above) and dragonflies (*Anaxemperator* sp. below).

the highest parts of the Berg but forage regularly at much lower altitudes. A few flocks of the extremely rare Cape Parrot are still to be found in the Yellowwood forest patches adjacent to the southern foothills.

The best time to watch birds in the Berg is in summer, from November to March or April. Numbers and species diversity are lower in winter when many move to friendlier places in the Midlands and coastal areas during 'altitude migrations'.

• See list of birds at the back of this book.

Insects

About 50 000 different insect species may exist in southern Africa alone. Insects are generally disliked and often persecuted as pests, as they loot crops and spread sicknesses such as yellow fever and malaria. Neither disease, however, is present in the Drakensberg region.

Among the Drakensberg's insects are many fly species, most of them endemic to the region. Associated with the ancient tarns and wetlands are 44 species of dragonfly. One highly specialized dragonfly has survived, apparently for millions of years, in ice and cold at the top of the escarpment. Of the 92 butterfly species recorded in the KwaZulu-Natal Drakensberg so far, 19 are classified as typical montane species and a few may occur only in the area. (A list of Drakensberg butterflies is given at the back of this book.)

Various species of arthropods occur in the Drakensberg. Visitors normally encounter a few widespread species such as red-ended millipedes and locusts. There are 32 species of millipedes, most probably endemic. Further research is needed to obtain more information about the different species.

Marsh acraea (*Acraea rahira rahira*).

Display in Main Cave, Giant's Castle Reserve (central KwaZulu-Natal Drakensberg), showing the way of life of the San, their hardships, crafts and pleasures.

The human tide

Archaeologically, the Drakensberg ranks as an important area in southern Africa. Excavations indicate that the region has been occupied by humans over the past million years and that hunter-gatherers lived there for at least 100 000 years. Evidence of human occupation in the uKhahlamba Drakensberg Park area goes back about 20 000 years, while Stone Age people moved into the central and southern Drakensberg foothills some 8 000 years ago. In the northern parts, including the Royal Natal and Golden Gate Highlands National Parks, humans have been present for at least 5 000 years.

They were the ancestors of the 19th century San, semi-nomadic hunter-gatherers who are regarded as the original inhabitants of the sub-continent. The San people (otherwise known as the Bushmen, a term that seems to be preferred by the last survivors elsewhere) lived in loose clans, hunting eland and collecting the fruits of the veld (grasslands). A deep understanding of the environment is revealed in their paintings, which can still be seen in the caves and overhangs of the Little Berg from the Royal Natal National Park to Barkly East, and in Lesotho and the Free State.

About 1 000 years ago Iron Age, Bantu-speaking farmers from the north settled in the fertile valleys of the Little Berg, at first living in relative harmony with the San. However, when the Mfecane (the wars of annihilation between the tribes) started during the first quarter of the 19th century, the San's livelihood was threatened. By 1828, the land south of the Zulu Kingdom, between the Thukela and Mzimkhulu Rivers, was devastated.

Environs of Kokstad, the capital of Adam Kok's short-lived republic.

Pressure increased when Shaka Zulu's 'impis' routed the local tribes and chased the survivors into the mountains. Some perished, others eked out a miserable existence on the high plateau until a leader with a mission, Moshoeshoe I, gathered them together to create the Basotho people. Moshoeshoe's military and diplomatic skills later foiled all attempts, British and Boer, to subdue him. The kingdom he established on the 'roof' of southern Africa exists today as Lesotho.

In 1862 a mixed tribe, the Griquas, moved eastwards under Adam Kok and his heirs from their native soil around Griquastad in the west. They crossed the Drakensberg with their 20 000 head of stock and 300 wagons, suffering fearful hardship before settling in the fertile 'No-man's-land' (as it was then known) that was to become Griqualand East in the Eastern Cape. They installed a *volksraad* or parliament in their capital, Kokstad, but by 1878 were forced to submit to British colonial rule.

At about the same time, the San were making their last stand against encroaching white settlers. Although they had lived for so long in harmony with their environment, they became the first victims of wildlife and habitat destruction. Vast stretches of the high region of the escarpment remain unspoilt to this day because of their way of life. Today, Ezemvelo KZN Wildlife (formerly the KwaZulu-Natal Conservation Service), guards the former hunting grounds of the Bushmen and remains the watchful custodian of the Berg's delicate ecosystem and magnificent biodiversity.

ROCK ART
a cultural heritage

In 1967 Harald Pager, a modern cave man and designer of Austrian origin, observed how rapidly San paintings were deteriorating. He became intrigued by the wealth of San art in the Didima Valley of Cathedral Peak and, with his wife Shirley Anne, took up residence in one of the rock shelters in the valley to take stock of what he described as the 'richest rock art area in the world'. Within two years he had copied some 4 000 rock paintings, hand-painting with infinite care life-size images of the originals, which he had photographed in black and white. Many of the copies found their way into his voluminous work, *Ndedema*. Since then, more than 20 per cent of the paintings at Didima have disappeared, while others are rapidly fading.

In the 1950s, only about 30 rock art sites were known in the KwaZulu-Natal Berg. Today, more than 30 000 rock paintings from 520 rock shelters are known, some only to the experts. Many, however, have already been vandalised and disfigured.

Harald Pager at work in Didima Gorge copying rock paintings through many a shower – almost a rain-making shaman himself in his own humourous description.

Caves

One must not associate rock paintings with dark underground caves. The San's open-air studios in the Drakensberg were open rock shelters or overhangs, mostly of eroding Clarens sandstone in the Little Berg. Some of these shelters, also used for daily living, were small and exposed to the elements, while others were quite large. Eland Cave in the Cathedral Peak area, for example, is about 100 m long and its walls are adorned with more than 1 600 painted figures.

Other well-known caves and artworks are the Bee Shelter in the Cathkin area, a 'Stone Age ballet' at a shelter of Mont Paul near Harrismith, and a painting of an elephant hunter wielding an iron axe to hamstring his quarry at the Elephant Shelter at Cathedral Peak. A cave near Royal Natal National Park depicts an 'elephant man' with a huge swarm of bees, a hunting method used by the Zulus, whereas San hunters used poisoned arrows. Dramatic pictures of the San's twilight years, dating back from around 1850–1870, have also been found in a shelter in East Griqualand.

Motifs

The Stone Age artists of the Berg seldom included landscapes or plants in their paintings, portraying mainly people and their tools, as well as the animals they lived with: baboon, black-backed jackal, dassie (rock hyrax), elephant, rhino, hyaena, lion, leopard, warthog, bushbuck, grey rhebok, hartebeest, oribi, reedbuck, roan antelope, birds, snakes and fish. The primary focal points, however, were the eland and the bee.

Later, pictures were added of horses, cattle, sheep, dogs and, in the southern Berg, ox wagons and colonial soldiers, as well as depictions of the San's response to the settler challenge during the clash of cultures. Scenes of mating animals are rare, although a depiction of two mating rhebok is known.

Surprisingly, the black wildebeest (gnu) played a minor role as a model for San artists, featuring in only one of more than 4 000 rock paintings registered by Harald Pager, although there must have been plenty in the foothills up to the 19th century. A traveller reported seeing 'stacks of wildebeest skulls near a deserted Bushman camp. It was as if one was looking at another Golgotha'. Perhaps they were not of religious importance? The San must have liked wildebeest meat, though, as shown by one of their prayers: *'Oh Lord, lead me to a wildebeest; I like much to have my belly filled . . . Lord, bring me a male wildebeest under my shafts."*

Interpretation

The modern three-pronged study of rock art by archaeologists, anthropologists and art historians has opened new perspectives of interpretation and led to fundamental changes in the understanding of San paintings. They are now acknowledged as artworks with an essentially religious character that – unlike the works of Rembrandt or Picasso in international galleries – should be admired in their places of origin.

The artists

If one accepts that most San rock paintings interpret the experience of healers or shamans in trances, it follows that it must have been the shamans themselves who recorded their experiences during their trance dances. These trances connected them to the spiritual world through altered states of consciousness. A shaman in a trance experienced nasal bleeding like a wounded eland, and his blood was rubbed on members of the clan in the belief that it would ward off evil and sickness. The eland was thus not only a source of food to the San, but also a potent religious force, important medium and symbol of well-being.

As can be inferred from their increased production of rock paintings in the 19th century, this San method of reducing social stress became more necessary, if less effective, with the growing contact between the San and European colonists that led eventually to destruction of the highly nomadic and egalitarian lifestyle that had cemented San society.

The paint

One of the last San in the area was a man carrying 10 small antelope horns around his waist, each containing a different colour of paint, much as a palette does. To make vivid reds, oranges and yellows, powders made from iron oxides were mixed, whereas burnt bone was used for black and fine clay for white. It is interesting to note that the colours were fast: it is usually the rock face that is disintegrating rather than the colours that are fading. Binding was probably achieved with plant sap, egg white or with human or eland blood. The painters used brush-like tools made from animal hairs or feathers, sticks, or pieces of bones, or simply used their fingers.

Main Cave at Giant's Castle (central KwaZulu-Natal Berg), easily accessible and much damaged by name writing on the walls.

kwazulu-natal
drakensberg

Eastern Buttress and Inner Tower (behind cloud) in Royal Natal Park, northern Berg.

KwaZulu-Natal Drakensberg

The heart of southern Africa's 'Great Escarpment', the
KwaZulu-Natal Drakensberg has been divided here into
northern, central and southern sections. Now a World
Heritage Site, the uKhahlamba Drakensberg Park contains
all the Berg's nature reserves and wilderness areas, offering
a vast zone of pristine wilderness with a good infrastructure
for visitors. The southern part of the province, a region known
as East Griqualand, forms the link with the north-eastern
Cape Drakensberg.

The KwaZulu-Natal Drakensberg is a narrow, crescent-shaped stretch of escarpment and foothills that runs along the KwaZulu-Natal and Lesotho border from Mont-aux-Sources in the north to Bushman's Nek in the south. Apart from the Mnweni tribal area between the Royal Natal National Park and the Cathedral Peak Mountain Reserve, the region falls under the jurisdiction of the former KwaZulu-Natal Conservation Service, now known as Ezemvelo KZN Wildlife.

The escarpment, otherwise known as the High Berg, varies greatly in altitude, its horizontal aspect interrupted by steep mountain passes and deep cutbacks. From its sheer basalt walls, grass-covered slopes and spurs lead down to the sandstone terraces known as the Little Berg where fast-flowing rivers have carved deep valleys.

KZN MOUNTAIN RESERVES
from north to south

Reserve (hectares)	Integrated wilderness areas
Royal Natal National Park (8 094)	none
Rugged Glen Nature Reserve (762)	none
Cathedral Peak (*)	Mlambonja & Mdedelelo
Monk's Cowl (*)	Mdedelelo
Injisuthi, part of Giant's Castle (*)	Mdedelelo
Giant's Castle (34 638)	none
Highmoor (*)	Mkhomazi
Kamberg (2 980)	Mkhomazi
Lotheni (3 984)	Mkhomazi
Vergelegen (1 159)	Mkhomazi
Cobham (*)	Mkhomazi
Garden Castle (*)	Mzimkhulu
Bushman's Nek (*)	Mzimkhulu
Himeville Nature Reserve (104)	none
Coleford Nature Reserve (1 272)	none
Mount Currie Nature Reserve (1 777)	none

* part of KZN Wilderness Area

Almost the whole area has been integrated into the Greater uKhahlamba Drakensberg Park and is protected as nature or mountain reserves and wilderness areas. Giant's Castle, proclaimed in 1903, was one of the first conservation areas in Africa.

The proclaimed wilderness areas Mlambonja, Mdedelelo, Mkhomazi and Mzimkhulu, covering 117 765 ha, have been formed from the state forests of Cathedral Peak, Monk's Cowl, Highmoor, Mkhomazi, Cobham and Garden Castle, which were proclaimed between 1927 and 1951 to protect the Drakensberg watershed.

World Heritage site

The 2 400 km^2 uKhahlamba Drakensberg Park, stretching from the Royal Natal National Park in the north to Bushman's Nek in the south, was declared a combined cultural and natural World Heritage site on 29 November 2000 – South Africa's fourth such site and the second in KwaZulu-Natal. The Greater St Lucia Wetland Park was the first.

With 690 cultural and natural sites already protected worldwide – only 23 combining two or more of the required aspects – the World Heritage Committee aims to ensure that future generations can inherit the treasures of the past. It is hoped that uKhahlamba Drakensberg Park's new status will foster renewed interest in the Berg region with its natural beauty and countless cultural treasures.

A chequered history

The central KwaZulu-Natal Berg must have been the focus of San spiritual life, as thousands of well-preserved paintings in the Didima Gorge and Valley testify.

Although some are several thousand years old, more recent paintings depict the coming of the end of the San clans. The paintings show men on horseback, with guns over their shoulders, and cattle – regarded by the San as the property of all, much like the eland, which they had hunted for thousands of years.

All this came to an end in the 19th century when pastoralists and agriculturalists, black and white, moved into the valleys and northern foothills, encroaching on the Berg and destroying the livelihood of the San forever. They were branded as cattle thieves and hunted until none remained.

The region quickly developed into one of South Africa's leading agricultural areas, with many villages and towns founded to serve farming communities. Once roads and railroads improved access, people flocked to the Berg for recreation and spiritual revival.

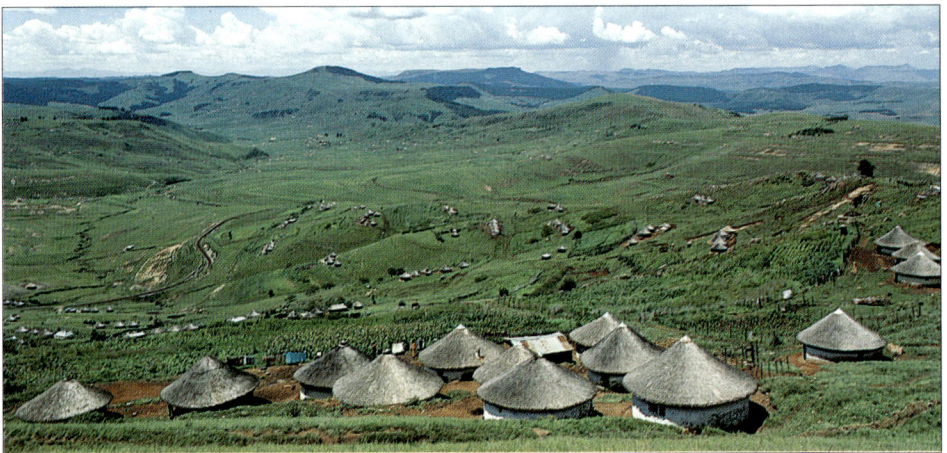

Road to the southern Berg, leading to paths trodden in the last century by European botanists and collectors.

The first hostel, the Gudu – later to develop into the Royal Natal National Park Hotel – was built in 1903. The first hotels were Champagne Castle (1930), and Cathedral Peak, built seven years later. At present, an extensive chain of stylish hotels, holiday resorts and retreats stretches across the Berg from north to south.

With unexpected foresight, measures were introduced at the beginning of the 20th century to protect catchment areas and pristine wilderness areas by declaring them nature reserves – just in time, too, as can be seen at places where human encroachment went too far. Today, provincial, national and non-governmental conservation agencies ensure that further development proceeds in an orderly fashion.

View of Cathedral range (central Berg) and Mlambonja Wilderness.

KwaZulu-Natal Berg wilderness areas

Largely untouched wilderness environments have been established only in the KwaZulu-Natal Drakensberg. They do not compete with national parks or traditional nature reserves, as they represent an entirely different concept in nature conservation.

In wilderness areas neither roads nor accommodation are provided and the number of visitors is strictly controlled. There is no radical managerial interference, although regular veld burning is carried out. Visitors have to make do with natural shelters such as caves, overhangs and habitat-friendly tents. They must carry whatever they need on their backs and leave no evidence of their visit behind them. Their reward is physical recreation and spiritual inspiration experienced in complete isolation from the high-tech world outside.

Officials of the Department of Forestry postulated many of these 'wilderness' principles in the 1960s. Since then about 1 180 km^2 of legally demarcated wilderness area have been taken under the control of KZN Wildlife.

NAME	MLAMBONJA	MDEDELELO	MKHOMAZI	MZIMKHULU
PROCLAIMED	1989	1973	1973/1989	1979
AREA (hectares)	6 270	27 000	56 155	28 340

SOME WELL KNOWN PEAKS
(in descending order of height)

PEAK	AREA	HEIGHT	FIRST ASCENT
THABANA NTLENYANA,	Sani/Lesotho	3 482 m	N/A (walk from Sani Top)
MAFADI	Injisuthi	3 446 m	Unknown
INJISUTHI	Injisuthi	3 410 m	Unknown
CHAMPAGNE CASTLE	Champagne	3 377 m	1861
KA-NTHUBA	Mkhomazi	3 355 m	Unknown
POPPLE PEAK	Injisuthi	3 325 m	Unknown
GIANT'S CASTLE	Giant's	3 316 m	1864
REDI	Mkhomazi	3 314 m	Unknown
MASHAI	Mzimkhulu	3 313 m	Unknown
MLAMBONJA PEAK	Mzimkhulu	3 309 m	Unknown
MOHLESI	Mkhomazi	3 301 m	Unknown
MONT-AUX-SOURCES	Royal Natal	3 282 m	1836
CLEFT PEAK	Cathedral	3 281 m	1936
HODGSON'S PEAK	Cobham/Sani	3 256 m	Unknown
INDUMENI DOME	Cathedral	3 255 m	1925
MONK'S COWL	Champagne	3 234 m	1942
IFIDI BUTTRESS	Mnweni	3 219 m	Unknown
INJISUTHI BUTTRESS	Injisuthi	3 202 m	1935
SENTINEL	Royal Natal	3 165 m	1910
COCKADE	Cathedral	3 161 m	1936
SADDLE, NORTH	Cathedral	3 153 m	1924
CATHKIN PEAK	Champagne	3 149 m	1912
MOUNT AMERY	Mnweni	3 143 m	1920
EASTERN TRIPLET	Injisuthi	3 143 m	1950
THE TENT	Mkhomazi	3 130 m	Unknown
WESTERN (BEACON) BUTTRESS	Royal Natal	3 121 m	Unknown
SADDLE, SOUTH	Cathedral	3 120 m	1947
ELEPHANT	Cathedral	3 109 m	1936
MBUNDINI BUTTRESS	Mnweni	3 100 m	1948
OUTER MNWENI PINNACLE	Mnweni	3 099 m	1948
INNER MWENI PINNACLE	Mnweni	3 096 m	1949
MPONJWANA	Mnweni	3 085 m	1946
NDEDEMA DOME	Champagne	3 078 m	1935
RHINO PEAK	Mzimkhulu	3 051 m	1953
EASTERN BUTTRESS	Royal Natal	3 047 m	1914
THABA-NTSU	Mzimkhulu	3 028 m	Unknown
ROCKERIES	Mnweni	3 027 m	1921
DEVIL'S TOOTH	Royal Natal	3 019 m	1950
HORN, INNER	Cathedral	3 006 m	1925
HORN, OUTER	Cathedral	3 005 m	1934
CATHEDRAL PEAK	Cathedral	3 004 m	1917
AMPHITHEATRE WALL	Royal Natal	2 972 m	1935

Vegetation

Three vegetation belts are apparent in the area of the KwaZulu-Natal Drakensberg: a montane belt of Afro-montane grassland (often invaded by Ouhout and Sagewood); a sub-alpine belt of high-altitude grassland; and an alpine belt of dwarf alpine fynbos.

Montane belt (*1 300 –1 800 m*)
Cliff and rock plants

Interesting plant communities have developed around the rock outcrops dotting the land-scape. They provide cover for animals and are important fire refuges. Characteristic species are Natal Bottlebrush, with its vivid scarlet flowers in September, Mountain Cypress, the Pompon Tree, and some Yellowwoods.

Most of the 1 000 km² of protea savannah in the Drakensberg is found in the northern and central Berg, usually on south-facing slopes between the sandstone cliffs and neigh-bouring grasslands. Common Sugarbush and Silver Sugarbush are the dominant species, easily identifiable by rounded crowns, black gnarled bark and flower heads. They grow in pure or mixed stands, seldom higher than 3–5 m. Drakensberg Sugarbush, Cloud Sugarbush and Dwarf Grassveld Sugarbush are also found.

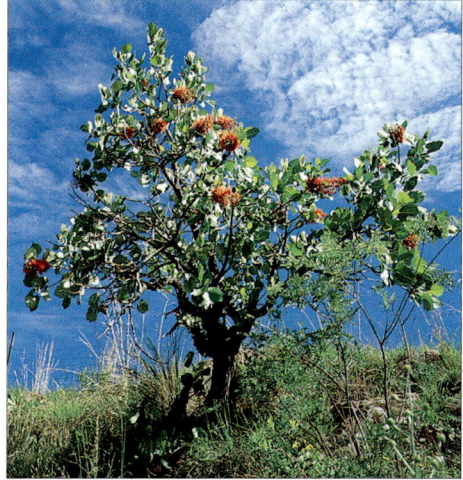

Natal Bottlebrush (*Greyia sutherlandii*).

Montane forest

Pockets of indigenous forest grow in sheltered valleys and kloofs on the south-facing slopes, up to the sub-alpine belt at about 2 000 m. Good examples of montane forest are: Gudu Bush (Royal Natal Park), Didima and Rainbow Gorges (Cathedral Peak Reserve), Giant's Castle Reserve, Hlathikulu (Biggarsberg) and Gxalingwena at the bottom of Sani Pass.

Characteristic species include Yellowwood, Wild Peach, Silky Bark, Cape Holly and the less common Mountain Hard Pear, Berg Bamboo and Cape Myrtle. All flourish in the warmer northern KwaZulu-Natal Drakensberg but grow less vigorously in the extreme climatic conditions of the southern Berg. The rare Drakensberg Cycad – a cone-bearing 'tree palm' which is neither palm nor tree – prefers the higher grassy slopes.

Montane forest slope at Gudu Bush, northern Berg.

Sub-alpine belt (*1 300–1 800 m*)
Fynbos scrub
This essentially transitory plant community includes grasses, small trees and scrubs typical of the Berg, and is quite similar to the fynbos of the Western Cape. Plants with small and hard leaves dominate, among them the Drakensberg Cycad and more common species such as Gannabas, Cape Myrtle and Mountain Cypress. Numerous ericas are found here and on the escarpment.

Basaltic region
The plant communities of the basaltic area consist predominantly of dwarf shrubs such as Grey-leaf Bush, ericas, cushion and rosette plants such as *Helichrysum sessile* and *Wahlenbergia montana*; forbs and herbs such as *Eucomis bicolor*, *Scabiosa drakensbergensis*, *Helichrysum scapiforme* and *Dianthus basuticus*; and some taller shrubs, such as *Leucosidea sericea* and *Cliffortia linearifolia*, in deeper valleys.

Alpine belt (*2 800–3 482 m*)
Dwarf alpine fynbos
This type of vegetation survives in the upper gullies, cliff faces and on the summit. It is dominated by everlastings and heaths, *Erica dominans* (a prominent member), Sedge Heath, and short hard tussock grasses and herbs. Bogs are common along the high plateau and in Lesotho.

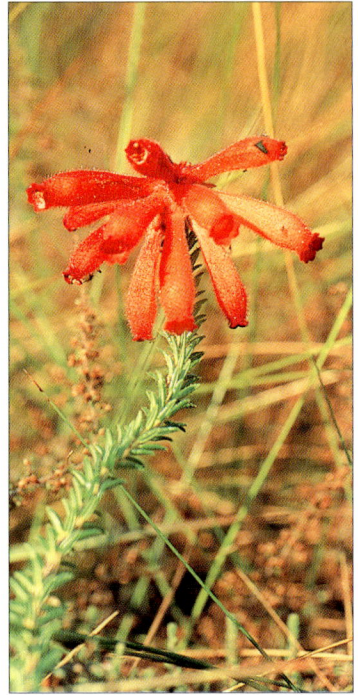

Hardy alpine-belt plant species: Red Hairy Heath (*Erica cerinthoides*) above, and Everlastings (*Helichrysum* species) below.

Walking, hiking, mountaineering

Countless paths and tracks stretch across the KwaZulu-Natal Berg, leading to meadows dotted with wild flowers or through steep passes to barren summits. A network of hundreds of walks, hikes and bridle paths has been created within the nature reserves.

Contour paths dating back to forestry times traverse the area from Bushman's Nek to the Cathedral Peak wilderness area. These facilitate long hikes along the Drakensberg range with overnight stays in caves, tents or old farm-houses, with many opportunities to cool down on hot days in mountain streams, which carry no risk of bilharzia or malaria.

KZN Wildlife controls access to most of the peaks. The plateau is reached quite easily by hiking and scrambling through passes located in all three sections of the KwaZulu-Natal Berg. Getting to the top of some of the 3 000 m peaks requires only fair to strenuous hiking and scrambling; others are the domain of experienced mountaineers, and require climbing equipment and some light to heavy rock climbing.

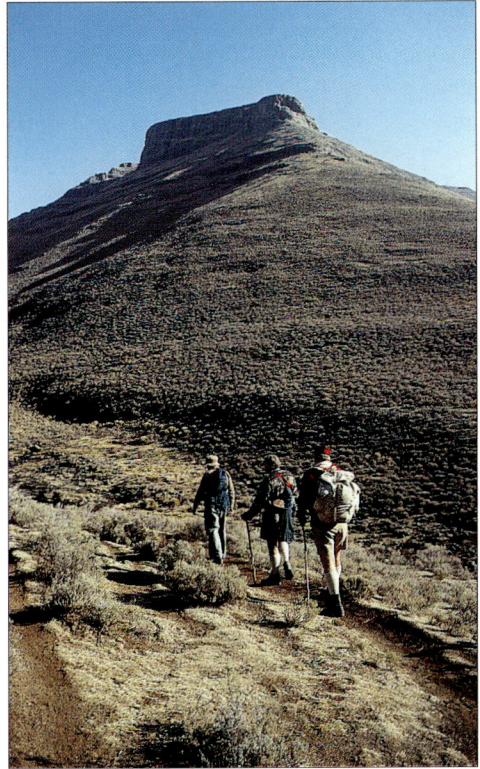

On top of the escarpment near Sani Pass in the southern Berg.

Well-known walks and hikes:

Northern Berg: Namahadi (Mont-aux-Sources), Chain Ladder (Mont-aux-Sources), Ifidi (Ifidi Buttress), Mnweni (Mnweni Cutback).

Central Berg: Umlambonja (Cathedral Peak), Organ Pipes (Cleft Peak), Ndedema (Ndedema Dome), Grey's (Champagne Castle), Leslie's (Injisuthi/Mafadi Peak), Bannerman (Popple Peak), Langalibalele (Popple Peak), Giant's Castle (Giant's Castle).

Southern Berg: Lotheni Pass (Carbineer Point), Sani Pass (Thaba Ntlenyana), Masubasuba Pass (Hodgson's Peak/Giant's Cup), Mlambonja Pass, Mashal Pass (Mlambonja Peak, Rhino Peak).

Some caves close to the summit:

Northern Berg: Crows (Mont-aux-Sources), Pin's (Mnweni), Fangs (Mnweni).

Central Berg: Twins (Cathedral Peak), Bell's (Cathedral Peak), Injisuthi Summit Cave (Injisuthi), Nkososana (Grey's Pass), Junction (Leslie's Pass).

Southern Berg: Mashal Shelter (Mlambonja Pass/Mashal Pass, Rhino Peak).

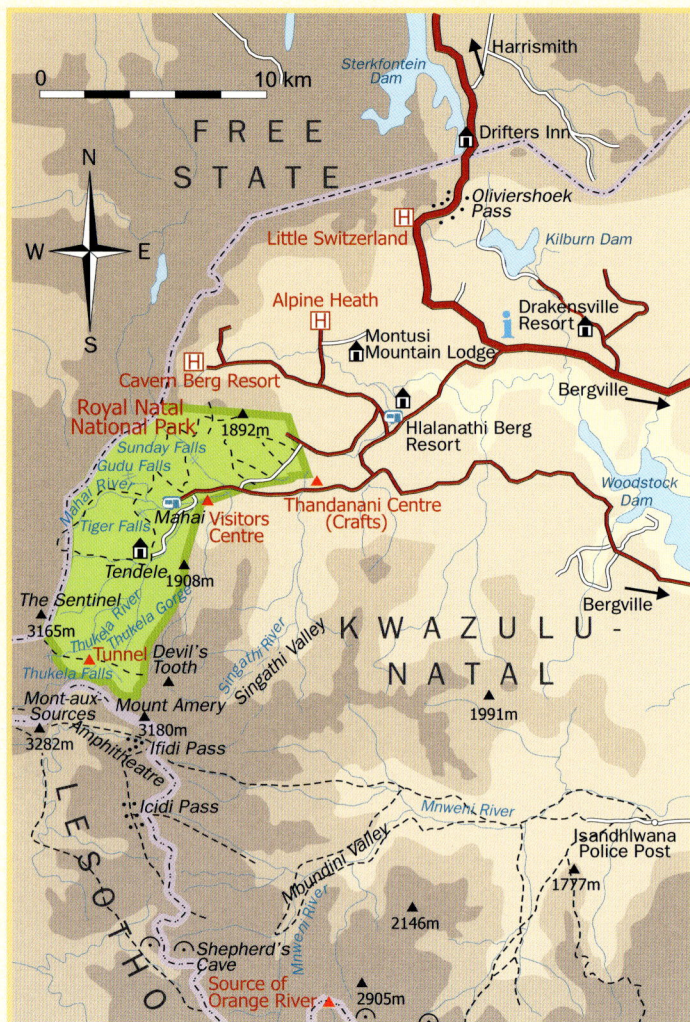

Northern KwaZulu-Natal Drakensberg

Two major natural areas – the world-famous Royal Natal National Park and the untamed Mnweni triangle to the south – shape the northern Berg, a region of high mountains, deep gorges, rivers and waterfalls that afford interest, inspiration and repose along with many opportunities for exploration.

The Northern KwaZulu-Natal Drakensberg begins south-west of Van Reenen's Pass. Its greatest assets are the gigantic Amphitheatre, the Thukela Valley and Gorge, its plant life and the number and variety of its fascinating yet undemanding walks and hikes.

The fact that the British royal family visited in the mid-20th century made the Royal Natal National Park the best known and most popular destination in the uKhahlamba Drakensberg Park. The high mountains of the Northern Berg are easily reached via Olifantshoek Pass or from Ladysmith-Winterton-Bergville.

By contrast, the Mnweni tribal area to the south, once part of the so-called Drakensberg Locations, lacks infrastructure and remains underdeveloped and inaccessible. The lordly mountains of the Mweni triangle overlook denuded, overpopulated valleys – the end result of policies that shunted people around to serve as a buffer between San hunter-gatherers and immigrant white farmers.

The solid face of the Amphitheatre, a major attraction in the Royal Natal National Park.

Towns and villages

Bergville, an agricultural and trading centre, lies about 50 km from the Royal Natal National Park. A blockhouse built by British forces during the Anglo-Boer War, now a national monument and museum, invites a short stop. The Drakensberg Tourism Association in Thatham Road (tel 036-444 1557) has information about the whole KwaZulu-Natal Drakensberg. **Winterton** boasts a museum devoted to the geology, fauna, flora and history of the San people of the Drakensberg, as well as other early inhabitants of the area. Information about the history of local farms is also available (tel 036-488 1885). The Purple House offers tourist information and a wide range of arts and crafts (tel 036-488 1025).

Royal Natal National Park

The Royal Natal National Park is by far the most famous destination of the northern Berg and KwaZulu Natal's only national park. The majestic highlight of the Drakensberg, it has it all: awesome vistas; deep gorges; glittering waterfalls; secret pools; cool forests; caves and rock paintings; exciting wildlife; beautiful flowers and trees, including the elusive Cloud Protea; and walks and hikes for everyone.

The western border of the park includes the Amphitheatre, a 500 m high rock face that stretches for 5 km. From afar, it looks like a solid basalt block, but it is actually deeply furrowed by erosion. Pinnacles, saddles and cutbacks are visible on closer inspection, while green 'spurs' (ridges that project outwards at right angles from the escarpment) descend towards the Little Berg.

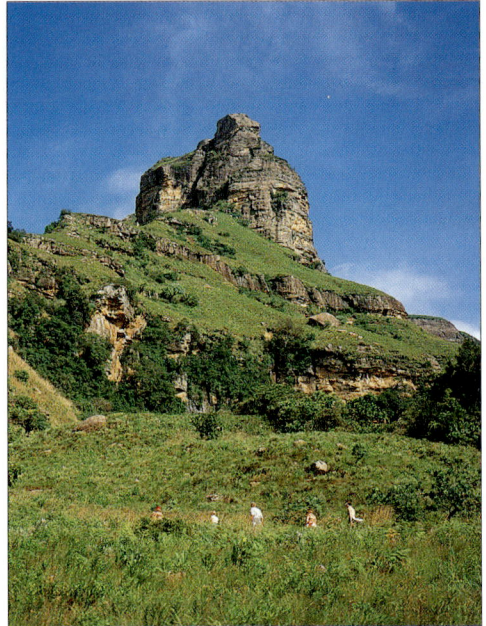

Plowman's Kop affords magnificent views for hikers who continue beyond the 'Crack' (see Walks, p. 54).

Framing this geological spectacle on the right are the flat-topped Sentinel (3 165 m) and Beacon Buttress (3 124 m), while the Eastern Buttress (3 121 m) stands guard on the left. Beyond lie the Mnweni tribal and wilderness areas.

The summit seems almost flat, with only a few hills and buttresses rising above it. One of them, an inconspicuous pimple about 3,5 km inland from the escarpment, is Mont-aux-Sources. It rises a mere 250 m above its surroundings and is therefore invisible from below the escarpment.

The Thukela, probably South Africa's most important river, and the less well known Bilanjil, have their source here. Thukela, the 'startling one', plunges 850 m into KwaZulu-Natal in five leaps, making it one of the highest waterfalls in the world.

Sunday Falls, down in the foothills and easy to reach (see Walks, p. 52).

Changing times

Mont-aux-Sources (3 282 m), which means 'the mountain of springs', was named in 1836 by two intrepid French missionaries who reached the summit above the Amphitheatre from Lesotho. Zulus and Basothos called the summit area the 'place of the eland' – emPhofeni and Pofung, respectively. Later, the region came under the jurisdiction of the colonial Natal government, which offered the first farms in the Thukela Valley for sale to white settlers.

The settlers urgently needed building material for homesteads and furniture and it did not take long before the first woodcutters arrived, among them a Mr Dooley, after whom a mountain in the Little Berg is named. One of the enormous saw blades used to cut down

One of the highest waterfalls in the world, Thukela Falls plunges 850 m from the top of the escarpment.

the centuries-old Yellowwood trees is still kept at the nearby Cavern Guest Farm. Some remnants of indigenous forest, like the impressive Gudu Bush, are within walking distance. Yellowwood trees here now seldom exceed 20 m in height. The tallest specimens can be found at Injisuthi and Normandien near Newcastle.

The area below the Amphitheatre was proclaimed a national park as early as 1906. When the government could not raise enough money, however, the project was abandoned and the land sold. It was finally

Dooley Ridge, named after a pioneer woodcutter.

Lovers of the Berg

'I would like every South African to see the Drakensberg Mountains, to know them as I know them, and to love them as I love them.'
Edith Pickwood, farmer's wife, 1878

'I have seen the Drakensberg Mountains and fallen in love with them,' noted Edith Pickwood, a spirited young woman of 19 who ran away from England to find her fortune in Natal in the latter part of the 19th century. She found it in Fenn Kidson, a farmer from Bergville in the Drakensberg. She married him and insisted they spend their honeymoon in the Drakensberg. In 1878, the adventurous young couple negotiated the upper Thukela Valley by ox wagon, camping in one of the wildest spots near the Thukela Gorge, collecting flowers on the grassy slopes during the day, listening to the call of the leopard at night. Edith was smitten from the first moment she set eyes on the Berg. 'And I shall remain in love with it till I die.'

proclaimed a nature reserve in 1916, and additional farmland has been purchased over the years. The park, which now extends over 8 000 ha, is still relatively small by South African standards. Its greatness lies rather in its diversity and attractions.

In 1941, the simple park hostel built in 1903 burnt down and was rebuilt as a proper hotel. After the British Royal family visited in 1947, the nature reserve was renamed the Royal Natal National Park and the hotel the Royal Natal National Park Hotel. The hotel's old-fashioned cosiness is now a thing of the past. In 2000, it was torn down and replaced by modern, upmarket self-catering units, However, the four Henkel's Yellowwood trees planted by the Royal couple and their two daughters remain as mementoes.

About 25 rock art sites in the Royal Natal National Park are all that is left of the first dwellers of the northern KwaZulu-Natal Berg. Some sites have been heavily vandalized; others are now in varying stages of conservation and are not currently accessible to the public. Only Sigubudu Cave is open to visitors, and anyone who visits the cave must be accompanied by an official guide.

Tendele Camp

Arguably South Africa's most enchanting mountain retreat, this quiet camp at the base of Dooley's Cliffs (2 170 m) offers spectacular views of the Amphitheatre and Thukela Valley from the luxurious lodge, self-catering chalets and cottages. A short walk through a forest patch around the corner provides an effortless opportunity to see many forest plants.

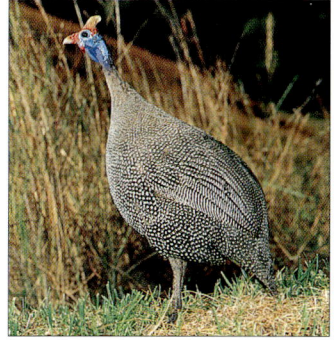

A Tendele treat – the Helmeted Guineafowl (*Numida meleagris*).

Noticeable among the forest flora are two *Streptocarpus* species – particularly *S. gardenii* – that flower throughout the summer, while Pompon Trees at the top end of the camp surprise visitors with glorious displays at Christmas. Sunbirds and butterflies are always around the showy pinkish flowers at this time, converting Tendele into a paradise for bird enthusiasts. From the comfort of a veranda, one can watch Helmeted Guineafowl, Redwinged Starlings and perhaps an Olive Woodpecker or shy Cinnamon Dove. Arrowmarked Babbler, Lazy Cisticola or Spotted Prinia also forage around the cottages. A Groundscraper Thrush or Pintailed Whydah is a common sight between the river, picnic site and the dam, which attracts Dabchick, Grey Heron and, sometimes, Egyptian Geese or a pair of Black Ducks – not to mention keen trout fishermen.

• Book accommodation (see 'Practical Tips' on p. 52) well in advance. Tendele is much in demand and places are allocated on a first-come, first-served basis. The management may be contacted directly to find out if a vacancy exists for the following day (tel 036-438 6411).

The lodge at Tendele Camp and all cottages and chalets afford beautiful views of the Amphitheatre.

An oasis for the soul, waterfalls in the landscape of the Berg, and the rich plant, bird and animal life, impart a feeling of well-being and happiness, easing tension and removing the complexities of daily life.

Wildlife
Mammals

As a rule, early morning and late afternoon are the best times to observe antelope like grey rhebok, mountain reedbuck and bushbuck. A young female bushbuck regularly visits the Mahai campsite and is quite tame.

Baboons are numerous and may become troublesome, largely because people ignore requests not to feed them. (Once they are used to being fed, baboons can be dangerous and may have to be destroyed – people, on the other hand, get away with fines of R500.) Carnivores are scarce and, with the exception of the the black-backed jackal, are seldom seen.

Visiting the campsite, a female bushbuck (*Tragelaphus scriptus*).

To see the Cape clawless otter that lives at the Mahai Dam, hide and keep quiet, or walk around the dam or along the river with a spotlight after about 10:00 p.m.

Birds

The Royal Natal Park is home to about 180 bird species. Quite a few LBJs ('little brown jobs') can be observed at Tendele. Helmeted Guineafowl, Olive and Groundscraper Thrush and Hadeda Ibis

Groundscraper Thrush (*Turdus litsitsirupa*).

are regular guests. Gurney's Sugarbirds and Malachite Sunbirds love the protea slopes, where hidden Redwing Francolins loudly herald the morning. The cool evergreen forests are preferred by Olive Woodpecker, Greater Doublecollared Sunbird, Chorister Robin, Emerald and Redchested Cuckoo.

A hike from Dooley's to Tiger Falls is worthwhile to spot Black Eagle, especially if they still nest at the top of Dooley's Cliffs. Look, too, for Lammergeier, Martial Eagle, Cape Vulture, Black Sparrowhawk and Jackal Buzzard. On the path next to the Mahai River between the camping site and reception area you may see Giant Kingfisher or Longtailed Wagtail. The locality next to the old bowling greens behind the dam is popular with 'twitchers'.

Reptiles

Snakes

At Royal Natal, which is frequented by visitors, snakes are seldom seen as most species take off when they sense human footsteps. An exception is the puff adder. Caution is advised.

Lizards

Many species are common and most can be easily spotted where there are boulders and rocks. This is true even in higher regions, as they are well adapted to harsh conditions.

Amphibians

Royal Natal's characteristic shallow waterfalls and dense vegetation provide an ideal habitat for amphibians, particularly the specialized frog species. (See lists of frogs at the back of this book.)

Common emperor moth (*Bunaea alcinoe*).

Insects

During summer, nightfall finds numerous insects, including hawkmoths and grasshoppers, gathering around the entrance to the ablution blocks in the Mahai campsite (see map). Some butterflies and moths, including impressive emperor moth species, might be encountered around the campsite during the day. Several butterflies and hawkmoths are easy to spot when proteas are in bloom.

While wandering through forest, visitors may occasionally be 'hit' by sticky droplets: these are invariably the product of the digestive process of harmless cicadas. The males' relentless, high-pitched love song (generated by a membrane that vibrates up to 400 times a second) can often be heard from hundreds of metres away.

Hawkmoth species, a conspicious visitor of proteas in bloom.

Thick-leaved *Gladiolus* species.

Flora

The Royal Natal National Park is very likely the best place to enjoy the Berg's plant diversity as most habitats are close together and easy to reach.

The vegetation of the park consists mostly of grassland, interspersed with patches of Afro-montane forest (as at Gudu Bush, Vemvaan Valley, Fairy Glen) in sheltered kloofs and expanses of protea savannah. Plant communities change considerably at different altitudes.

Grasses

Wire Grass, Weeping Lovegrass and Common Thatchgrass are found on the moist cool mountain slopes and escarpment. Endemic species occur at high altitudes, among them Blackpatch Lovegrass and Toothbrush Grass. Tussock grasses predominate in the alpine region but other grasses, such as Mountain Wiregrass and Drakensberg Danthonia, grow here too.

Wildflowers

In spring, flowering plants change the winter-brown grassland into a riot of colour. Modest euphorbias, gardenias and black-eyed susans are among the first to bloom. In September and October, members of the amaryllis and daisy families follow, joined by showy affiliates of the iris family. Many of the better-known, tall species of the lily family begin their flowering cycle around the middle of summer when smaller species are hidden in the tall grasses. Look for the Suicide Gladiolus that grows along a narrow strip between Mont-aux-Sources and the Giant's Castle area. One or two orchid species are found in the forests where they use other plants as hosts (epiphytes), but are not parasitic. Ground orchids occur mainly on top of the Little Berg and its slopes.

Proteas

All six protea species of the KwaZulu-Natal Berg grow within the Royal Natal Park. They include the extremely rare, only recently discovered, Cloud Protea or Cloud Sugarbush (Protea nubigena). To find it is a major undertaking, although it is easily identified by its multi-branched stems and very small globular flowerheads (40–50 mm across).

More common and widely spread over the whole of the Berg are Dwarf Grassveld Sugarbush and Waterlily Sugarbush. Only the fire-resistant Common Sugarbush and Silver Sugarbush grow up to 8 m tall. Both form extensive stands on south-facing slopes. A fine example of protea savannah is found on the way between Mahai campsite and Tendele hutted camp.

Cloud Sugarbush

Common Sugarbush, Drakensberg Sugarbush, Cloud Sugarbush and Dwarf Grassveld Sugarbush, collectively known as grassveld proteas, are distinguished from the mountain and savannah proteas by their hairless or near-hairless bracts. The slender, bushy Waterlily Sugarbush (or Lip-flower Protea) has easily recognized creamy-white flowers, and can grow into a 4-m high tree. It is occasionally found on stream banks, but is more abundant in sheltered areas of sub-alpine fynbos. Like most other local proteas, it flowers between December and March.

Jewel in the clouds

Nubigena *remains every botanist's dream. The Cloud Protea or Cloud Sugarbush,* Protea nubigena – *unassuming star of the proteas – is so rare one can see almost its entire habitat from the cottages at Tendele Camp. For centuries the world's rarest protea flourished in obscurity, hidden in the clouds. To this day, only a handful of people have seen its glory, and its chances of survival remain uncertain.*

More beautiful proteas can be found, especially in the Cape, but none at the altitude of P. nubigena. *Because of cloud, mist, thunderstorms and annual rainfall as high as 1 500 mm, sunlight is rare on these cliffs, even in summer. In winter, they are covered by snow and blasted by icy winds.*

Elsie Esterhuysen, one of South Africa's most distinguished botanists, discovered the unexpected botanic treasure during a winter camp in the 1960s. The plants were not flowering but she gathered a few branches bearing dried fruiting heads.

What were they like in full flower? Dr John Scotcher, then a keen young Natal Parks Board scientist, tracked down a small population of about 50 of the elusive plants, which were not in flower either. In the mid-1970s, some 18 months and many climbs later, Scotcher finally saw the plants in all their glory on a south-east-facing, almost vertical, cliff above Policeman's Helmet.

Elsie Esterhuysen had clearly discovered a new species, but for the next 10 years another of these plants was not found. Today, the Cloud Protea is known only from a single site between Policeman's Helmet Ridge and The Witches, facing Thukela Gorge at about 2 300 m.

P. nubigena *remains as mysterious as ever.*

Tourist attractions
Walks and hikes

Charming waterfalls, pockets of indigenous forest in hidden kloofs, meadows awash with flowers, San paintings in caves of bright sandstone, crystal-clear pools and streams, breath-taking panoramas and historic places await the eager explorer. The Royal Natal National Park has a well-developed infrastructure. It has over 30 walks and hikes, painstakingly mapped, marked and well maintained. A list of 22 of the best walks and hikes is given overleaf, graded according to their level of difficulty. Starting points are Mahai campsite or the Visitors Centre. Add to or subtract from the given distance if you set off from Tendele Camp.

Hiking towards Beacon Buttress and Devil's Tooth in the Royal Natal Berg.

Horse trails

Most of the terrain can be explored on horseback. The stables at Rugged Glen, which borders Royal Natal National Park, organize day rides and shorter outings. Book at the Visitors Centre.

Mountain bike trails

Mountain biking is a new activity gaining momentum in all regions of the Berg but at present still being developed. Bikers will probably be allowed on some walking paths in future. Ask at the Visitors Centre.

Drives

Route around the Berg: A trip by car from Royal Natal National Park leads to the summit of the Little Berg (2 200 m) near Witsieshoek via Oliviershoek Pass, Sterkfontein Dam and Phuthaditjhaba. Beyond Phuthaditjhaba, the sheer sandstone cliffs of the Qwa-Qwa Mountains are visible on the right and the Drakensberg range on the left. The never-ending Maloti Mountains can also be seen in the distance. Witsieshoek Mountain Resort, the highest of its kind in South Africa, offers good hospitality and accommodation. The management maintains a hide where the Bearded Vulture (Lammergeier) and other raptors, such as the Black Eagle and Jackal Buzzard, come to feed in winter. The road leads past the Witsieshoek Resort to a parking lot below the Sentinel. A short walk from here leads to a magnificent view over Royal Natal National Park to the far end of the Amphitheatre, with the Sentinel, Beacon Buttress, Eastern Buttress and Devil's Tooth straight ahead.

A footpath to the right leads to the 100 rungs of the chain ladder, from where it is a short climb to the plateau. The sweeping view from the summit over the foothills, the Thukela Valley, and the KwaZulu-Natal Midlands in the distance to the cascading Thukela Falls will be the experience of a lifetime – weather permitting. The trip can be completed in a day.

• To avoid possible theft of your equipment do not camp overnight on top of Mont-aux-Sources.

PRACTICAL TIPS

How to get to Royal Natal Park
From Harrismith via Oliviershoek Pass, or via Winterton-Bergville.

Where to stay
Tendele Camp is one of the most popular camps in South African nature reserves, offering accommodation in a lodge, cottages and chalets. Book well in advance. There is a huge caravan and camping site with modern facilities at Mahai and a smaller camp at Rugged Glen. Royal Natal has no wilderness areas, and camping outside the official campsite is not allowed. Several hotels and holiday resorts nearby.

Where to eat
There are currently no services inside the park, but a number of restaurants and hotels nearby offer good to excellent food.

Facilities
Small shop at Tourist Office and a supermarket in Bergville (50 km from the park).

Local weather
Rainfall varies from 1 000–1 300 mm at Tendele Camp to nearly 1 800 mm near the edge of the escarpment. At least 75 per cent falls between October and March, with Jan–Feb the wettest months. Snowfalls are usually expected between April and September. Insiders regard April and May as the best time to visit the reserve.

Shopping
Beautiful traditional handcrafts by local people are on sale at the park entrance and at the Thandanani Centre a few kilometres further on the road to Bergville. A traditional amaZizi kraal has been developed, tel 036-438 6653.

Information/bookings
Book hutted accommodation through Central Reservations, Box 13069, Cascades 3202 tel 033-845 1000, fax 033-845 1001. Book camping and caravan sites directly through KZN Wildlife's local office, tel 036-438 6310, fax 036-438 6231 For general information, telephone 033-845 1000/2.

ROYAL NATAL NATIONAL PARK WALKS
(return distance unless stated otherwise)

EASY TO AVERAGE	INTERMEDIATE TO DIFFICULT	DIFFICULT TO EXTREME

1 QUEENS CAUSEWAY AND CASCADES: 1,5 km

Relaxing atmosphere. Cascades gush into beautiful pools where children like to swim. A little further up, the Mahai River follows an intake point for drinking water. From here swimming and wading in the river is not allowed. An easy stroll from the campsite, trodden in 1947 by princesses Elizabeth and Margaret with their parents and General Smuts.

2 FAIRY GLEN: 1,6 km

Beautiful scenery; delightful picnic spot on hot days. After crossing the bridge opposite the Visitors Centre, a path to the left leads through bush to the Broome Hill stream. After crossing the stream twice, the path leads through the bush to the glen and waterfall.

3 OTTO'S WALK: 3 km

Extends one's knowledge of trees and ecology of the Berg. This self-guided 'educational trail' starts at the Visitors Centre and winds along the Mahai and Thukela Rivers to the park's entrance. Some trees are marked for easy identification.

4 SUNDAY FALLS: 3 km

From the Mahai crossing below the casual car park, the path leads in the direction of Surprise Ridge. The turning to the right after the first intersection leads to the falls.

EASY TO AVERAGE	INTERMEDIATE TO DIFFICULT	DIFFICULT TO EXTREME

5 SCRAMBLE UP THE LION: 4 km

Spectacular views of the Amphitheatre, Thukela Falls and Sentinel from the top (2 000 m). Across the Thukela at the gorge car park a path winds anti-clockwise up to the ridge, zigzagging through proteas and leading along the fence to the cliffs. After crossing the fence, a steep, grassy gully next to a cave leads to the top of the ridge. This walk leads outside the park and is not sign-posted.

6 MCKINLAY'S POOL VIA CASCADES: 5 km

Relaxing atmosphere, with a chance to cool off in clear water. An easy path leads from the Cascades to the pool where the Gudu stream meets the Mahai.

7 SAN PAINTINGS IN SIGUBUDU VALLEY: 6 km

Fascinating legacies of the past in congenial surroundings. The short path branches off to the left just after the bridge over the Sigubudu Stream from the tarred road to the entrance gate. Information at the Visitors Centre.

8 DEVIL'S HOEK VALLEY: 6 km

Forest walks, heart-warming scenery. Follow the gorge path from the car park. After a 10-minute walk through bush, a sign-posted path turns right up the valley. After another 10 minutes you will come to a large rock on the right. The path then leads through a large patch of forest and uphill across an open section, followed by a second patch of forest where it ends. Heavy scrambling from here on. Shortcut: start from Tendele Camp.

9 DOOLEY WATERS AND MAHAI VALLEY: 7 km

The path leads to the upper end of the Gudu Bush (see Route 11) and links up with the main bridle path overlooking the Mahai stream for about 2,5 km. Where it crosses the stream is an attractive picnic spot. The path then leads up the north-facing slope and reaches a junction: the path to Dooley Waters branches off to the left.

10 TIGER FALLS: 7 km

Magnificent waterfall surrounded by indigenous forest. From the camping grounds: bypass the Cascades and follow the very steep concrete path leading up to the viewpoint on a mighty boulder. This boulder is home to one of the many cliff and rock communities of plants scattered on the grassland. The falls are sited at the first large stream and forest patch, right under the cliffs of Dooley. Look for raptors and vultures above. Return by crossing the Mahai and going through the Gudu forest. An easier, direct path (3 km) leads from behind the historic hotel site to the Tiger Falls.

11 GUDU FALLS: 9 km

Excellent example of indigenous forest. Impressive waterfall in cool, relaxing surroundings. The falls are reached after a wild scramble through the dense Gudu Bush around the Gudu stream. Some large Yellowwood trees grow here, as well as an impressive Cabbage Tree on the left side at the foot of the scrambling path. Take a dip in the cool pool at the end of the scramble.

kwazulu-natal/northern

ROYAL NATAL NATIONAL PARK WALKS (contd.)
(return distance unless stated otherwise)

EASY TO AVERAGE	INTERMEDIATE TO DIFFICULT	DIFFICULT TO EXTREME

12 VEMVAAN VALLEY/POLICEMAN'S HELMET: 9 km

Breathtaking views from the ridge in all directions. Make an excursion to higher ground to search for the elusive Cloud Protea. Follow route 8 for about 1 600 m where a path branches to the left, crosses a stream, and leads up into the Vemvaan Valley. Proceed further into the valley or follow another sign-posted path leading to the erosion-carved Clarens sandstone of the Policeman's Helmet. Shortcut: start from Tendele Camp.

13 TENDELE CAMP VIA TIGER FALLS: 10 km

Magnificent view of Amphitheatre with Policeman's Helmet and Vemvaan Valley in foreground. The path from behind the historic hotel site to the Tiger Falls passes through grassland where antelope sometime forage. It then branches to the left and leads through beautiful Protea groves to Tendele Camp on the back slopes of Dooley. Easy route: follow the tarred road to the gorge parking lot.

14 THE GROTTO: 10 km

Walk through protea savannah. Explore two splendid gorges of the Little Berg. Connect from Mahai campsite or cross the Mahai River below the casual car park and follow the path towards Surprise Ridge. Soon after passing the four-path junction, turn left and proceed up Broome Hill Valley. Continue climbing to the left and walk the last 10 minutes to the Grotto, which consists of two enormous gorges.

15 SIGUBUDU RIDGE: 10 km

Principal walk to spot some of the smaller antelope. From the path to the San paintings (see Route 7), take the path branching to the right a short distance before the krantz and walk up to the plateau. Search for the path leading up the ridge between Sigubudu and Forgotten Valley. Start early, take your time and you will be rewarded.

16 RUGGED GLEN FOREST WALK: 11 km

From the park gate, go left onto the tarred road serving the resort on the left before joining the road to Bergville again. Pass the riding stables on the right and turn left to the Rugged Glen campsite. From here a short circular walk leads to several patches of indigenous forest. You could visit the nearby resort, formerly the Mont-aux-Sources Hotel, for a drink or meal.

17 CRACK AND MUDSLIDE: 11 km

Daring, slightly arduous excursion. Proceed through Gudu Bush (see Route 9) for another 1 200 m to the path leading towards the Crack. Climb the steep path to the top - very slippery when wet - using the short chain ladder to assist you. At the top keep on the high ground overlooking the Mahai Valley. Walk to the top of Gudu Falls and cross the Gudu River some 50 m upstream. This is a good place for a swim and picnic. You can scale Ploughman's Kop if you still yearn for magnificent views, or return straight down the difficult Mudslide if you do not suffer from vertigo. The descent from the far corner of Ploughman's Kop is very steep and can be slippery. Use the short chain ladder at the start. Once you have reached the foot of the cleft, it is easy going home.

EASY TO AVERAGE	INTERMEDIATE TO DIFFICULT	DIFFICULT TO EXTREME

18 CASTLE ROCKS: 13 km

Take the path to the Grotto (see Route 15), but turn right before entering the main bush. Turn left shortly after crossing the stream. When you reach the trees below the krantz, turn left and follow the sandstone. A sign points to a hole in the rock face. Walk through and scramble up the steep grassy slope to the top. Start your trip early to give you enough time to explore the unspoilt surroundings. Return by the same route.

19 SURPRISE RIDGE AND CANNIBAL CAVE: 22 km

Excellent views. Various Protea species. Mountain reedbuck is quite common here. Head for Sunday Falls (see Route 4), but keep to the main path leading over Sunday Falls and Sigubudu stream to the ridge and the park boundary. On a clear day the view extends as far as Cathedral and Cathkin Peaks, even Champagne Castle. A track to the left of the ridge leads to the immense Cannibal Cave, where cannibals allegedly feasted. They may even have used the big slab of rock in the middle of the cave as a butcher's block. San paintings can still be admired on the inner side of the boulder. Return home via the Grotto (see Route 14).

20 MAHAI FALLS AND BASOTHO GATE: 22 km

Picnic spot and tranquil waterfall with great views down the valley. Turn right at the Basotho Gate/Dooley Water junction and continue up the valley to the Mahai Falls. From here, the path leads up to Basotho Gate and the Witsieshoek Mountain Resort. It is now only a short walk over the ridge into the Free State, with superb views of the Maloti Mountains.

21 THUKELA GORGE: 23 km

Probably the most attractive excursion of the whole Berg. Scramble and boulder-hop through the Thukela Gorge. At the upper end dive through a deep, ice-cold pool, climb the rocks at its end and you will be rewarded with a view of the Thukela Falls cascading from the summit. Or climb the chain ladder leading to equally spectacular views of the Amphitheatre. The path follows the Thukela through patches of indigenous forest, protea savannah and, for the last 1 600 m, through the gorge forest. A good picnic spot and pictur-esque scenery wait at the end. From here a chain ladder bypasses the 60 m long tunnel and leads straight into the Amphitheatre.

Thukela Valley, view from gorge path.

22 AMPHITHEATRE SUMMIT AND MONT-AUX-SOURCES: 45 km

This is a long and strenuous hike, but very rewarding. At least two days are needed. A night under stars on the sum-mit is a must. Check bookings in advance and security status at the Visitors Centre where the Mountain Register has to be signed! Beware of thieves! Many visitors favour the much easier 'Route around the Berg' (see 'Drives' below) in an undemanding two-hour car journey. The parking lot near the Sentinel can be reached by normal sedan car.

kwazulu-natal/northern

Mnweni Triangle

This is one of the most impressive areas of the Drakensberg, offering unspoilt wilderness in its higher reaches, as well as hikes to the source of the Orange (Gariep) River. It is a paradise for mountaineers and has great potential for tourism.

Mnweni, the 'place of the finger', is an area where pinnacles, pillars, spines and columns abound to form a spectacular backdrop to the most remote part of the Drakensberg. It begins just south of the Royal Natal National Park, with Eastern Buttress and Middle Tower marking its northern limit. The P388 gravel road from the Mnweni bridge ends after about 15 km of bumpy driving – to be negotiated by a normal sedan only with the utmost care – just after Moliva's Store, famous for decades among hikers and mountaineers distancing themselves from modern amenities.

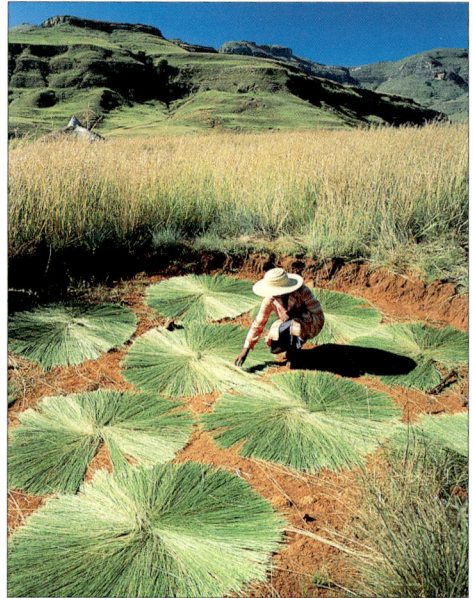

AmaZizi woman preparing grass for basket weaving.

The Mnweni triangle (formerly known as the Upper Thukela Location) is about 30 km long and 10 km wide at places, the largest tract of tribal land in the Drakensberg region. Mount Amery, the Singathi Wall, Thaba Endanyazana and Ifidi Buttress form its upper boundary in the west. To get to its northern tip, take the gravel road branching off from

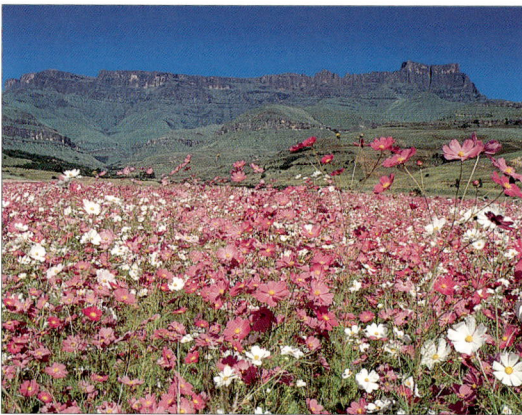

Cosmos (*Cosmos bispinnatus*), a harmless invader from Mexico, has reached the northernmost Mnweni region.

the main Bergville road just before the Royal Natal National Park, running parallel to the Singathi River through the village of Busingatha. The road ends after about 10 km, between groups of traditional homes. From here, only hiking through the as yet little-known rough country is possible.

The amaZizi, their dialect distinguished by click sounds, have lived for centuries in the Singathi Valley, and are said to be descendants of Iron Age pastoralists. The women specialize in plaiting and weaving indigenous grasses into baskets, bowls and mats, and face the challenge of selling their ingenious handiwork at a good price.

Traditional lifestyles

Further to the south and accessible only via the Isandhlwana Police Post lies the greater part of the Mnweni triangle, guarded by giants like Ifidi Buttress (3 218 m), Mponjwana (3 117 m), Mnweni Pinnacles (3 100 m) and the Saddle (3 153 m). These are the backdrops of the amaNgwane tribal area, where a rapidly growing population of some 10 000 lives in the green valleys, venturing into the upper reaches in search of grazing or firewood. Dagga (cannabis) has become an important crop and an increasingly important source of income. To avoid detection, it is mostly planted in remote areas, sometimes on steep slopes right under the giants of the high Berg.

The amaNgwane probably settled in the Mnweni area after fleeing from Shaka's warriors, and were later used as a buffer between cattle-raiding Bushmen and white stock farmers. Their settlements, culture, rituals and material life are little different from what they were a century or two ago.

Although a few roads and bridges make the area more accessible, this is a place where one expects to encounter hardy mountaineers, cattle rustlers and police patrols searching for dagga smugglers coming down steep passes; a place from which loners return with tales about huge dagga fields, unknown peaks and San caves.

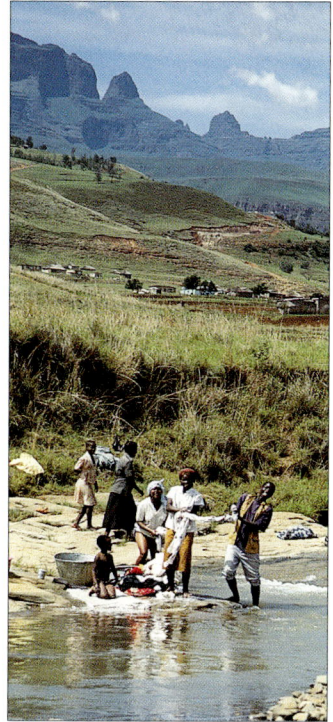

Washerwomen at the Mnweni River.

Traditional homes enjoy spectaclar views in the foreground of the lofty Mnweni Pinnacles.

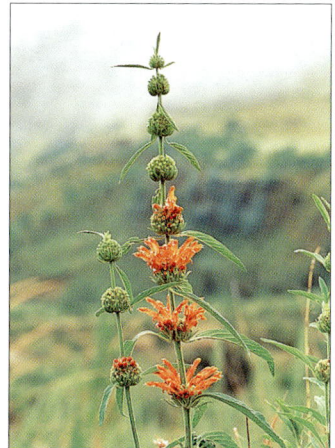

Wild Dagga (*Leonotis ocymifolia*) – not the real thing.

Woodstock Dam – a link in the Thukela-Vaal water management scheme – amid unspoilt wilderness.

Plans for ecotourism

The amaZizi and amaNgwane share the Berg watershed with Lesotho. The Mnweni River and its tributaries form one of the most important high-water catchment areas in South Africa. Like the Thukela, the Mnweni flows into nearby Woodstock Dam. This is linked to Spioenkop Dam and Kilburn Dam and most of its water finds its way to the highveld, transferred there via the daring Thukela-Vaal Water Scheme. Until now, the local people have benefited little from the scheme but plans are afoot at last to improve their living conditions, as well as to secure urgently needed environmental and cultural conservation.

Cultural and nature-based tourism is envisaged by the tribal council, assisted by non-governmental organizations and the KwaZulu-Natal Tourism Authority. Plans include a cultural craft and rock art centre, hiking base camps, hiking and horse trails, cultural tours and guided trails to rock-art shelters – all run by the community. A programme to remove alien plants is already in progress.

As soon as the necessary infrastructure is in place and the area's scenic wonders are properly accessible – with the catchment/wilderness areas remaining protected and the pitfalls of the past being avoided – the Mnweni wilderness will be without equal. Among the 10 or more peaks, all over 3 000 m high, and the dozen or so caves, many with priceless San paintings, there is a wealth of unspoilt nature waiting to be explored.

Wildlife and flora

Once developed to its potential, wildlife viewing should be similar to that in the Royal Natal National Park. To date, however, the area has hardly been researched, and detailed lists of the creatures to be found in the higher regions are not available.

In the lower valleys, the natural vegetation has declined sharply and has been infiltrated by a variety of exotic species. Surprisingly, imposing Paperbark Thorn Trees still grow in healthy numbers and seem largely to have escaped the axe of the seeker of firewood.

Paperbark Thorn (*Acacia sieberiana*).

Tourist attractions
Walks and hikes

Countless footpaths on the slopes are interwoven into a fine network leading to the central Mnweni plateau. However, they are not always easy to follow, and hikes through the wilderness are long, arduous, and sometimes dangerous. The time when Moliva's Store nearby was the starting point for all hikes is long over: Moliva Livay Hlongwana has rested since 1981 facing the mountains, a few paces behind his store.

Nowadays, a trip along the Mnweni River, usually starts from the Isandhlwana Police Post, where the mountain register has to be signed. With one exception, all hiking trails up to the majestic peaks of the Mnweni area start here. Cars may be parked under a tree inside the fenced compound. 'Be careful,' warns the policeman on duty, 'especially close to the Lesotho border. There are many dagga smugglers about.'

Moliva's store – once the universal starting point of hikes into the wilderness.

EASY TO AVERAGE	INTERMEDIATE TO DIFFICULT	DIFFICULT TO EXTREME

23 SINGATHI CAVE AND SINGATHI WALL (3 010 m)

The only route that starts from the end of Busingatha Valley near Royal Natal National Park.

24 EXPLORATION OF THE INTONYELANA RIVER

This river flows into the Mnweni just 1 km beyond Moliva's. Alternatively, follow the path turning left near the school, about 1,5 km beyond the police post. It skirts along Scramble Kop (1 777 m) and leads to Makhawela's Kraal where the river splits into iNtonyelana empumalanga and iNtonyelana entshonalanga. The path along the latter, the 'setting sun', leads to the right, up Scaly Cave (2 356 m) and further to Rockery Pass.

25 IFIDI PASS AND PINNACLES (3 200 m)

The path follows the Mnweni River to its junction with the Ifidi River and proceeds through the valley, past Cycad Cave, to the escarpment. The route requires some dangerous rock climbing and should be led by competent mountaineers. Minimum three days.

26 ICIDI PASS AND BUTTRESS (3 243 m)

The route leads through the Mnweni Valley past Mlambu's Kraal and Shelter up into the Icidi Valley and past Grasscutter's and Jubilee Cave to the escarpment. Potentially dangerous rock scrambling required.

27 MBUNDINI BUTTRESS AND STIMELA PEAK (3 232 m)

Same as route 26 but after Mlambu's Kraal follow the path to the left, which joins the Mnweni Valley near 5-Star and Shepherd's Caves after about 4 km. Take a right turn into the Mbundini Valley and the fork to the right after a further 3 km to the Mbundini Cave and escarpment.

28 FANGS AND FANGS PASS (3 050 m)

Follow route 27 but take the fork to the left and proceed through the pass to Fangs Cave and the Lesotho border at the top of the escarpment. A 1 km long path on Lesotho soil joins the route past Mont-aux-Sources to the chain ladder and Sentinel car park. Passport required.

29 THE TRUE SOURCE OF THE ORANGE (GARIEP) RIVER

Up Rockeries Pass, past Mponjwana or Rockeries Towers (3 117 m) and the quadruplet pinnacles Eeny, Meeny, Miny, Mo (3 000 m) leads to the true source of the Orange River, the river Senqu or Sinque. The path along iNtonyelana empumalanga, the 'rising sun', continues to Waterfall Cave (1 842 m) and proceeds into Lesotho via the iNtonyelana Pass. The distance from Moliva's to the pass is about 15 km as the crow flies. Return via Rockeries-Saddle path past Hlongwane's Kraal to the police post. The source can also be reached by walking along the escarpment from Royal Natal National Park or by following route 27, but proceeding straight past 5-Star and Shepherd's Cave to Chichi Bush Camp. The Mnweni Pass is about 2 km further on.

Note: *Exact distances are not available at present. Please consult a map of the Berg to work out your route.*
(Reliable maps at a scale of 1:50 000 are readily available, see page 172.)

PRACTICAL TIPS

How to get to the Mnweni area

amaZizi country is easily reached from the Royal Natal National Park. Turn into the gravel road (very slippery when wet!) to Busingatha opposite the Thandanani Handcraft Centre. The road ends after about 10 km. A path for herding cattle follows the Singathi Valley up to Singathi Cave. After that, it is heavy-going through the Singathi Valley to Mount Oompie (2 871 m) Ifidi (3 219 m), Ifidi Cave and Ifidi Pass. To get to the amaNgwane tribal area: from Bergville, take the Rookdale fork, the turn-off right before the Mnweni bridge to the left (P388). Proceed along the Mnweni River until you arrive at the Isandhlwana Police Post. Another 6 km further and you come to the famous Moliva's Store.

Where to stay

No accommodation is available in the area, except in caves. Follow the rules when sleeping in caves (see 'Cave etiquette', page 171). Alternatively, bring your own tent.

Where to eat

Bring your own food.

Facilities

None, except for small stores and bottle stores.

Local weather

Similar to Royal Natal National Park's.

Information

KwaZulu-Natal Tourism Authority, Box 2516, Durban 4000; tel 031-304 7144, fax 031-305 6693 email: info@tourism-kzn.org

Bookings

Bookings not necessary at present for hikes or caves.

• Good hiking maps of the area (see page 172) and a compass are essential. All hikers should report at the police post and sign the mountain register there. It is also the best and safest place to park your car, as a few trees provide some shade. You could also use it as an emergency camping ground.

Warning

Extreme caution is advised! Most of the routes in the Mnweni area are long to very long and can be dangerously difficult. All excursions should be planned and executed with great care. There is no contour path linking up to the Royal Natal National Park and the Cathedral Peak wilderness area. Only caves or your own tents provide shelter, some of the caves at lower altitudes being permanently occupied by the local people.

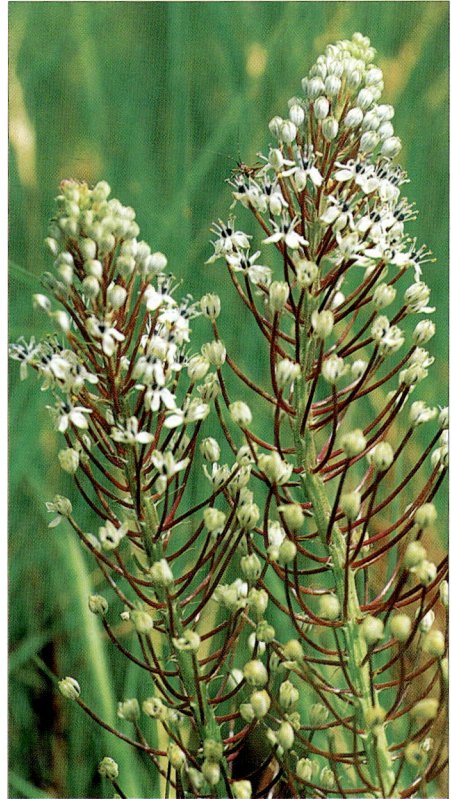

White Scilla (*Scilla nervosa*).

Bergville

0 15 km

N E W S

Winterton

Berghaven
Mountain Splendour

R600

Drakensberg
Sun Hotel

Inkosana Lodge

Dragon's Peak

Jacobs Ladder

Dingaan's Cave

Manzimahle

LITTLE BERG

Stable
Cave

Monk's Cowl

Champagne Castle

Monk's Cowl
Mountain Reserve

Injisuthi

Didima Special
Conservation Area

Blind Man's Corner

Cathedral
Peak

Mike's Pass

Leopard Cave

Cathkin Peak

Upper Ndedema

3148m

Champagne
Castle

Cathedral Peak

Arendsig

3245m

Cathedral Peak
Mountain Reserve

Mdedelelo
Wilderness Area

iNkosazana Cave

Old Woman
Grinding Corn

Battle Cave

Cathedral
Peak

Tseketseke

Windsor
Castle

Little Sugarloaf
Saddle

2986m

Outer
Horn

Inner
Horn

3004m

3011m

2723m

Triplets

The Bell
2928m

3005m

Cleft Peak

3065m

3071m

3187m

Injisuthi
Dome

Didima
Buttress

Didima
Dome

Mafadi
3446m

3450m

3277m

L E S O T H O

Central KwaZulu-Natal Drakensberg

The Central Berg begins beyond the Mnweni triangle and ends
about 60 km further south at Giant's Castle. It includes many mountain
reserves – Cathedral Peak, Monk's Cowl/Champagne Valley, Injisuthi
and Giant's Castle Game Reserve – connected via the contour path that
runs between Little Berg and Escarpment. These reserves are also
gateways to huge wilderness areas – a paradise for the spirited hiker
and mountaineer and protection for innumerable caves and overhangs
that shelter the rich legacy of San rock art.

Map labels:
White Mountain Holiday Resort
Estcourt
Mooi River
Hillside Gate
Bushman's River
Witteberg Gate
World's View
Lammergeier Hide
Meander Hut
Giant's Castle Game Reserve
Giant's Hutted Camp
Main Cave Museum
pple Peak
31m
The Thumb
Mountain Huts
Vulture Hide
Bannerman Pass
Mt Durnford
Kambue
Giant's Hut
Giant's Castle 3316m
Giant's Castle Pass

At the foot of Monk's Cowl mountain, Champagne Valley has the densest and most wide-ranging spread of modern tourist facilities. A drive of about 60 km from Monk's Cowl brings the traveller to Injisuthi, past the world's most varied potholes, and into a rural lifestyle that contrasts sharply with that of neighbouring Champagne Valley. Injisuthi is actually part of Giant's Castle, the last of the central reserves and one of Africa's oldest conservation areas. It still protects precious San rock art and the once-doomed eland, herds of several hundred of which can sometimes be seen here in summer.

Until the mid-1970s, parts of the central Berg were the mecca of only serious hikers and mountaineers. More recently, the area has been discovered by others yearning for peace and tranquility, or simply looking for fun – walking, swimming, overnight hiking, mountain biking, adventuring, star-gazing, art and food appreciation, as well as golfing, tennis, horse riding and angling.

Accommodation ranges from campsites without facilities to increasingly stylish hutted camps. Traditional caravanning, five-star hotels, holiday homes and timeshare chalets are among many available options.

Truly the core of the Berg, the central escarpment boasts some of South Africa's highest peaks, including a range of monumental free-standing peaks. Hidden valleys conceal caves filled with precious San rock art, Didima Gorge in the Cathedral Peak area containing the greatest concentration of San rock art in the entire Drakensberg region. The central Berg is also known for its thriving Drakensberg Cycads.

Past and present in the central Berg (from left to right): Ground Hornbill (*Bucorvus leadbeateri*); rock art in Main Cave, Giant's Castle Reserve; traditional craft in the hands of a friendly vendor.

Towns and villages

Estcourt, the hub of the KwaZulu-Natal midlands, was founded in 1848 as a military post to control the cattle raids by San people. Fort Durnford, built in 1874 after the Langalibalele rebellion (see 'A black day at the pass', page 91), is now the town's local history museum. It has models of the Langalibalele clash near Giant's Castle Game Reserve and local battles during the Anglo-Boer War. An amaNgwane Zulu kraal and a fine collection of bird's eggs are also on display. The Moor Park Nature Reserve – administered by KZN Wildlife – is situated at the head of the nearby Wagendrift Dam, which offers good fishing, water sports and swimming. **Mooi River**, 30 km south of Estcourt, is known for some of South Africa's finest stud farms. It also has the shortest tarred road to Giant's Castle Game Reserve. **Rosetta** and **Nottingham Road**, known as the place where the first trout were introduced to KwaZulu-Natal in 1884, are reached from the N3 off-ramp 12 km south of Mooi River. They form gateways to both the central and southern Berg.

Cathedral Peak Mountain Reserve

The Cathedral range inside the Mlambonja Wilderness Area forms a bulwark of basalt jutting eastwards from the escarpment. It has been eroded to form the impressive 4-km line of peaks called Mponjwana, the 'place of little horns', which includes Cathedral Peak, the Bell and the Outer and Inner Horns.

The Cathedral Nature Reserve and the north-eastern part of the Mdedelelo Wilderness Area, including the Didima Special Conservation Area, make up the 32 000 ha Cathedral Peak Mountain Reserve (once known as the Cathedral Peak State Forest), which ends at the Monk's Cowl part of the Mdedelelo Wilderness Area.

From Cathedral Peak: the outlines of (from left) Sterkhorn, Cathkin Peak and Champagne Castle.

The Cathedral range in the early morning.

Two rivers, the Mlambonja and the Didima, have carved deep valleys across the area. The Mlambonja rises somewhere between the escarpment and Cathedral Ridge, cutting through the beautiful Rainbow Gorge. Just below the entrance gate to the reserve, the Mlambonja is joined by the Didima, the valley and gorge of which are even bigger and more impressive than Rainbow Gorge, and shelter a treasure house of San rock art.

The Cathedral Peak conservation area grew out of the need to protect the sparkling waters of the Drakensberg watershed, as well as the remaining indigenous forest patches, from further over-exploitation. As early as 1880, concern was expressed in reports submitted to the colonial government. However, timber resources were further depleted in the Berg region until issuing of permits was stopped in 1922. Five years later three areas were demarcated as state forests: Cathedral Peak and the Cathkin Forest Reserve, Monk's Cowl and Cobham State Forests.

The rugged terrain along the escarpment, 1 800 m and higher, remained crown land hired out for grazing. Concern about the effect of plantation forestry on water supplies led to the establishment of a research station in the Cathedral Peak State Forest in 1938. The famous Cathedral Peak Hotel was built on private ground within the protected area in the Mlambonja Valley in the same year, and remains an enclave of luxury in the wilderness.

As late as 1948–1951, large areas such as Garden Castle, Highmoor and Mkhomazi, also became state forests, making protection of the most important water resources of the Drakensberg catchment area a reality at last. Meanwhile, KZN Wildlife (formerly the KZN Conservation Service) was entrusted with management of the consolidated area now known as the uKahlamba Drakensberg Park.

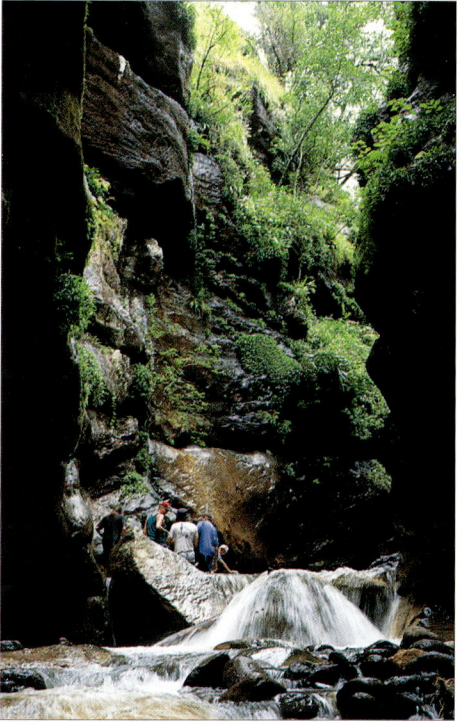

Rainbow Gorge, carved by the Mlambonja River.

How high you stand

The mountains of the Cathedral Peak conservation area contain some of the highest peaks in the region. From a bench at Arendsig at the top of Mike's Pass, an impressive row of peaks in line with the escarpment meets the eye.

From north to south, they are: the Saddle, Mlambonja Buttress, Xeni Pass Rock, Elephant, Cockade, Castle Buttress, Ndumeni Dome (which appears like an inconspicuous hillock, seemingly planted on the edge of the high plateau as an afterthought), Windsor Castle, Didima Dome and Didima Buttress.

A number of high peaks in the Cathedral Peak area, some of them rising above 3 000 m, remain unnamed.

Surprisingly, Cathedral Peak is one of the least difficult peaks to ascend and the hike to its summit is a popular excursion. However, the 8–10 hour round trip is quite strenuous and should be attempted only by those who are fit. The final assault involves a hard scramble but is worth it for the view of the deep valley of the Mlambonja River at your feet and the mountains of the escarpment that, on a clear day, seem to go on forever.

The weather

Summer rains come down in torrents, accounting for more than 50 per cent of the area's 1 000 mm annual rainfall. The wettest months are normally from January to March. Summer days are warm, though seldom hot, whereas increasing altitude turns pleasantly cool winter days into cold, frosty nights. Snowfalls occur mostly in the winter months but are possible at any time of the year in areas above 2 000 m.

As always, proceed with caution, especially in wet weather.

View of Champagne Castle range with flat-topped Cathkin Peak (on the left).

TABLE OF HEIGHTS

Nature Conservation Office	1 400 m	Cathedral Peak	3 005 m
Cathedral Peak Hotel	1 470 m	Inner Horn	3 006 m
Mushroom Rock	1 850 m	Mitre	3 023 m
Tryme	1 887 m	Castle Buttress	3 053 m
Baboon Rock	1 948 m	Windsor Castle	3 065 m
Contour Path	2 000-2 200 m	Elephant	3 109 m
Camel	2 651 m	Saddle, North	3 120 m
Pyramid	2 914 m.	Saddle, South	3 153 m
Bell	2 930 m	Cockade	3 161 m
Column	2 926 m	Ndumeni Dome	3 206 m
Outer Horn	3 005 m	Cleft Peak	3 281 m

Mike's Pass

A drive up Mike's Pass in a normal sedan car gives a sweeping view of the High Berg from the footpaths at the top of the pass or from Arendsig Hill to the right of the parking lot. Materials for road building used to be quarried from the hill, but the scar left by the old quarry is now being rehabilitated.

The scenic beauty of Mike's Pass and Arendsig outshines almost anything South Africa has to offer. Between 1947 and 1949, the Italian road engineer, G R Monzali, built the winding road along steep slopes and vertical sandstone cliffs. Although he broke his back on the first day of construction and courageously supervised construction from his wheelchair, the pass was named after Mike de Villiers, a forestry research officer who had been instrumental in establishing the research station on the Little Berg's summit in 1938.

The 10,5 km long gravel road climbs 600 m to the summit of Arendsig Hill (1 876 m) for panoramic views of the main escarpment, Cathedral Peak, the Cleft and Ndumeni Dome. In November, wildflower enthusiasts need wander only a short distance along the old jeep track to find themselves surrounded by a blaze of spring flowers. The same route can be used to look out for Ground Orchids between January and March.

Arendsig is linked to the contour path. Its parking lot serves as a starting point for hiking trails to the Organ Pipes (3 000 m) and Organ Pipes Pass, along the escarpment or down the Thuthumi River to the famous Didima Valley and Gorge (see routes 47 and 50, p. 75).

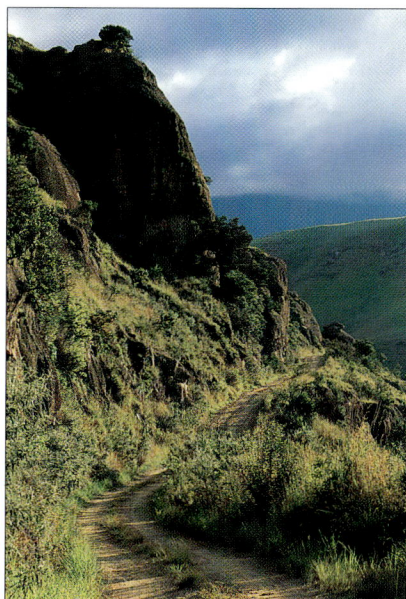
Winding up Mike's Pass.

Winter wonderland

A visit to the Berg in winter is a must.

. . . the atmosphere is crisp and invigorating, while the peaks, escarpment and grassy slopes may be blanketed in snow. To experience snow in the Berg listen to the daily weather report and be ready to depart at short notice. Recommended destinations are Himeville-Sani Pass, Giant's Castle and, especially, Cathedral Peak. The top of Mike's Pass, usually free of snow, can be reached easily in a normal sedan car for a glimpse of the spectacular winter wonderland below. The ultimate snow adventure with ski and sledge awaits the patient winter sports enthusiast around Barkly East and Rhodes in the north-eastern Cape highlands (see page 145).

• Do not forget to take warm clothing, including gloves or mittens, waterproof shoes and something to warm you from the inside. Fortunately, hotels and holiday resorts in snowy areas are usually well heated.

Didima Valley and Gorge

The Didima, 'river of reverberations', tumbles over the Didima Falls and thunders through the famous 5,5 km Didima Gorge, which is surrounded by the largest patch of indigenous forest in the KwaZulu-Natal Berg. In this unspoilt paradise, at least 17 rock shelters accommodate close to 4 000 San rock paintings, making one of the world's greatest wilderness art galleries.

KZN Wildlife has declared Didima Gorge and its environs a Special Conservation Area (SCA) because of the concentration of rock art sites. The SCA is clearly demarcated on the new hiking map for Cathedral Peak. Although hikers continue to be given access to the area, new management procedures have been initiated. Hikers may, for example, visit painted shelters only in the company of an accredited guide. Community guides operate from the Cathedral Peak gate, but hikers who obtain

Shamanistic rituals such as rainmaking are depicted in the treasure trove of rock art in Didima Gorge.

individual accreditation may lead groups without a guide. No overnighting is allowed anywhere in the SCA unless you are accompanied by a guide.

An easy 10 km walk from Arendsig brings you directly to the head of the Didima Valley, from where the path follows the upper edge of the gorge for about 5 km, with splendid views of the forest on the south-facing slope. Sebayeni Cave, the first shelter in the band of Clarens sandstone on the southern side of the valley, contains more than 1 100 paintings. Many have faded beyond

The Cathedral Peak area is known for its indigenous forest (seen here in Rainbow Gorge).

recognition since the late Alex Willcox rediscovered the cave in the mid-20th century. Among several hundred depictions of human figures, a scene of 30 antelope-headed figures attracts particular attention. It was initially thought to represent 'foreigners', but the antelope heads are now believed to depict shamans in a trance.

Two other cave-like shelters near the forest on the gorge's southern slope are ideal for overnighting, provided a guide is at hand. Poacher's Cave boasts about 200 paintings, including a rare picture of a grey rhebok resting. Leopard Cave, which can sleep about 12 people, takes its name from a painting of a cat-like figure chasing a man. Over 100 other paintings, many only fragmentary and fading rapidly, depict human figures and animals such as eland, bushbuck and rhebok.

Honour the unknown masters

Careless campers used to light fires in painted rock shelters, allowing the smoke to blacken ceilings and walls adorned with priceless San paintings. Keen photographers have been known to wet the images, using even soft drinks or urine to bring out the colours. Others have scratched the paintings or added their names to the originals, while one guide is known to have pointed out picture details by throwing stones at them.

KZN Wildlife claims that such risks to these matchless works of art have been significantly reduced in the KwaZulu-Natal Drakensberg region. The conservation service strictly controls access and, with rare exceptions, prohibits camping in painted caves. The locations of most sites no longer appear on maps available to the public. A few sites, such as Main Cave at Giant's Castle, Game Pass at Kamberg and Battle Cave at Injisuthi, have been declared national monuments and are fenced. They can only be visited in the company of a guide, a rule that now applies to any shelter containing rock art.

A rock art interpretive centre will be opened by the end of 2002 as part of the proposed upmarket Didima Camp at Cathedral Peak. It is hoped that it will create awareness of the value of rock art, and the need to protect it for future generations.

An example of rock art thought to represent shamans in trance carrying antelope.

Wildlife
Mammals

During the era of forestry administration, which came to an end in the 1980s, there was increased pressure on wildlife from hunting. With the takeover by the Natal Parks Board, the situation began to change. Where it was deemed necessary, game was re-introduced, bringing animal populations back to their former levels.

Grey rhebok (*Pelea capreolus*).

Healthy herds of eland can often be seen in summer. Shy bushbuck graze around the KZN office, and reedbuck frequent the wetlands along the Masongwane River below. Mountain reedbuck and grey rhebok are common, but the grey duiker is a rare bonus. Higher up, oribi may sometimes be sighted in isolated pockets of short grassland.

Sporadic sightings confirm that leopards still occur in the area. Small predators like genet, caracal and black-backed jackal are also present, but seldom seen. Rock hyrax (dassie) and baboon are more frequently encountered, as are both the Cape clawless otter and spotted-necked otter, which can be seen swimming and catching fish in the late afternoon at the Cathedral Peak Hotel's trout farm.

Black Eagle (*Aquila verreauxii*).

Birds

The Cathedral Peak area is good for observing raptors such as Black and Longcrested Eagle, Jackal Buzzard, Lammergeier and Cape Vulture. So far, about 130 bird species have been recorded.

When summer begins, a number of intra-African migrants return from their winter visit to other African countries. Black, Diederik and Klaas's Cuckoo, Paradise Flycatcher and Lesser Striped Swallow can be spotted quite easily around the Cathedral Peak Hotel. Four sunbird species – Malachite, Black, Lesser and greater Doublecollared – as well as Gurney's Sugarbird can be seen in the hotel gardens or at forest edges and in riverine bush and protea savannah.

The Drakensberg Siskin's sweet song is heard in alpine grassland and montane scrub. Pairs may be spotted during the breeding season from November–January; during the rest of the year, small flocks appear.

Tourist attractions
Walks and hikes
A grid of more than 120 km of footpaths makes the area famous for its walks, hikes and climbs at all levels of difficulty and duration. During holiday season, 350 to 400 hikers visit the area daily and honorary officers who know the area well will assist in working out sensible routes. (The Arendsig area on top of Mike's Pass is an excellent spot for wild flower enthusiasts.)

Trips can be started from three parking areas: at the park entrance; behind the reception office; and at the entrance boom to the Cathedral Peak Hotel. (Note that the hotel is on private property and a fee is charged for parking. Backpackers are allowed on the grounds only if they have booked accommodation.)

Dangerous camping at the edge of the escarpment.

PRACTICAL TIPS

How to get to Cathedral Peak Reserve
From the north, travel via Harrismith-Oliviershoek Pass and Bergville onto a tarred, well sign-posted district road. From the N3, turn left at the Winterton-Colenso off-ramp to Winterton. Proceed on a well sign-posted district road.

Where to stay
A caravan and camping site with 21 stands is situated under huge poplar trees outside the entrance to the Cathedral Peak Mountain Reserve. No electricity is available, and security is questionable. By the end of 2002, a new caravan and camping site inside the reserve should be open. Ten rock shelters (caves) can be booked in advance: Barker's Chalet, Bell, Ndumeni One and Two, Outer Horn, Ribbon Falls, Schoongezicht, Sherman's, Twins and Xeni. For those who want to experience the Berg in comfort, there is the Cathedral Peak Hotel in the Mlambonja Valley (tel 036-488 1888, fax 036-488 1889). Nowhere else is it possible to wine and dine so close to the High Berg – or get married in a quaint Molteno sandstone chapel with a magnificent view of the Berg. The hotel has a gym, golf course, 'cold' and heated pools, and offers horse riding, trout fishing, tennis, etc. Guided walks are organized daily, and there is a weekly day-trip to the summit of Cathedral Peak.

Where to eat
Bring your own provisions or book a table at the Cathedral Peak Hotel.

Facilities
Fuel is available at the Cathedral Peak Hotel. The nearest supermarket, bank and garage for car repairs are at Winterton (40 km).

Information/bookings
Book for for camping, caravan sites or overnight caves through the local KZN Wildlife office, tel 036-488 1880.

San rock art

Trained 'community guides' take individuals and groups on a first come, first served basis to specific rock art sites that were previously inaccessible to the general public. These guides also know numerous other sites and are prepared to lead clients on day or overnight hikes to any destination, such as the top of Cathedral Peak, Organ Pipes Pass, Cleft Peak, Didima Gorge, Rainbow Gorge and Botha's Cave. Porters can also be hired. Like the guides, they bring their own equipment and food. Get more details or make a booking at the main gate or through the KZN Wildlife office at Cathedral Peak.

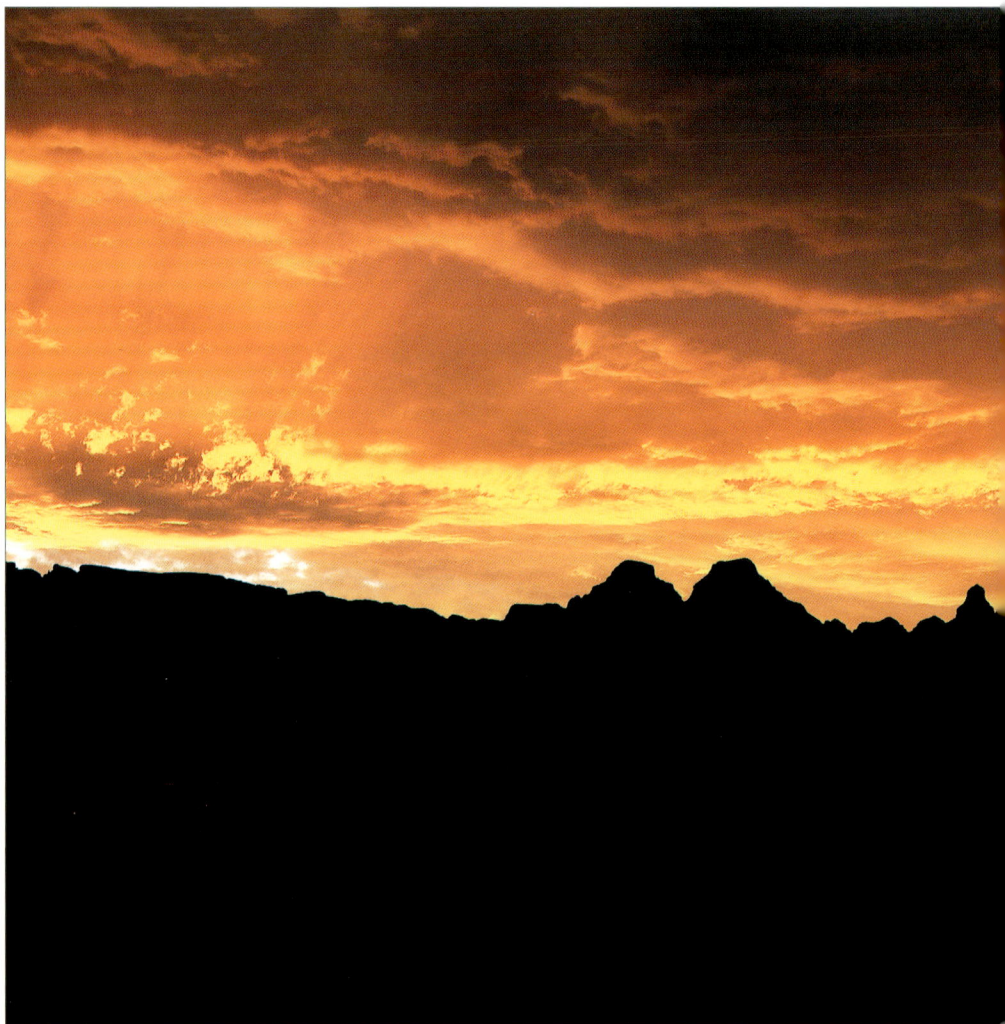

Mountain biking

Using tracks dating back to the 1960s, a 35 km route for mountain biking was laid out at Cathedral Peak from the foot of Mike's Pass to the top, and on to Didima Gorge. It offers awe-inspiring views of the escarpment. The route is also used by official and private vehicles. Further information from KZN Wildlife.

Sunset over the Cathedral range.

CATHEDRAL PEAK WALKS
(return distance unless otherwise stated)

EASY TO AVERAGE	INTERMEDIATE	DIFFICULT TO EXTREME

30 BELINDA FALLS: 1 km

A family walkabout of about 10 minutes. Ideal for a picnic while listening to the soothing sounds of a waterfall, or for a swim in the adjacent pool.

31 MUSHROOM ROCK: 5 km

Start behind the hotel complex. The hike is quite steep but relatively short and leads to the famous mushroom-shaped rock. After crossing the Nhlonhlo Stream turn right, cross a stream, turn left up a steep zigzag path. At the sandstone cliff a sign points towards Mushroom Rock, an odd example of weathering.

32 DOREEN FALLS: 5 km

Naturally picturesque. Starting at the hotel, take the path to Nhlonhlo Stream but do not cross the stream. A pathway on left leads up the river. Turn right at the sign and cross the river. Take a sharp turn left up the steps. Hire a guide to accompany you to the San paintings in a cave nearby.

33 CONTOUR PATH TO DIDIMA GORGE: 10 km

Start at the hotel. The path leads southwards below Cathedral Range to the contour path.

34 UMHLONGO VALLEY: 10 km

Lovely pools and waterfalls in the forest. A stone cairn points to Mushroom Rock. The path zigzags to the first layer of Clarens sandstone, from which there are spectacular views. About 1,2 km behind Mushroom Rock towards the main Berg there is a small tarn (dry in winter). You will be rewarded with views of the whole Cathedral range.

CATHEDRAL PEAK WALKS (contd.)
(return distance unless otherwise stated)

EASY TO AVERAGE	INTERMEDIATE TO DIFFICULT	DIFFICULT TO EXTREME

35 RAINBOW GORGE: 10 km

One of the most picturesque yet relatively easy hikes in the area. Start at the hotel or the hairpin bend below the Nature Conservation Office and follow the path to the sign at the base of the hill. After about 3 km, the path follows the Ndumeni River through lush forest with impressive Yellowwood trees, into the gorge, past rock pools, rapids and waterfalls. Another highlight is the boulder wedged between two rock faces of the gorge, which is very narrow here.

36 BLUE POOL, MARBLE BATH, NEPTUNE'S POOL AND XENI CAVE: 10 km

Start at the hotel and follow the signs.

37 CONTOUR PATH VIA ONE TREE HILL: 11 km

Set off through the Oqalweni forest, follow the zigzag path to the left and climb up the hill. From here a 30 minute walk leads to the contour path and to Royal Natal National Park.

38 BLUE POOL AND NYOSI GROTTO: 11 km

Start at the hotel and follow the Nyosi River in a southerly direction.

39 OQALWENI FOREST WALK: 11 km

Start at the hotel. The route leads past the trout hatchery along the Oqalweni Stream to one of the crystal-clear waterfalls.

40 MLAMBONJA VALLEY TO NEPTUNE'S POOL AND MARBLE BATH: 11 km

Start at the hotel and follow the Mlambonja River past the trout hatchery.

41 ROUND TRIP BETWEEN TRYME AND TARN HILL: 12 km

Allow at least half a day for this excursion, which offers spectacular views of the escarpment and its pinnacles, spires and buttresses. Explore the forest patches around Ribbon, Albert and Doreen Falls.

42 DIDIMA HIKE AND CAMPSITE: 16 km

The jeep track leads up to Solar Cliffs. Cross the Mhlwazini River below the game guard outpost. The path leads further up river to the campsite (no facilities).

43 OQALWENI VALLEY, ROUND TRIP: 17 km

Regarded as the grand tour of the valley. Start at the hotel and follow the route to the summit until the path branches off to the left beyond Sherman's Cave. Turn left here and return via One Tree Hill.

44 TSEKETSEKE HUT AND CAMPSITE: 18 km

Start at KZN office or the hotel. Path leads up from under Cleft Peak, between Cathedral Peak and Champagne Castle.

CATHEDRAL PEAK WALKS (contd.)
(return distance unless otherwise stated)

EASY TO AVERAGE	INTERMEDIATE TO DIFFICULT	DIFFICULT TO EXTREME

45 CATHEDRAL PEAK SUMMIT: 18 km

Start from the hotel or the hairpin bend near the KZN Wildlife office. The path leads up to Cathedral Ridge. Cathedral Peak is supposedly one of the easiest free-standing peaks to climb, but the last few hundred metres are extremely difficult! Rock scrambling requires a high level of fitness. Trips are regularly organized by the Cathedral Peak Hotel.

46 MLAMBONJA PASS-TWINS CAVE: 22 km

Start at the hotel and follow the Mlambonja River past the trout hatchery. Climb the Little Berg near Neptune's Pool and Marble Bath above the river.

47 DIDIMA GORGE: 27 km

Start at Mhlwazini Store. Either take a day trip to the top of the gorge and back via the same route, or a more rewarding round trip of 2–4 days, including camping en route. Do not leave your car at the Store parking area!

48 DIDIMA TO MONK'S COWL CONTOUR PATH: 28 km

A difficult 2-day hike. Distance is calculated from the contour the path at the upper end of the Didima Valley. Follow the contour path in a southerly direction through the Mdedelelo Wilderness Area.

49 MIKE'S PASS TO CATHEDRAL PEAK HOTEL VIA ORGAN PASS, ROUND TRIP: 49 km

This hike takes at least 3 days. It leads through the steep Organ Pipes Pass, traverses the escarpment and descends through Mlambonja Pass. It requires a high level of fitness and should only be attempted by those who are well equipped and under expert guidance.

50 ESCARPMENT VIA ORGAN PIPES PASS: 41 km

From Arendsig, follow the path to Didima Gorge. A sign-posted path branches off to the right at The Nek, about 2,5 km before Didima Gorge. After passing the old fire lookout, the path rises about 900 m, passing Qolo la Masoja, the 'Ridge of Soldiers'. The peak called The Column is known for its strong echo, allegedly used to maintain contact between Zulu and Basotho. Return via The Nek or the Camel (2 410 m) and Tryme Hill. The first section from Organ Pipes Pass/Windy Gap includes a dangerous section where a rope may be required.

Warden's tips

- *Rainbow Gorge gives a good idea of what the Drakensberg is all about. This walk is recommended for families, elderly people and first-time visitors.*
- *Organ Pipes is popular and calls for only reasonable fitness. Follow the route from the Nek, spend the night in the cave and sample the glorious view next morning.*
- *Walk to the 'Valley of Pools' from Solar Cliffs via Hospital Spruit to Stable Cave. Return the same way or use the circular route.*

Monk's Cowl Mountain Reserve and Champagne Valley

An exceptional feature of Monk's Cowl is that the mighty free-standing peaks and the base of the escarpment are less than 15 km away. Monk's Cowl is also a major breeding site of the Cape Vulture. According to the latest count, about 50 pairs nest in the area, most of them at the famous Vulture's Retreat (see route 76, p. 85).

Monk's Cowl Mountain Reserve lies at the upper end of Champagne Valley. It comprises the greater south-eastern part of the extensive Mdedelelo Wilderness Area and provides easy access to the Cathedral Peak Mountain Reserve. On the north west the contour path enters the reserve near the famous Gatberg Mountain (2 408 m) and connects on the reserve's southern flank with a trail to Camp.

Here, the escarpment reaches dizzying heights, with some peaks well over 3 300 m. As the scene of the first fatal climbing accident in the Berg, Monk's Cowl (3 229 m) is one of the most infamous mountain peaks. Together with the rounded dome of Champagne Castle (3 377 m) and the free-standing Cathkin Peak 3 149 m, it is among the most prominent peaks in the area. Bulky Cathkin Peak is also known as Mdedelelo, which means 'make room for him', a Zulu paraphrase of 'bully'. It almost obscures the taller Champagne Castle and, from a greater distance, hides the Matterhorn-shaped Monk's Cowl from sight. Other well-known peaks are Amphlett, Tower and the jagged Sterkhorn (2 973 m). Further to the south-west are the highest peaks in South Africa, Injisuthi Dome (3 410 m) and Mafadi (3 446 m). The odd-looking peak is Gatberg or Intunja ('the eye'), a reference to the huge hole in its basalt cap.

The well-developed Champagne Valley sparkles with facilities: Bellpark Dam; Culfargie Reserve; self-catering and B&B establishments like Champagne Cottages, Graceland and Berghaven; Dragon Peaks and Mountain Splendour caravan parks; Inkosana Lodge, which caters for back-packers; and the Drakensberg Sun and Champagne Sports Resort. It is home to the world-famous Drakensberg Boys' Choir School, and the historic Champagne Castle Hotel, founded in 1930.

The peak of Monk's Cowl (centre) between Champagne Castle (left) and the bulky Cathkin Peak (right).

Masters of the Berg

Few animals are as adaptable as the doughty baboon, which survives in deserts, between hostile farm communities and is found in many harsh and dangerous environments. It has also found a niche in the high mountains.

The findings of scientists studying the behaviour of baboon troops in different parts of the Drakensberg challenge the traditional interpretation of baboon existence and confirm that living beings are the product of their environment. Living in the Berg has considerably changed the lifestyle of baboons. Winters are very cold and mortality rates high, despite the absence of predators. Food is relatively scarce, especially at high altitudes, so that they sometimes have to forage for twice as long as their comrades in the bushveld. This leaves little time for grooming, generally used by baboons to foster team spirit.

Chacma baboon (*Papio ursinus*).

Drakensberg baboon troops seldom consist of more than 20 animals. According to a group of scientists who hiked through the Berg from the Royal Natal National Park in the north to Cobham in the south, finding and observing 330 baboon troops, the total Drakensberg population consists of an estimated 7 000 animals.

Wildlife

Mammals

Grey rhebok and mountain reedbuck stick mainly to the Little Berg, while rock hyrax (dassie) frequent sandstone cliffs. Forest-dwelling bushbuck are hard to find, but occasionally browse at the reserve's campsite, which is sometimes also invaded by cheeky vervet monkeys and baboons. Klipspringer visit the Stable Cave area but are hard to spot. On the summit, the rare Natal rock rabbit comes out to feed at dawn.

Impressive herds of eland can be spotted crossing from Injisuthi or the Cathedral Peak Reserve, and porcupine quills on the footpath hint at the presence of these nocturnal creatures. Most small predators are secretive. Not so the large spotted genet living at Keith's Bush Camp, which is quite tame.

Pieces of crab shell left by the Cape clawless otter are often found along streams and rivers but the chances of seeing this sleek and wary animal are small, unless you wait patiently at the water's edge late in the afternoon. Slogett's rat, commonly known as the ice rat, can be seen basking in the sun near iNkosazana Cave.

'Most people prefer to enjoy the Berg without too much interference by man-made noise. Many animals are stressed by constant noise pollution, too: it puts them in a constant flight mode which can lead to sickness, infertility, cannibalism and even death.'

(Anonymous)

Malachite Sunbird (*Nectarinia famosa*).

Birds

About 170 bird species have been identified at Monk's Cowl, Mdedelelo and Culfargie Nature Reserve, including most of the typical Berg species such as Bearded Vulture, Drakensberg Siskin, Malachite Sunbird and Gurney's Sugarbird. Many 'garden' birds, including Barratt's Warbler, Forest and Cape Canary, Olive Bush Shrike, Black Cuckoo-Shrike, Chorister Robin and Redchested Cuckoo, are fond of the Ouhout hedges bordering individual camping sites. In protea savannah (see routes 58 and 63, page 83), mighty boulders on scree slopes provide a habitat for Sentinel Rock Thrush, Ground Woodpecker and Bokmakierie. Local forests attract Swee Waxbill and Bush Blackcap. Crowned Eagle and other raptors may nest in Yellowwood canopies in summer.

A variety of waterbirds frequent the pond at Dragon Peaks Park. The Dragon Peaks Holiday Resort maintains a vulture feeding area. A nesting site of the endangered Cape Vulture and Bearded Vulture is hidden behind the Dragon's Back range in 300 m high cliffs of the main escarpment known as Vulture's Retreat.

Falcon Ridge, a couple of kilometres downhill, offers daily flight displays of a number of typical Drakensberg raptors, among them Black Eagle and Lanner Falcon. Contact Greg or Allison, cell 082-774 6398. These raptors can also be watched in the wild around Keith's Bush Camp.

Reptiles
Snakes

All three dangerously poisonous snakes of the Berg (puff adder, Berg adder and rinkhals) are present, as well the less dangerous Rhombic skaap-steeker. Puff adder and skaapsteeker occur up to 2 200 m on top of the Little Berg. Even the Berg adder survives on the top of the escarpment. Some harmless montane grass snakes and eastern green snakes have been spotted at lower altitudes.

• Look out for the secretive puff adder. Use a walking stick in summer and avoid shortcuts.

Spotted or rhombic skaapsteker (*Psammophylax rhombeatus*).

Lizards

Some lizard and skink species such as the relatively common Drakensberg crag lizard survive at high altitudes.

Flora

The forests of the area contain excellent specimens of Real and Outeniqua Yellowwood, White Stinkhout and Forest Num-Num. Easy-to-reach forest patches occur around Nandi Falls at the entrance to the Sterkspruit Gorge and Hlathikulu Forest. (Hlathikulu means 'tall tree' in Zulu.) Large colonies of the endangered Drakensberg Cycad grow in the sheltering iMhlwazini Valley, among them several that are 500–800 years old. Single cycads grow near Stable Cave and there are two exceptionally large ones about 2 km from Monk's Cowl camp en route to Keartland's Pass.

Red-hot Poker, Pineapple Flower and Wild Dagga grow in the tall montane grassland along the contour path. Tree Ferns predominate in open grassland and along water courses, growing up to 5 m tall. Ouhout is the only tree species that grows up to an altitude of 2 200–2 300 m, even if somewhat stunted.

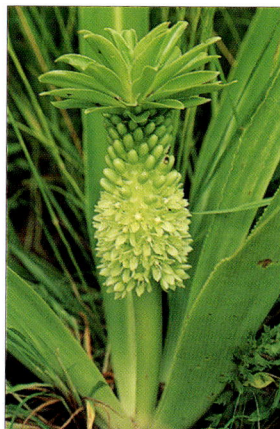

Pineapple Flower (*Eucomis autumnalis*), above. Red-hot Poker (*Kniphofia ichopensis-caulescens*), below.

Waterfall Bush

Nestled in a 14 ha mist-belt forest patch below Sterkspruit Falls is a little gem called Waterfall Bush, officially known as Bush Reserve Number 2. It can be reached by a short walk through surrounding private property, possible only if you are accompanied by one of the local guides and at a small fee. The walk leads across the boulder-strewn Maklhulumane River into the forest, which has fine examples of montane tree species embellished by delicate ferns, lichens and mosses. Watch out for the Cinnamon Dove, Chorister Robin, Starred Robin and Yellowthroated Warbler.

Saw pits dating back to the Voortrekker era some 150 years ago are still visible in the dim, green forest. Man-sized holes were excavated under the felled giants to assist in the work of carving them up by hand with immense saw blades. A few enormous Outeniqua Yellowwoods, among them one measuring 2 m in diameter at the base and bearing a Crowned Eagle's nest in its canopy, have survived the onslaught of the early woodcutters.

At Dingaan's Cave, situated on private land adjoining the reserve but linked to the trail, are San paintings depicting the arrival of the Nguni people and their livestock. They are possibly about 800 years old. An Nguni cow is clearly visible on a rock panel that also depicts eland and other game.

Tourist attractions
Walks and hikes
Monk's Cowl camp is an ideal starting point for a number of popular day walks to viewsites, cliffs, streams, waterfalls and forest patches, and for overnight hikes into the Mdedelelo and Mlambonja Wilderness Areas and to the top of the escarpment.

Useful info for hikers:
- Hikers' all-hours emergency telephone number for Monk's Cowl wilderness areas: 036-4681103.
- Beware of unexpected snowfalls, especially in the higher regions.
- Day visitors wishing to walk beyond Blind Man's Corner or Jacobs Ladder (Culfargie) are requested to fill in the mountain register.
- Distances from the campsite: Blind Man's Corner: 5,5 km; Hlathikulu Nek: 8 km; Keith's Bush Camp: 13,5 km; Gray's Pass: 16 km; iNkosazana Cave: 17 km; Champagne Castle: 19 km; Cathkin Mountain Pass: 20 km.
- Mountain campsites like Keith's Bush Camp and Cowl Fork offer no facilities.

San rock art
San rock art and other cultural sites within the conservation area can be visited only if you are accompanied by KZN Wildlife accredited guides. The guides are also available for other day or overnight hikes, and offer popular outings to nearby Zulu villages where you can meet local people and sample traditional meals. Discounts are negotiable according to the size of the group. Direct contact: cell 082-216 9974; or through the Monk's Cowl office, tel 036-468 1103. Some guided walks can be undertaken directly from Dragon Peaks Resort or the Drakensberg Sun Hotel.

The largest Paperbark Thorn (*Acacia sieberiana*) in the southern hemisphere – at Cathkin Farm.

Other attractions

- **Thokozisa Indigenous Nursery and Mountain Café** offers the opportunity to acquire some indigenous flora and plenty of information. The owner is a fundi on Drakensberg flora. You will find the nursery at the crossroads between the R600 and the district road Estcourt to Bergville, with the access road to Cathedral Peak. The first 5 km after the crossroads are gravelled and very dusty. tel 036-488 1492.

- Immediately after the turn-off to Bell Park Dam is **Cathkin Farm** where an enormous Paperbark Thorn is preserved, the canopy measuring 33 m across. It is the biggest in the southern hemisphere, claims the farm owner, who will give you the gate key to the piece of land where it stands. tel 036-468 1630.

- **Meadowsweet Herb Farm lies** about 7 km from The Nest on the road to Cayley Lodge/Bellpark Dam. View, taste and buy a variety of herbs as well as their selection of herbal ointments. tel 036-468 1216.

- **Sunset Cruises** are offered by Cayley Lodge, situated near Bell Park Dam. tel 036-468 1222.

- **Scenic Helicopter Flights** promises trips below the sheer rock faces of Champagne Castle and sunsets overlooking Wonder Valley from the Matterhorn. You may contact the pilot, cell 082-572 3949.

- Listen to performances by the famous **Drakensberg Boys' Choir.** The choir usually performs at the school every Wednesday at 15:30 during term time. tel 036-468 1012.

PRACTICAL TIPS

How to get to Monk's Cowl Reserve

Take the tarred R600 from Winterton (35 km), which leads directly to Monk's Cowl camp.

Where to stay

A caravan and campsite with 15 stands (maximum 90 persons) has ablutions with hot/cold water but no electricity. The lower section of the campsite is marked for 4x4 vehicles, as the steep road is tricky in wet weather. There are several hotels, self-catering and B&B establishments nearby: Champagne Castle Hotel, tel 036-468 1063; Dragon Peaks Resort, tel 036-468 1037; Champagne Sports Resort, tel 036-468 1088; and Inkosana Lodge, ideal for backpackers, offering B&B and advice on walks and trails, tel 036-468 1202.

Where to eat

Fast food outlets, restaurants and upmarket hotels are to be found in the area.

Facilities

Firewood, charcoal and ice are sold at the reserve's office. There are two well-stocked supermarkets nearby.

Local weather

Late March and April are the best times for overnight hiking as they are free of hail, thunder and lightning experienced from December to February. May to August is very dry. In winter blizzards are a danger at the upper levels, where temperatures can drop to -20°C, especially in September when high winds blow from the Lesotho highlands. Thermal gear is advised for hikers.

Information/bookings

Campsites, caves and overnight hikes are booked directly through Monk's Cowl's officer-in-charge, Private Bag X2 Winterton 3340; tel 036-468 1103. Community guides: cell 082-216 9974 or tel 036-468 1103.

A hike on the summit leads from Amphitheatre (right) via the Mnweni escarpment to Monk's Cowl and Champagne Vall

MONK'S COWL & CHAMPAGNE VALLEY WALKS
(return distance, starting at Monk's Cowl camp, unless otherwise stated)

EASY TO AVERAGE	INTERMEDIATE TO DIFFICULT	DIFFICULT TO EXTREME

51 FERN FOREST: 1 km

A short and easy walk which starts at the Drakensberg Sun Hotel and leads to a picnic spot next to a waterfall.

52 THE GROTTO: 15 km

Start at the Drakensberg Sun Hotel and follow the path through the golf course. This walk is only for the fit, involving much climbing over rocks and streams. The first half is through indigenous forest, while the return trip is through the fern forest.

53 SAN PAINTINGS FOR VISITORS IN A HURRY: 15 km

Start at Dragon Peaks Resort for a short walk to an easily accessible rock art cave with 15 or more paintings.

54 THE CASCADES: 2 km

Start at the Drakensberg Sun Hotel. Steep slopes, wonderful views.

55 STERKSPRUIT FALLS: 2,5 km

Well sign-posted from the camp, this is an easy round trip to an enjoyable waterfall but is not an ideal spot for photographs as the falls are fenced in and the viewpoint is above them.

56 CRYSTAL FALLS AND SPHINX: 3 km

Follow the sign-posted path southwards, turn west to the Sphinx and continue to Breakfast Stream. This is a popular route into the Little Berg, with good views from the summit of Hlathikulu Forest and Sterkspruit Valley.

EASY TO AVERAGE	INTERMEDIATE TO DIFFICULT	DIFFICULT TO EXTREME

57 MAKLHULUMANE ROCK: 5 km

Take the route to the Mpofana (Sterkspruit) River, cross the river and head up the first rocky ridge. Follow path for about 2 km. The huge boulder with forest behind it is Maklhulumane Rock. Return by the same route.

58 STEILBERG: 6 km

Follow route 57 past the rock and walk along the Little Berg's slope and through some forest patches, close to the eastern border of Monk's Cowl Reserve. The end of the spur is known as Steilberg.

59 HLATHIKULU FOREST TRAIL: 7 km

The circular route leads into the Mpofana River Valley. Boulder hopping or wading is required when the path crosses the river. The path soon enters the forest, which is ideal habitat for forest birds. During the hike almost every important Berg habitat type, from protea savannah to grassland and riverine shrub can be seen. Return via the direct path from Nandi Falls and Gorge to the camping site after crossing the river again.

60 BARRY'S GRAVE AND THE GROTTO: 7 km

Short round trip starts at Drakensberg Sun Hotel outside the protected areas and leads through grassland, a wattle plantation and Fern Forest, past Barry's Grave towards the Grotto. Ensure you carry your permit (available at Hotel reception) if you want to scramble up to the Grotto, which is part of the Monk's Cowl Reserve.

61 SUNSET TRAIL: 8 km

This is a popular self-guided medium-distance hike to Little Berg viewpoints. Take the route past the Sphinx and Breakfast Stream. Allow for a short detour to a ledge overlooking Wonder Valley with its magnificent forests and cliffs. Return through protea savannah and riverine bush, descending a hill known as Matterhorn (1 995 m). Still time to proceed to Champagne Castle Hotel for a sundowner?

62 STABLE CAVE AND JACOB'S LADDER (VIA STEILBERG OR GROTTO): 9,5 km

This day walk starts at the Drakensberg Sun Hotel. Starting from the camp adds about 4 km to the trip. The path, steep in parts, leads along ridges and down slopes to the top of the Little Berg past Van Damm's Cascades and Jacob's Ladder, where it zigzags through sandstone cliffs and protea savannah before reaching Stable Cave, which has been extensively used by local people. Look for vultures roosting in the cliffs. Permit available from hotel reception.

63 SPHINX TO SHADA RIDGE: 10 km

Follow the route past Blind Man's Corner via Crystal Falls and the Sphinx. The path takes you to the top of the Little Berg and through protea savannah to Blind Man's Corner, with the escarpment towering ahead, Cathkin Peak on the left and the Amphlett on the right. Return via Keartland's Pass below mighty sandstone cliffs. About 2 km from the camp, are two large Drakensberg Cycads growing very close to the path.

EASY TO AVERAGE	INTERMEDIATE TO DIFFICULT	DIFFICULT TO EXTREME

64 BLIND MAN'S CORNER TO INJISUTHI: 15 km

Take the path via Shada Ridge and Van Heyningen's Pass. The path from the camp links up with the contour path leading southwards to Shada Ridge, from where Monk's Cowl and Champagne Castle can be seen at close range. Injisuthi Mountain Reserve camp lies about 10 km to the south.

65 NANDI GORGE AND NANDI FALLS: 25 km

The return trip from the falls via the Mpofana (Sterkspruit) River leads into the gorge. Some boulder hopping is required. A different return route runs eastwards across the Little Berg and down the Sphinx. Nandi's Falls is a beautiful place to relax and forget the world.

66 ASCENT OF CHAMPAGNE CASTLE: 21 km

Follow the route to Gray's Pass. The contour path leads around Cathkin Peak, Sterkhorn and the Tower, and continues to Amphlett and Hlathikulu Nek. The ascent is steep but no rock climbing is required. The path is eroded in many places. The alternative route via Ship's Prow is strenuous and treacherous.

67 GATBERG VIEW: 22 km

Take the path to Blind Man's corner via Crystal Falls. Turn right onto the contour path and continue towards Hlathikulu Nek (2 650 m). The Gatberg can be seen at the end of the range known as Dragon's Back. A sweeping view down the iMhlwazini Valley reaches as far as Eagles and Didima Gorge.

68 ZULU CAVE AND SAN ROCK ART: 22 km

A moderate overnight hike. Take route 67 to Hlathikulu Nek and turn right onto the path to Zulu Cave along the iMhlwazini River.

69 IMHLWAZINI VALLEY: 24 km

Follow the route to the Sphinx, ascend and follow the contours to the top of Hlathikulu forest. From here continue downwards into the iMhlawazini Valley and along the river.

70 MONK'S COWL TO DIDIMA GORGE: 24 km

One-way trail around Hlathikulu Forest along the bridle path to Blind Man's Corner. Follows contour path to Hlathikulu Nek. Left into iMhlwazini Valley to Eagle Gorge. Path criss-crosses iMhlwazini River to Lower Didima campsite.

71 ROCK ART TOUR TO DIDIMA GORGE: 24 km

One-way trail. Spend the first night in Zulu Cave (see route 68). On the second day pass through the iMhlwazini Valley down to Didima Gorge. The second night can be spent in Leopard or Eland Cave. This trail must be booked through community guides, who will provide return transport.

EASY TO AVERAGE	INTERMEDIATE TO DIFFICULT	DIFFICULT TO EXTREME

72 MONK'S COWL TO INJISUTHI: 25 km

Weekend walk for the reasonably fit. Take the path to Blind man's Corner via Crystal Falls or Keartland's Pass and follow the historic contour path for about 4 km to Shada Ridge or proceed down Van Heyningen's Pass to Injisuthi Camp.

73 CLIMB UP GATBERG (INTUNJA): 25 km

Take route 63 to Blind Man's Corner and proceed along the contour path past Hlathikulu Nek around Amphlett to Keith's Bush Camp. Spend the first night at the camp and the second at Zulu Cave.

74 TRAIL AROUND CATHKIN PEAK: 28 km

Take route 67 to Gatberg View. Turn left up the iMhlwazini Valley between Dragon's Back on the right and Sterkhorn on the left (2 973 m) to Keith's Bush Camp. From here it is quite strenuous going down the watershed between Monk's Cowl (right) and Cathkin Peak and Champagne Castle (left). After 4 km a well-defined link path leads back to the contour path between Shada Ridge and Blind Man's Corner. The views are breathtaking. Turn left for Blind Man's Corner and take the path back to the camp.

Cathkin Peak, Sterkhorn, Amphlet and Tower.

75 GRAY'S PASS AND INKOSAZANA CAVE: 30 km

Follow route 73 to reach Keith's Bush Camp at the back of Sterkhorn after 15 km. Gray's Pass and the cave are situated about 3 km from here. Heavy scrambling is involved!

76 VULTURE'S RETREAT AND CHAMPAGNE CASTLE: 35 km

A steep climb up Gray's Pass ends at the upper iNkosazana River where a waterfall freezes solid in winter. Good view of Vulture's Retreat. Look across a cutting to The Litter to see the large colony of Cape Vulture 200 m away. Finally, slog your way to the top of Champagne Castle. Overnight in iNkosazana Cave near the top of the pass, about 3 km from Champagne Castle.

77 CLIMB TO THE TOP OF STERKHORN: 35 km

Plan as a 2-day hike. The route leads from Blind Man's Corner along the contour path past Hlathikulu Nek around the Amphlett to Keith's Bush Camp on the western site of Sterkhorn.

78 CLIMBING CHAMPAGNE CASTLE: 40 km

Take route 73 to Keith's Bush Camp. Proceed next day up Gray's Pass and turn left after reaching the escarpment. Walk along the South African border with Lesotho for about 2,5 km when you will see the 3 377 m summit in front of you. Watch out for Ship's Prow Pass if you want to proceed further on a circular route. It is extremely steep and dangerous, especially in the rainy season. Attempt only with experienced hikers during dry weather.

Injisuthi Mountain Reserve

Solitude and breathtaking views from the campsite and mountain paths are two of the Injisuthi Mountain Reserve's trump cards, but perhaps its best feature is its proximity to sparkling rivers crossed by wooden bridges originally built by Howick Boy Scouts.

Injisuthi, as the name 'well fed dog' suggests, must once have been rich in wildlife, its remoteness helping to preserve the game. The reserve still offers the quiet seclusion that was its trademark during its period as the private Berg resort 'Solitude'. When it was taken over by KwaZulu-Natal Nature Conservation, it was renamed Injisuthi and incorporated into the northern part of Giant's Castle Game Reserve, although it has kept its own access road and facilities.

The Injisuthi Valley offers some of the most spectacular scenery of the KwaZulu-Natal Drakensberg range. Overseas visitors

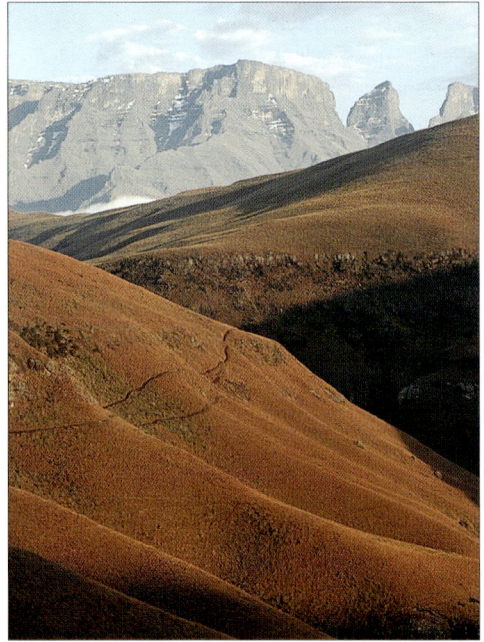

Champagne Castle and Monk's Cowl, within a day's walk from Injisuthi Valley.

Crossing the Injisuthi River.

have declared the view from the Little Berg next to Van Heyningen's Pass to be the 'best in the world'. The excellent contour path, extended by forester Van Heyningen to Wonder Valley, links the resort with Giant's Castle Reserve and the neighbouring Mdedelelo Wilderness Area. This serves to expand walking and hiking opportunities, although the routes to the summit from Injisuthi are a challenge intended for serious hikers.

To the north the towering Champagne Castle, Monk's Cowl and Cathkin Peak are within a day's walk. The panorama of the giants continues southwards with Old Woman Grinding Corn (2 986 m) at the northern border, followed by the Ape (3 096 m), Leslie's Pass (3 104 m), the Greater Injisuthi Buttress (3 202 m), Red Wall (3 212 m) and Pople Peak (3 315 m). South Africa's highest peak, Mafadi (3 446 m), and Injisuthi Dome (3 410 m), the second highest, are close by.

Wildlife

Mammals

Eland are often encountered during walks and hikes. They visit the camp in winter, knocking over dustbins, and making short work of newly planted shrubbery and trees. Reedbuck, duiker, rhebok and the elusive oribi are also found in the area, while klipspringer can sometimes be seen close to the escarpment. Cape clawless otter frolic now and again in Poacher's Stream.

Birds

A comprehensive birdlist is not yet available. Possible sightings include Chorister Robin, Gurney's Sugarbird, Redcollared Widow, Pintailed Whydah, Kurrichane and Olive Thrush, Buntings and Rednecked Francolin, as well as Lammergeier, Jackal Buzzard and Longcrested Eagle. A little magic for children is that the (reintroduced) Helmeted Guineafowl may be fed. Seed is sold in aid of the Ezemvelo KZN Wildlife Conservation Trust.

Flora

The patch of indigenous forest near the Injisuthi campsite harbours spectacular Real Yellowwood trees, some around 1 000 years old. The Common Cabbage and Mountain Cabbage Tree can be seen on short walks along rivers and streams.

Many wild flowers find ideal habitats along the Injisuthi River, and a walk along the river from the camp-site to the reserve's entrance is rewarding at almost any time of year.

Yellowwood (*Podocarpus* sp.) in indigenous forest at Injisuthi.

How to get to Injisuthi Reserve

Take the R600 from Winterton. After 14 km, turn left to Loskop and then right to Injisuthi. From the N3 outside Estcourt take the road to Loskop and after 24 km, take the road to Injisuthi. Maps show this road as tarred for the 30 km to the entrance gate of the reserve, but the potholes are so bad in places that you yearn for a simple, solid gravel road.

Where to stay

Hutted camp has 16 six-bed cabins, fully equipped and self-contained. Electricity is switched on from 17:30 to 22:00 but only one plug point is available (at the camp office) for emergency recharging, etc. There are two dormitory cabins with eight beds each. Camping and caravan site accommodates 100 persons. Hot/cold water available, but no electric light.

Where to eat

Bring your own food, but beer, braaipacks and bread are sold at the office shop. The nearest supermarkets and other facilities are at Estcourt (60 km).

Facilities

Freezer space and day rucksacks are available for hire.

Bookings

Bookings for hutted camp and dormitories through Central Reservations, Box 13069, Cascades 3202 tel 033-845 1000, fax 033-845 1001. Camping and caravan bookings through camp manager, tel 036-431 7848, fax 036-431 7849.

Tourist attractions

Walks and hikes

Several short and long hikes can be undertaken from the camp. Especially recommended is a tour to Wonder Valley, which is more easily reached from here than from Monk's Cowl Camp. Visitors can stay overnight at Lower and Upper Injisuthi Caves, Grindstone Cave about 3 km away in the Mdedelelo Wilderness Area, and Marble Bath Cave.

San rock art

A highlight of the area is a guided tour of Battle Cave (see route 86), famous for its rock painting of a massive battle. The guided walk to Battle Cave starts at 08:30 from the office, where bookings must be made and paid for a day in advance.

INJISUTHI MOUNTAIN RESERVE WALKS
(return distance, starting at camp, unless otherwise stated)

EASY TO AVERAGE	INTERMEDIATE TO DIFFICULT	DIFFICULT TO EXTREME

79 YELLOWWOOD FOREST AND OLD KRAAL: 2,5 km

These sights are best tackled on a short circular walk. From the office take the Cowl Stream fork and turn left to the walls of the Old Kraal at the top of the incline.

80 GORGE POOLS: 5 km

The three pools in the Injisuthi River, enhanced by a waterfall and a cool forest patch, are ideal places for a splash on lazy summer days. They are reached by two paths branching off from the tar road at the guardhouse near the entrance.

81 LITTLE BERG: 8 km

After about 3 km a path branches off to the right from the direct route to Van Heyningen's Pass and leads to a spectacular view over the escarpment of the central Berg. Most of the surrounding peaks can be seen.

82 MARBLE BATHS AND CAVE: 26 km

Choose the route to Fergy's Cave. Take the right fork shortly before Island camp and follow the path along Old Woman Stream in a northerly direction along the boundary between Giant's Castle Game Reserve and Monk's Cowl Wilderness. A path branches off to the left at Junction Cave, reaching Marble Baths after about 2,5 km. Return or stay overnight in Marble Bath Cave.

EASY TO AVERAGE	INTERMEDIATE TO DIFFICULT	DIFFICULT TO EXTREME

83 CENTENARY HUT: 22 km

Take the route to Fergy's Cave and go 4 km beyond it to the hut at the base of the contour path. It is one of three hikers' huts strategically placed along the contour path.

84 WONDER VALLEY AND CAVE: 20 km

Go up Van Heyningen's Pass to the viewpoint, then on to Wonder Valley and Wonder Cave 3 km further. Return or stay overnight in the cave.

85 GRINDSTONE CAVES VIA CATARACT VALLEY: 13 km

Walk through Yellowwood Forest, cross the bridge and follow the path climbing out of the forest. Turn left at the next junction, leading into Cataract Valley. Turn left again at the next fork and continue up to the band of Clarens sandstone where the caves are situated. Proceed on the circular route past the Grindstone Caves back to camp (see route 87).

86 BATTLE CAVE AND INJISUTHI CAVE: 14 km

This guided tour must be booked in advance. Entry is only in the company of official guides. Overnight stays are not allowed in these caves, but are possible in Lower Injisuthi Cave, about 2,5 further up the Injisuthi River.

87 CATARACT VALLEY: 15 km

Start as for route 85, but continue on the path in front of Grindstone Caves, round the bend and scramble down to cross Old Woman Stream above the waterfall. The path then rises and zigzags to the second waterfall and further on to the top of the ridge, from where it winds down again into Cataract Valley.

88 POACHER'S STREAM: 15 km

Take the tarred road and turn to the right after crossing the 'new bridge' spanning the Injisuthi River. The path joins the Battle Cave route (see route 86) after about 1,5 km, climbing through a narrow band of sandstone. Cross Poacher's Stream and turn left onto the path running along the stream. The last section before turning right at a T-junction is rather poorly defined. Proceed west until joining the path from Centenary Hut. Return home past Battle Cave along the Injisuthi River.

89 LESLIE PASS TO SUMMIT: 22+ km

Take route 82 and stop overnight at Marble Baths before the final assault on the summit. Proceed on the less well-defined path past Buttress Fork (2 062 m) to the escarpment (3 104 m) through Leslie's Pass, with Molar and Ape (Mahlabatshaneng) to the right. This is a difficult and potentially dangerous hike and should be undertaken only in the company of experienced mountaineers.

Manager's choices

- *Viewpoint via Van Heyningen's Pass*
- *Grindstone Caves*
- *Poacher's Stream*

kwazulu-natal/central

Giant's Castle Game Reserve

This is the heart of the Central Berg region, dominated by the free-standing basalt block of Giant's Castle (3 316 m) over-looking the Bushman's River. The Giant's Castle conservation area extends from Old Woman Grinding Corn (2 986 m) in the north to the Giant's Castle Ridge in the south. Injisuthi in the north-west, though part of Giant's Castle Reserve, is not directly connected to the reserve's main camp.

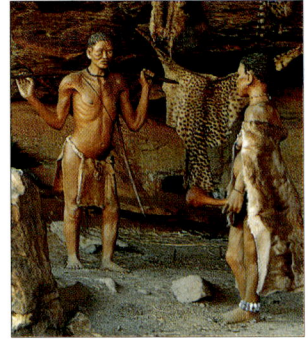

San models at Main Cave.

The Bushman's River starts at the upper end of the ka-Langalibalele Pass and cuts vigorously through the plateau below the escarpment along the Langalibalele Ridge, allowing glorious views all around. Major ecosystems of Giant's Castle Reserve include open montane grassland and patches of indigenous forest. There are also some marshy areas and tarns in the reserve.

Giant's Castle Game Reserve is one of the oldest conservation areas in Africa, first proclaimed by the Natal colonial government in 1903, with the goal of protecting the area's magnificent scenery and the last remaining eland of the Berg. The early conservationists took their mission very seriously, hunting down every predator perceived as a threat to the eland.

A large Clarens sandstone rock shelter near the main camp has been converted into an open-air museum interpreting the way of life of the San hunter-gatherers who once lived there. The area around Giant's Castle was one of their favourite hunting grounds as eland were plentiful before farmers and fences stopped their migrations.

The Bushman's River cutting through the plateau below the escarpment, at the heart of the central Berg.

Wildlife

Mammals

Huge herds of eland are seen in summer at the top of the Little Berg. The reserve has more than 300 mountain reedbuck, occupying steeper terrain than the 100 common reedbuck, and about 400 grey rhebok. Oribi are common as their typical habitat, open montane grassland, is widespread in the reserve. For a chance to see bushbuck, wait patiently in the forest in the late afternoon. Klipspringers are seen only on the high, steep slopes of the main Berg. Black-backed jackals are usually heard at night rather than seen. Serval, caracal and African wildcat are very scarce, making a sighting a major scoop.

• Winter is probably the best time to see animals.

Bushbuck (*Tragelaphus scriptus*).

A black day at the Pass

The 4th of November 1873 is remembered as 'the day of the smoke on the Pass' and a black day for the 75th Natal Carbineer Regiment, which rested at Giant's Castle on its way up the Bushman's River Pass to quell a rebellion spearheaded by Chief Langalibalele (meaning 'the sun is burning').

Langalibalele, branded a habitual troublemaker, had dared to defy the British by refusing to register the guns of his Hlubi followers. Declared an outlaw, he was pursued by colonial troops, including a unit of the Carbineers led by Major Anthony Durnford. Their brief was to block the then Bushman's River Pass (now ka-Langalibalele Pass), but they took a wrong turn as their maps were faulty and – like most of the 16 000 white settlers in Natal at the time – they had little knowledge of the Berg.

Like the famous Italian mountaineer who said: 'Let a drop of water fall directly from the summit and that is the line I want to follow,' Durnford led his men directly to the top. When they arrived at the lip of Bushman's Pass 24 hours late, completely exhausted, they were attacked by Hlubi tribesmen and fled. Three Carbineers and two loyal Zulu scouts were killed in the skirmish and are buried at the top of the pass. Their grave, marked by a stone cairn and aluminium cross, has become a landmark for hikers (see route 107).

Chief Langalibalele was apprehended and banished to Robben Island for life, although the terms of imprisonment were later modified. The Carbineers took savage revenge on the Hlubi, killing at least 150 men, women and children, and driving the tribe away from the slopes of the Drakensberg, where they had been settled as a buffer against San raiders.

In 1874 Durnford returned with a detachment of Royal Engineers and blew up the mountain passes between Oliviershoek and Giant's Castle to make them impassable for the San. It was possibly at this time that the 75th Regiment's number was carved into 'Rock 75', which hikers pass on the way to Main Cave.

The year of the eland

Until the end of the 19th century, huge herds of eland trekked in winter from the slopes of the Berg deep into the lower bushveld areas like the Thukela Valley. They were cut off from their feeding grounds when the fertile valleys were divided into fenced farmland and settlements, and have since been restricted to the low winter grazing of the uKhahlamba Drakensberg Park. Eland cannot survive on the grasses of the 'suurveld' alone, as their nutritional value is poor in winter.

Eland still congregate in spring and, by the time the calves are born in September and October, they have massed into large herds of 200–300 animals. To take advantage of the fresh green growth of burnt grassland, the herds trek up towards the summit in search of summer grazing. In autumn, they break up again into bachelor groups or small herds of females with their calves.

By mid-winter the eland have moved into the sheltered valleys of the Little Berg, where they browse on Ouhout and Sagewood, as well as other woody plants and leaves.

Birds

A comprehensive birdlist of the area includes more than 170 species, including raptors such as Bearded Vulture, Cape Vulture, Black Eagle and Jackal Buzzard. The indigenous garden at the reserve's campsite is one of the best spots for birdwatching, particularly in spring and summer, when many songbirds and other small birds (Passeriformes) live, feed and nest in the trees and undergrowth. Watch for Spotted Prinia, Fairy Flycatcher, Broadtailed and Yellow Warbler, or even the Ground Woodpecker.

Other ecosystems support specialized bird communities, Forest patches and stream banks, for instance, are home to the Malachite

Bearded Vulture (*Gypaetus barbatus*).

Kingfisher. Open grassland above the campsite supports Greywing Francolin, Yellow-breasted Pipit and Blue Crane. Still higher up, energetic hikers may encounter Drakensberg Siskin, Sickle-winged Chat or Orange-breasted Rockjumper. The walk to the nearby San Shelter passes through habitat suitable for Malachite and Doublecollared Sunbirds, Gurney's Sugarbird, Ground Woodpecker and Yellowrumped Widow.

Tourist attractions
Walks and hikes
Giant's Castle has a very well-developed grid of walking and hiking paths. These include a variety of self-guided walks through the lower parts of the reserve, many overnight trails and even some thrilling ice climbing in winter.

A short walk to Main Cave, a memorial to the world of the San.

Lammergeier Hide

The well-camouflaged Lammergeier hide on a spur in the central Berg offers excellent raptor viewing from May to September. Black Eagle, Cape Vulture, Jackal Buzzard and Lanner Falcon are regulars. The highlight of any visit is the sudden arrival of one or two Bearded Vultures (Lammergeiers), attracted by bones laid out on top of the cliff in front of the hide. Photographers from all over the world queue up for a chance to photograph such rarities close up. To share this wonderful experience, book as early as possible as the hide is often fully booked up to a year ahead.

Contact the camp manager, tel 036-353 3718, fax 036-353 3775.

Mountain biking
The Mountain Bike Challenge is probably South Africa's toughest mountain bike event. With the Drakensberg as majestic backdrop, it is held annually on the last Sunday in April. The aim is to raise funds for the Ezemvelo KZN Wildlife Conservation Trust.

Contact KZN Wildlife information, tel 033-845 1000/2.

San rock art
At Main Cave, the reserve boasts one of the most impressive rock art sites in the country and features a three-dimensional exhibition of the San way of life in an original shelter above the Bushman's River. (See routes 91 and 95 in the list of walks on page 95).

Approach to the well-known Giant's Castle – a 3 316 m high block of Drakensberg lava.

PRACTICAL TIPS

How to get to Giant's Castle reserve

Easy access from the tarred road from Mooi River or Estcourt, or use the signposted N3 off-ramp near Estcourt. From Estcourt, it is about 60 km to the entrance gate and 7 km to the camp.

Where to stay

The traditional hutted camp has comfortable, self-contained cottages and chalets for 76 visitors. The fully serviced Giant's Lodge, built into the hillside beside the camp, is one of the most luxurious KZN Wildlife has to offer. It accommodates up to seven people in three en suite bedrooms and has its own cook. Recently 28 two-bed self-catering chalets with fireplaces were added. Three mountain huts, Bannerman's, Giant's and Centenary (with no facilities except bunkbeds and mattresses) are strategically placed along the 30 km section of the contour path that passes through the reserve at a

height of 2 200–2 400 m. Each hut sleeps eight. A fourth, Meander, near Lammergeier Hide, sleeps four.

Where to eat

The newly built 50-seat restaurant, with braai-area and licensed bar, provides for those in the cottages or chalets who do not want to prepare their own meals.

Facilities

The camp's shop sells a wide range of supplies. The nearest town is Estcourt (65 km from main camp).

Local weather

Weather changes are frequent during summer when heavy afternoon thunderstorms occur regularly. Temperatures tend to be lower than in northern Berg.

Bookings

Chalets and mountain huts must be booked through Central Reservations, Box 13069, Cascades 3202 tel 033-845 1000, fax 033-845 1001.
Lammergeier hide booked through camp manager tel 036-353 3718, fax 036-353 3775.

GIANTS CASTLE GAME RESERVE WALKS
(return distance, starting at main camp, unless otherwise stated)

EASY TO AVERAGE	INTERMEDIATE TO DIFFICULT	DIFFICULT TO EXTREME

90 MEANDER HUT TO SKOPONGO RIDGE, ROUND TRIP: 2,5 km

A pleasant short walk from Meander Hut in an easterly direction along the jeep track to the Skopongo Ridge airstrip, with beautiful views of Ncibidwane River, Meander Stream and towering Giant's Castle.

91 MAIN CAVE VIA DURNFORD'S CAMP: 3 km

A sign-posted path leads along the river and close to the forest edge towards Main Cave with its San exhibits. After approximately 1 km the path winds down the hillside to some large boulders where a sign reading 'Rock 75' indicates the site of Major Durnford's camp during the Langalibalele rebellion. The main path crosses a rustic bridge (Two Dassie Stream) and continues up a concrete path to Main Cave. The entrance gate is opened on the hour every hour between 09:00 and 15:00.

92 CHAMPAGNE POOLS: 4 km

The circular walk starts 1 km from Giant's Castle main gate. The secluded pools are ideal for swimming and trout fishing.

93 BUSHMAN'S RIVER WALK, ROUND TRIP: 4,5 km

The path leads past 'Rock 75' to the river walk, which is signposted just before the rustic bridge. The path continues on the east bank of the Bushman's River, then cuts through low-lying grassveld and light bush, where it forks. Take the path to Bannerman's Bridge/picnic site through thick bush. On reaching the pool at Bannerman's Bridge, take the path that reads 'picnic site' (a fairly steep climb). At the picnic site, join the main road to the hutted camp.

94 BERG VIEW, ROUND TRIP: 5 km

Take the main road to the conservator's house. Turn right behind the house and follow the sign-posted walk, continuing up a steep slope until the path crosses a stream and leads to one the most magnificent views of the Drakensberg. A jeep track leads back to main camp.

95 MAIN CAVE'S FOREST: 5 km

The sign-posted path leads to Main Cave's Forest and then to Giant's Hut. After about 2,5 km the path enters a beautiful forest below the sandstone cave overhangs, which shelter San paintings. Deep pools in Two Dassie Stream along the way offer the prospect of a cooling swim.

96 GRYSBOK BUSH: 8 km

The path past Main Cave leads to Grysbok Bush and further to the ka-Langalibalele Pass. The stretch through a fairly swampy grassland (during summer) has been cemented to cope with the wet patches. A rustic bridge marks the entrance to the largest indigenous forest at Giant's Castle. A series of pools follows after about 20 minutes. Swimming is allowed but beware of whirlpools after heavy rains. Do not cross the first rustic bridge ahead; take instead the path to the left, signposted 'Grysbok Bush'.

GIANTS CASTLE GAME RESERVE WALKS (contd.)
(return distance, starting at main camp unless otherwise stated)

EASY TO AVERAGE	INTERMEDIATE TO DIFFICULT	DIFFICULT TO EXTREME

97 BANNERMAN'S HUT: 18 km

From the picnic site, take the path down to Bannerman's Bridge and cross the river. Follow the path marked Bannerman's Hut. At first it climbs steeply through the cave sandstone but levels out before reaching the contour path. Follow the contour path to the right, passing a small pan after about five minutes. From here the path crosses numerous small streams and passes beneath The Thumb and Bannerman's Face. Bannerman's Hut is sited at the foot of Bannerman's Pass.

98 SPARE RIB CAVE: 6 km

A rock shelter, reached from Bannerman's Hut. It is situated on the left side of the path near the top of the escarpment.

99 BANNERMAN'S: 20 km

The ascent starts behind Bannerman's Hut, goes up the stream and passes a huge rock in the narrowing gully. The path is generally well defined, with small piles of stones (cairns) acting as markers wherever difficulty may be experienced. Scrambling up the end of the pass becomes difficult. Boulder scree in the steepest sections hampers progress.

100 MEANDER HUT TO GIANT'S HUT VIA LOTHENI JEEP TRACK: 11 km

The old jeep track leaves Meander Hut and travels west, climbing steeply to the trigonometric beacon on the spine of the ridge (2 020m) before descending to the Lotheni jeep track. Turn left and climb a series of steep inclines until you reach the old Lammergeier hide. From here a level path continues to Giant's Hut. Return distance from Giant's Hut to main camp via the Lotheni jeep track is 11 km.

101 MEANDER HUT TO VIA BEACON RIDGE, ROUND TRIP: 14 km

Start as for route 94 above, but follow the sign to Meander Hut. This track follows the spine of ridges and includes two steep ascents. At the top of the second is a trigonometric beacon. From here, the track descends to Meander Hut, situated above the cliffs overlooking Meander Stream. To return, climb the short steep hill behind the hut and follow the footpath below the beacon until it links up with a jeep track leading to the main road to the rest camp.

102 WORLD'S VIEW, ROUND TRIP: 14 km

Cross Bannerman's Bridge and take the path to the right marked 'World's View'. It climbs a short hill, crosses a stream and follows an elongated plateau then splits at a huge rock. The lower path leads to World's View. Ahead lies Sugar Loaf Hill, to the west is the main Drakensberg escarpment with The Thumb, to the south is ka-Langalibalele Pass, and to the north is Bannerman's Pass. Walk along the base of Sugar Loaf Hill until the path peters out. Walk straight to the top of World's View to find the escarpment from Giant's Castle to Champagne Castle stretched out in front of you, the Umtshezana and Bushman's Rivers sparkling below, and the Chimney Pot ahead.

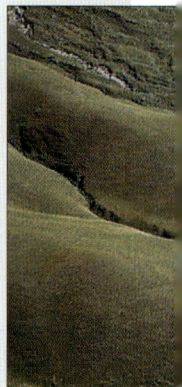

EASY TO AVERAGE	INTERMEDIATE TO DIFFICULT	DIFFICULT TO EXTREME

103 THE LAKES, ROUND TRIP: 15 km

Walk on the jeep track towards Meander Hut. After climbing up the steep slope through the sandstone, turn left at the fork sign-posted 'The Lakes'. Again the track climbs steeply, with concrete strips in places. Pass an old quarry and continue along the old jeep track until you reach a huge basalt shelf containing a series of large water-filled potholes. From the edge, a magnificent view of the Drakensberg range unfolds. Continue along the track, which leads back onto the original jeep track.

104 CONTOUR PATH AND LANGALIBALELE PATH, ROUND TRIP: 16km

Take the route to Bannerman's Hut. On reaching the contour path, turn left and continue, crossing several streams. Turn left again into Langalibalele path (marked by two stone cairns). Proceed down the spine into Bushman's Valley below. After crossing two streams (and a rustic bridge) the path continues back to main camp.

105 GIANT'S HUT TO BANNERMAN'S HUT VIA CONTOUR PATH, ONE-WAY: 18 km

This fairly easy walk at an altitude of about 2 260 m becomes a little rough when crossing the mountain streams. The escarpment and a range of local peaks are in full view, as are the foothills below.

106 GIANT'S HUT TO GIANT'S PASS AND GIANT'S CASTLE SUMMIT, ROUND TRIP: 19 km

At Giant's Hut a cairn on the contour path marks the path to the north. After crossing four streams, a long track up the side of the hill leads to a break in the cliffs at the bottom of the pass. The scree-covered slope is difficult to negotiate. A path to the right, marked by a small cairn, finally leads to the summit. Gullies branching off to the left are impassable.

107 KA-LANGALIBALELE PASS, ROUND TRIP: 27 km

A clearly sign-posted path leads past Main Cave to ka-Langalibalele Pass via the contour path. Continue up from the contour path, negotiating the steep incline to a stone cairn. Another three short but steep inclines follow. The path then

continues up the ridge to a final stone cairn, then veers to the left along level ground and gradually descends to the river, crossing at the base of ka-Langalibalele Pass. The path is clearly defined all the way to the summit, but becomes very steep in places. At the top of the pass, look up to the left to see the Carbineers' grave (see 'A black day at the Pass', p. 91).

Bannerman's Hut.

0   25 km

N   W   E   S

Giant's Hut
Giant's Castle
The Hawk 2356m
Highmoor Mountain Reserve
Lammergeier Hide
Mool River
Kamberg
2288m

Thabana Ntlenyana
Highest point in southern Africa 3482m
Mlahlangubo Peak
3071m
3301m
Lotheni
Lotheni Nature Reserve
2234m
Mkhomazi Nature Reserve

Nlangeni
3068m
Mkhomazi River
The Pyramid
Vergelegen Nature Reserve

Kotisephola Pass

L E S O T H O

Mangauing Pass
3249m

Sani Pass

Menga River
1935m
1820m

Mkhomazi River

Cobham Nature Reserve

Mzimkhulu Wilderness Area
Little Bamboo
2384m
Mzimkulwano
Rhino Peak
Mashai 3056m
3310m

Ndlovini
Prolela River
Mkomazana
Sani Pass
Sani Lodge

Himeville
Himeville Nature Reserve

Swiman
Lake Naverone
Drakensberg Gardens
Garden Castle Nature Reserve
Taylor's Lodge
The Banks
Underberg
Underberg Inn

Mashai River

Walker's Peak
Bushman's Nek
Bushman's Nek
Bushman's Nek Hotel
Penwarn Country Lodge
Bushman's Nek Pass
Sehlaba-Thebe National Park

R617
R617
Ixopo
Kokstad

Southern KwaZulu-Natal Drakensberg

The least developed and coolest section of the KwaZulu-Natal Drakensberg, the southern Berg extends to the Lesotho border and neighbouring Sehlaba-Thebe National Park. The latter, along with other parts of the Lesotho escarpment, may soon merge with KwaZulu-Natal's giant uKhahlamba Drakensberg Park to form an international 'Peace Park'.

Larger than northern or central regions, the southern KwaZulu-Natal Drakensberg stretches from Giant's Castle in the north down to Bushman's Nek and East Griqualand in the south, after which the Berg fades into the north-eastern Cape. This section, with the Drakensberg's best guarantee of snow in winter, is the least developed. Its potential has hardly been tapped, its majestic scenery and solitude left largely untouched.

Impressive peaks tower over the spreading Mkhomazi Wilderness Area south of Giant's Ridge, from the Tent (3 130 m) to Mlahlangubo Peak (3 071 m), ka-Nthuba (3 355 m) and the Twelve Apostles (2 914 m) jutting out at right angles from the escarpment. Beyond, just north of the Sani Pass road, the Mzimkhulu Wilderness Area begins at Phinong (2 905 m). Many hiking paths connect with the wilderness areas but most destinations are reached only after long, arduous hikes from the camps in the reserves.

The climate is generally harsher than in the northern or central sections, the winters colder and snowfalls more widespread and predictable. Plant life is also less lush than further north, with forest patches decreasing in size and number.

Mountain passes and caves, some with excellent rock art sites, abound in the region. A comprehensive management plan is in progress to make these sites accessible to the public and to provide guides trained through special awareness courses.

Cobham Nature Reserve, Phoelela River valley, where herds of eland gather on the river bank in summer.

Towns and villages

The small towns and villages of the midlands and foothills are ideal starting points for visits to the southern Drakensberg. To get there, follow the scenic R617 from Pietermaritzburg through the Mkhomazi River Valley to **Bulwer** (90 km), a little town surrounded by forest plantations. The historic Yellowwood Chapel, the only one of its kind in the world, is a direct link to the remaining forest patches in the Berg. Continue on the tarred road to **Underberg** (40 km) for other historical sites such as the Reichenau Trappist Mission (more than 100 years old) and the old Water Mill. Turn right at the sign pointing to the Mission and 'Gästehaus', which offers reasonably priced accommodation. The village of **Himeville**, 6 km from Underberg, is known for its hospitality. It is the gateway to the Sani Pass and has the last filling station before Mokhotlong, 60 km away in the Lesotho highlands.

The R617 continues from Underberg via Swartberg and Franklin to **Kokstad** (95 km), the southern-most point of the KwaZulu-Natal Drakensberg. Kokstad, the former capital of East Griqualand, is the centre of a thriving farming community. Mount Currie Nature Reserve is the sole drawcard in this area for nature lovers, although Kokstad can be regarded as the kick-off point for expeditions into the north-eastern Cape Drakensberg region.

Highmoor Mountain Reserve

Situated between Giant's Castle in the north and Lotheni in the south, Highmoor Mountain Reserve is the most northern access point to the Mkhomazi Wilderness Area, which covers 56 155 ha from Giant's Castle down to Sani Pass. Although Highmoor offers little high-altitude hiking, it does have the highest KZN Wildlife office in the Berg. At 2 000 m on the top of the Little Berg, it is one of few points where the summit above the Clarens sandstone can be reached by family car.

The Ipofane Nature Reserve is part of the Highmoor section of the greater Drakensberg Park. Ipofane, Zulu for 'eland', are quite common here, as are viable populations of black wildebeest.

Some minor patches of wetland add to the stark beauty of the Highmoor plateau. A short drive through a striking mountain pass winds to the top of the Little Berg, from where it is possible to walk along the summit for panoramic views from Giant's Castle to Cathkin Peak.

Dominating the Highmoor landscape, monumental Giant's Castle.

Black wildebeest (*Connochaetes gnou*), a rare sight in the foothills.

Wildlife

Mammals

This is one of the few Berg areas where blesbok occur. There are healthy numbers of eland, black wildebeest and baboon; reedbuck, bushbuck, grey rhebok and oribi are seen less often. By 1960, when the red hartebeest became extinct in the province, a small breeding herd at Giant's Castle had been built up to about 30 animals. Although the reintroduced hartebeest seemed to do well at first, they later declined and the few surviving animals were relocated to Highmoor.

Birds

Highmoor has a single nesting site of Wattled Crane and the largest breeding colony of Bald Ibis in the Berg. Lammergeier, Cape Vulture, Jackal Buzzard and other raptors thrill visitors with their occasional presence. Three dams – all stocked with trout – are noted for their variety of waterbirds, including the nomadic Whitebacked Duck, known for its melodic whistling.

Flora

Among noteworthy plants are four protea species: Common and Silver Sugarbush, Drakensberg Sugarbush and Waterlily Sugarbush.

Poaching

'Poaching is ongoing and happens all over the place where eland occur,' says a KZN Wildlife spokesperson. This means that the Berg from Giant's Castle to Garden Castle is the area worst affected by plundering of wildlife. Although eland are the main target as they provide a sizeable amount of meat, mountain reedbuck and oribi are also poached.

On nights when the moon is full, groups of up to 10 men with dogs enter the area stealthily , brandishing automatic weapons or spear-like iron rods, the sharpened points prepared with 'muti' (medicines), to shoot or spear their quarry and cut its throat. If it should escape, the dogs will run it down. The meat feeds the hungry while the fat, bones, skin and horns are sold as potent 'muti' to inyangas in Durban, Gauteng or elsewhere.

White poachers also hunt at night, often in 4x4s, and some farmers take their share of unsuspecting antelope crossing the borders of protected areas. Not all poachers are from South Africa. Basotho tribesmen are also involved. Upset by effective counter measures, they are known to have started Berg fires that ravage the region.

HIGHMOOR MOUNTAIN RESERVE WALK

EASY TO AVERAGE	INTERMEDIATE TO DIFFICULT	DIFFICULT TO EXTREME

108 AASVOELKRANTZ CAVE, RETURN: 11 km

This walk is a favourite with hiking clubs and families as it is not very strenuous. It offers plenty of fresh water as it is close to a spectacular waterfall. From the local KZN Wildlife office the path leads past the three fishing dams to a lookout post. Pass it on your left and proceed downwards into the gorge to the cave and waterfall, which is one of the Berg's largest.

Approach to Kamberg Mountain Reserve.

Kamberg Mountain Reserve

This conservation area lies far from the escarpment at the western end of the lush farming valley of the Mooi River. With distant views of Giant's Castle, Kamberg is named after a mountain that looks like the comb of a Guineafowl. The 2 232 ha reserve is quite close to Lotheni, Vergelegen, Highmoor and Giant's Castle, and affords relatively easy access to the Mkhomazi Wilderness Area.

Hutted camp at Kamberg.

Adding to the serenity of the area are seven clear trout dams and a number of Weeping Willow trees along the Mooi River. Although the exotic, ornamental willow generally invades watercourses, it is welcomed here for the shade it affords trout. Apart from their uses in erosion control and as fodder, willows are associated with African 'muti' and superstition.

The trout hatchery run by KZN Wildlife breeds brown (European) and rainbow (American) trout, and supplies all KZN Wildlife reserves with fingerlings and trophy-size specimens. The trout hatchery is open daily to the public.

Smoke from winter fire disturbs wildebeest and blesbok in Kamberg.

Wildlife
Mammals

Eland are often seen in winter, when most of the grasses lose their nutritional value and the eland depend on Ouhout and other woody plants. In summer, large herds of 150–300 animals move between Giant's Castle and the Kamberg area.

Other species thrive in the fertile mist-belt grassland: black wildebeest, grey rhebok, as well asred hartebeest, duiker, oribi and reedbuck. Bushbuck are often seen along the Mooi River Trail.

Kamberg Mountain Reserve is probably the best place to see the Cape clawless otter and spotted-necked otter, which visit the trout dams regularly, especially in winter. Caracal and serval also occur. The porcupine is best seen at night with the aid of a powerful spotlight.

Birds

Two pairs of Wattled Crane breed at Stillerust Vlei. Crowned Crane and Blue Crane also occur at Kamberg. A reasonable number of other species can be observed in the reserve, though keen birders will find the untarred access road from Himeville, which winds through farmland, forest and wetland, more rewarding. Sightings include Stanley's Bustard, Jackal and Steppe Buzzard, African Marsh Harrier, Secretary Bird, Gurney's Sugarbird, Rufousnaped Lark, Orangethroated Longclaw, Wailing and Lazy Cisticola and Goldenbreasted Bunting. White Storks visit the area from about Christmas. Bearded and Cape Vultures nest in the cliffs of the Little Berg.

Insects

Water insects at the dams are of special interest. Little whirligig beetles are common, and float on water, using surface tension to support themselves. They move their legs rapidly, like oars, to reach dead or decaying insects, which they detect with the bottom half of their eyes on the water while the other half scans the air for enemies. The streamlined Water Beetle usually swims under water but surfaces to trap an air bubble that serves as its aqualung.

Wattled Crane (*Bugeranus carunculatus*).

Tourist attractions
Walks and hikes
Many well-maintained paths starting at the camp (1 700 m) allow short walks and self-guided trails to caves, waterfalls or the summit of the Little Berg (2 200 m). Game Pass Cave can also be visited if you book a guide in advance at the KZN Wildlife office. The Mooi River Trail (see route 110) was the first interpretative trail of its kind developed by KZN Wildlife. Important characteristics of the reserve and the Drakensberg as a whole are explained in detail along the path and in a booklet obtainable from the office.

San rock art
Shelter Cave is famous for its stylized shaman figures in trance state. Large, polychrome eland adorn the wall-like rocks. The Department of Tourism has granted R1,2 million towards the preservation of the priceless San rock art, as well as the surroundings, including the culturally important Waterfall Cave where sangomas collect water that has special healing powers. The access path will be upgraded and an audiovisual interpretation centre built. Shelter Cave is a 40-minute walk from the camp, reached by a steep climb from Waterfall Cave. You must be accompanied by a local guide. Enquire at the KZN Wildlife office. A guided walk to the rock art shelter at the end of Game Pass path is conducted every Sunday morning from the office at 08:30. Book in advance.

Polychrome painting of eland and human figures in Shelter Cave.

KAMBERG MOUNTAIN RESERVE WALKS
(return distance, starting at camp unless otherwise stated)

EASY TO AVERAGE	INTERMEDIATE TO DIFFICULT	DIFFICULT TO EXTREME

109 CYPRESS CAVE: 9 km

Short and easy hike in the Mkhomazi Wilderness. Good for beginners to experience a night in a rock shelter. Running water nearby.

110 MOOI RIVER TRAIL: 4-6 km

Self-guided trail to highlAight some of Kamberg's and the Drakensberg's natural history features. The trail has been divided into short segments so that physically disabled and elderly people can cope with it easily. Most of the interpretative information is given in the first section. Start at the picnic site and follow the pointers.

111 GLADSTONE'S NOSE TRAIL: 8 km

This extension of the Mooi River Trail may be one of the most beautiful walks in the KwaZulu-Natal Berg region. It leads through grassland and indigenous forests.

112 GAME PASS CAVE AND SAN ROCK ART: 7 km

The trail provides spectacular views of the valley, the trout hatchery and dam. The return walk follows a contour path through grasslands. You must be accompanied by a local guide in order to visit Game Pass and Shelter Cave.

Mkhomazi Nature Reserve

Very near to the largest, most remote and least developed Drakensberg Wilderness area, the 6 000 ha Mkhomazi Nature Reserve is ideal for self-reliant people who want to come face to face with untainted nature. A few hiking trails criss-cross the grassland of the Little Berg, connecting to caves, valleys and the distant escarpment. There are also links from Mkhomazi to the Kamberg and Highmoor Mountain Reserves in the north and Lotheni Mountain Reserve in the south.

Entrance to bucolic Mkhomazi Nature Reserve.

Wildlife
Mammals

Almost all the mammals found in the entire Drakensberg region are present, from aardwolf to zorilla. Quite a few are active at night, among them caracal, genet and porcupine.

The Longcrested Eagle (*Lophaetus occipitalis*) is solitary like the Bearded Vulture, but more common.

Birds

Apart from the Lammergeier and Cape Vulture, birders may also spot Whitebacked Vulture, Longcrested Eagle and Jackal Buzzard.

There is a Lammergeier nesting site in the cliffs of the Little Berg about 5 km from the KZN Wildlife office. Seasonal visitors include the White Stork, Yellowbilled Kite, several species of Swallow and a host of LBJs. An official birdlist is not yet available.

Flora

Vegetation varies according to altitude, ranging from grassland to alpine tundra flora. Although Mkhomazi Nature Reserve has not been widely researched, its flora appears to differ very little from the flora of other sections of the KwaZulu-Natal Drakensberg.

Bone breaker

*The Bearded Vulture or Lammergeier is regarded as an evolutionary link between eagle and vulture. The first eyrie of this elusive bird ever found in the Drakensberg was in an inaccessible cliff along the road from Sani Pass to Mokhotlong in Lesotho. A group of lucky birders made the discovery in 1959 and subsequently presented the first photographs of this endangered southern African sub-species (*Gypaetus barbatus meridionalis*) to the public. They returned repeatedly with their moun-taineering gear to watch an egg hatch and the nestling grow up during the mercilessly cold Lesotho Plateau winter.*

This highly specialized mountain-dweller (see pages 92–93), with a wingspan of up to 2,8 m, depends heavily on a diet of bone fragments and marrow. As long as Basotho pastoralists continue to herd their stock on the ice-cold Drakensberg escarpment, the huge birds will find enough bones to survive. As their beaks are surprisingly weak, they splinter bones by dropping them from a height of 15–50 m onto a chosen rock, called an ossuary. The scoop-shaped tongue is used to extract the marrow before the splinter is swallowed whole

Southern Africa's breeding population is estimated to be about 200 pairs, with 122 pairs in Lesotho and approximately 40 along the Drakensberg escarpment. The highest breeding density occurs in the Giant's Castle area. Intensive studies and a new population census are underway. The best time to undertake Lammergeier counts is between May and July when the birds are nesting. Although they are still under threat of extinction, the establishment of 'vulture restaurants' seems to have alleviated the situation. Most internationally famous is the Lammergeier hide at Giant's Castle. The reopening of a hide at Cobham is under consideration and a new vulture hide is planned for Cathedral Peak.

Tourist attractions
Walks and hikes
Although the main escarpment is at some distance, local walks with overnight stays in caves have a special appeal. A number of caves with San rock art are off-limits: the new policy allows access only to people accompanied by an accredited guide and none are available here because demand is minimal. It is possible, however, to visit some caves if a field ranger is available.

As there is no sales point at the office, it is essential to bring a good hiking map with you (see page 172).

(see page 172).

PRACTICAL TIPS

How to get to Mkhomazi
Take the country road from Nottingham Road to Underberg, which is tarred for the first 29 km. After about 15 km on gravel watch out for the well sign-posted turn-off at the bridge over the Mzinga River. The warden's camp is about 1 km off the road.

Where to stay
Open space without shade is demarcated near the office for parking and camping. A water tap and a simple toilet are the only amenities.

Where to eat
Bring your own food.

Facilities
None. The nearest shops and petrol stations are at Nottingham Road (42 km).

Information/bookings
The Warden, Mkhomazi Wilderness Area, Box 105, Nottingham Road 3280 tel 033-263 6444.

MKHOMAZI NATURE RESERVE WALKS
(return distance, starting at parking area, unless stated)

EASY TO AVERAGE	INTERMEDIATE TO DIFFICULT	DIFFICULT TO EXTREME

113 FOREST WALK: ± 6 km

A short walk to a patch of indigenous forest with very good opportunities to swim in clear, secluded pools.

114 CYPRUS CAVE: 8 km

Children from the age of about five can manage this easy hike. The cave sleeps 6 people. Plenty fresh water is available.

115 MCKENZIE'S CAVE: 22 km

The path, which leads to the Makungana mountain range, is quite steep in parts. Fresh drinking water is scarce all along the path, as well as at the cave, which sleeps up to 12 people.

116 SINCLAIR'S CAVE: 22 km

Experience is required for this hike to White Rocks (2 150 m) at the northern border as the gradient is steep to difficult. To make it easier one could extend the hike to two days, sleeping overnight at Cyprus Cave. Water can be scarce around Cyprus cave, which sleeps up to 6 people.

Enjoying the Mkhomazi River.

kwazulu-natal/southern

Running through the reserve, the Lotheni River.

Lotheni Mountain Reserve

Situated in the undulating foothills of the southern Berg, Lotheni Mountain Reserve is a place to relax amid scenic beauty. It is almost entirely surrounded by the Mkhomazi Wilderness Area and by the escarpment south of Giant's Ridge, with its row of monumental peaks such as the Tent (3 130 m), the Hawk (3 077 m), Redi (3 314 m), Hlathimbe Buttress (2 935 m) and Duart Castle (2 910 m). All are in demand among local hikers, as well as by those keen to practise ice climbing in winter.

Vegetation consists mainly of mist-belt and montane grassland, interspersed with natural forest patches in sheltered valleys and kloofs. Fairly easy walking trails are laid out inside the core reserve, but Lotheni has also long been a starting point for serious hikers and mountaineers. Several mountain paths lead through the adjoining Mkhomazi Wilderness Area to caves, mountain passes and the escarpment about 12 km away as the crow flies. The caves include at least 23 rock art sites, which at this stage cannot be visited by the public, as there is not yet enough demand for permanent expert guides.

Wildlife
Mammals
Lotheni rangers have prepared a comprehensive list of mammals in the reserve, including: black-backed jackal, black wildebeest, blesbok, bushbuck, caracal, Chacma baboon, civet, common and mountain reedbuck, eland, grey duiker, grey rhebok, klipspringer, leopard, Natal red rock rabbit, oribi, Cape and spotted-necked otter, red hartebeest and serval.

Birds

The area is rich in bird life, with 172 species recorded. Those most likely to be seen include Orangethroated Longclaw, Ground Woodpecker, Redwing Francolin, Stonechat, Cape Rock Thrush, Wailing Cisticola, Jackal Buzzard and Black Eagle. The region also protects a number of Wattled Crane breeding sites.

Tourist attractions

Mountain biking

A simple trail has been designed for the average family biker. The single-track route of 14 km leads to the top of the historic Gelib Tree site (see route 119 below) and past the inviting Cool Pools before returning along the tarred road.

Trout fishing

Book the rustic cottage, which has a small trout-stocked dam for occupants' use only.

LOTHENI MOUNTAIN RESERVE WALKS		
(return distance, starting at rest camp, unless otherwise stated)		
EASY TO AVERAGE	INTERMEDIATE TO DIFFICULT	DIFFICULT TO EXTREME

117 ASH CAVE: 16 km

A fairly easy path leads along the Lotheni River to this sandstone cave. Enjoy the forest patches at the river.

118 EAGLE EDUCATIONAL TRAIL: 12 km

This circular route starts on a steep incline and includes boulder hopping when crossing streams. It leads through two scenic valleys with patches of indigenous forest and a mixture of protea savannah and grassland. It is well marked and easy to follow. A booklet with details is available from the office shop.

119 GELIB TREE: 4 km

This well marked trail leads through the Bhodla River Valley and a natural forest patch. It includes a few gentle climbs and a steep, short ascent out of the valley. It offers magnificent views and is of historical interest, commemorating the Royal Natal Carbineers killed near the village of Gelib in East Africa in World War II. Shorter routes start near the Settler's Homestead Museum and at the main gate. The 'Gelib Incident' booklet is available from the office shop.

120 HLATHIMBE PASS AND CAVE: 16 km

From Lotheni, follow the Ngodwini River to the contour path (2 350 m). Turn left and follow the contour path south-wards to Hlathimbe Cave (which sleeps 4) near the top of the pass (2 842 m). A relatively short hike leads from here to Thabana Ntlenyana in Lesotho, southern Africa's highest peak.

121 DUART CASTLE ALONG THE ESCARPMENT, AND BACK TO CAMP: 16 km

Short walk from the top of Hlathimbe Pass (route 120). Head to Duart Castle and Lynx Cave (sleeps 6) or walk 6 km due north on the summit past Redi Peak to Ka-Masihlenga Pass and back to camp via Yellowwood Cave (sleeps 8).

How to get to Lotheni

From the south on the N3, take the turnoff to Bulwer/Underberg on the R617. From the north, take the Nottingham Road off-ramp and follow the signs through the village to the reserve, 62 km away (the last 30 km on good gravel road).

Where to stay

12 self-contained chalets with the usual facilities. Electricity only between 17:00 and 22:00. There is also a rustic cottage, and a 12-site camping ground, which lacks shade and electricity, but has hot/cold water.

Facilities

A small shop at the KZN Wildlife office sells groceries and curios.

Information/bookings

Chalets must be booked through Central Reservations, Box 13069, Cascades 3202 tel 033-845 1000, fax 033-845 1001. Book camping sites, caravan sites and caves through the local office, tel/fax 033-702 0540.

Jacobs Ladder.

LOTHENI MOUNTAIN RESERVE WALKS (contd.)
(return distance, starting (except 125) at rest camp)

EASY TO AVERAGE	INTERMEDIATE TO DIFFICULT	DIFFICULT TO EXTREME

122 YELLOWWOOD CAVE, TARN AND WATERFALL: 20 km

Although the hike is not difficult, plan to take at least 2 days. Yellowwood Cave is the favoured stopover on the way to the escarpment and Redi summit. Follow the Lotheni River and turn left at the Masinhlonga fork. The south-facing cave is very cold in winter. The next stop is a campsite (with no facilities except drinking water) a few km ahead, next to the contour path that links through to Buttress Pass (2 950 m), Redi Pass (2 900 m) and Ka-Masihlenga Pass (3 140 m).

123 CIRCULAR EMADUNDWINI TRAIL: 12 km

This well sign-posted trail offers spectacular views of the surrounding Berg. Cross the Lotheni River at the Tebetebe suspension bridge and walk through protea savannah, montane forest and grassland. A number of small streams must be crossed and some steep inclines traversed.

124 FALLS TRAIL: 0,5 km

This extension of the Eagle Trail (see route 118) takes you to a scenic waterfall and river pools for swimming. Follow the markers from the Eagle Trail.

125 CANYON TRAIL: 14 km

Start about 500 m from the museum and head past the Gelib Tree up the mountain in a very steep climb. The path then levels out along the grassland plateau and continues up the Bhodla River Valley, giving superb panoramic views of the Lotheni Valley and escarpment, especially Hawk, Tent and Hlathimbe Buttress. About 5 km beyond the Gelib Tree, you reach the canyon, where you are rewarded with another waterfall.

126 JACOBS LADDER: 4 km

This short walk is ideal for family groups planning a picnic. It crosses the Lotheni River at the suspension bridge and heads downriver. The 5-section falls are part of Jacobs Stream as it joins the Lotheni. The pool at the bottom is perfect for swimming. Be prepared to cross the stream a few times.

127 HIKE TO HIGHMOOR CAMP, ONE-WAY: 20–25 km

This long, relatively arduous overnight journey through the Little Berg is an ideal way to discover the Mkhomazi Wilderness Area but needs careful planning. The path is not very well defined at places.

A 'far away' place with a river (the Mkhomazi) running through it.

Vergelegen Mountain Reserve

The Mkhomazi River rises at the top of the Mkhomazi Pass and carves its way through this reserve from west to east, adding a soft touch to the rugged beauty of Vergelegen, which means 'far away' place. Steep slopes and deep valleys are covered by montane grassland, with patches of indigenous forest in ravines and sheltered places. Some imposing peaks include Mlahlangubo Peak (3 071 m), Nhlangeni (3 068 m), Mohlesi (3 301 m), Ka-Nthuba (3 355 m) and Mqatsheni (3 249 m).

The 20 000 ha reserve is part of the Mkhomazi Wilderness Area, which begins near Giant's Castle Game Reserve in the north and adjoins the Mzimkhulu Wilderness Area in the south, along a line close to the road between Sani Pass Hotel and Sani Top.

Most of the San rock art in the area is, unfortunately, in a poor state.

Wildlife
Mammals
All Drakensberg antelope species occur here, including the rare and secretive oribi, which can sometimes be seen near the camp. Ask the officer-in-charge for details.

Birds
A new bird list is in preparation. So far, the species appear to differ little from those at neighbouring Lotheni Mountain Reserve (see page 109).

vergelegen: wildlife

How to get to Vergelegen

From the south, take the road from Himeville in the direction of Sani Pass but when the tar ends continue on the gravel for another 12 km, where a road branches off to the reserve, which lies 19 km further on. At the Mqatsheni supermarket, the road follows the Mkhomazi River to the camp. From the north, follow the directions from Nottingham Road past Mkhomazi Wilderness Area to the turnoff to the reserve. The access road may be flooded or partly washed away during the rainy season (October to March).

Where to stay

There are four shady camping sites, as well as some unshaded sites, with hot/cold water (donkey boilers). Six caves are open for overnight stops.

Bookings

All camping sites and caves can be booked through the local officer-in-charge, tel 033-702 0831.

Top of southern Africa's highest mountain – Thabana Ntlenyana.

Tourist attractions
Walks and hikes

Although Vergelegen has the advantage of being the closest point from which to walk to the top of Thabana Ntlenyana, the highest mountain in Africa south of Mount Kilimanjaro, its camp is set at a greater distance from the Drakensberg escarpment and catchment area. The paths leading to caves, passes and peaks traverse some of the Berg's most remote areas, making hiking here a truly natural adventure. The lush valley, with marshy areas and huge reedbeds, is ideal territory for birders.

VERGELEGEN MOUNTAIN RESERVE WALKS (return distance, starting at camp, unless otherwise stated)		
EASY TO AVERAGE	INTERMEDIATE TO DIFFICULT	DIFFICULT TO EXTREME

128 ROOIBESSIES: 8 km

aTake the path from the office in a northerly direction to reach this beautiful patch of forest.

129 KAULA CAVE: 28 km

Follow the Mkhomazi River from the camp for about 5 km before turning left onto a less well defined path. Follow the path for 9 km along a stream bed to the cave at the end of the escarpment spurs. (A 14 km hiking path connects Kaula Cave to the Sani Pass road about 4 km above the border post.)

130 NHLANGENI CAVE AND PASS: 40 km

This long, arduous trail follows the Mkhomazi and Nhlangeni River from the camp right into a deep cutback. Plan to spend at least 3 days on the trail, with possible stopovers at Bridge Cave or Small Cave.

131 SUMMIT OF THABANA NTLENYANA: 40 km

Follow route 130 and spend the night at Nhlangeni cave before the final assault on the escarpment. Enjoy the magnificent views as you walk to the top of the peak, aptly named 'beautiful little mountain'. This is the easiest part.

132 MOHLESI PEAK: 38 km

Take route 130 to the summit but instead of turning left to Nhlangeni Pass turn to the right at the last fork and reach the summit via Mohlesi Pass. Plan for at least 2-3 days, with possible stopovers at Small and Bridge Caves.

Sani Pass–Himeville–Underberg

The only road crossing the escarpment from KwaZulu-Natal into Lesotho takes you within less than an hour from the charming green foothills of the Berg (1 400 m) to a harsh alpine world called, not inappropriately, the 'Tibet of Africa' or the 'roof of Africa'. The escarpment plateau can be reached fairly easily via the road to Sani Pass (2 874 m). Once a narrow track for sure-footed Basotho ponies, this is now the highest destination in southern Africa reachable by car.

Looking down Sani Pass.

The road to Sani Top.

Historical note

The name Sani refers to a Basotho chief and is not linked to the San, who inhabited the southern Berg from about 8000 BC. They probably used Sani Pass as frequently as members of the Bhaca tribe, whose descendants still live around the southern foothills. The main body of this Nguni tribe, however, took refuge from Shaka's warriors during the expansion of the Zulu kingdom in the first half of the 19th century and settled in nearby East Griqualand.

The Bhaca subsequently established an independent chiefdom in the Mount Frere district, from where they constantly raided their Mpondo neighbours. The supposedly peaceful relationship between Nguni pastoralists and San hunter-gatherers came to an end when settlers of European descent moved in, putting pressure on both groups.

Entering the town of Underberg, Hodgson's Peaks in the background.

Towns and villages

Underberg and Himeville, a quaint place named after Sir Alfred Hime, the prime minister of Natal in 1889, actively promote their own brand of ecotourism. Several operators offer daily trips up to Sani Top and Africa's highest pub. Others specialize in birding trips to the summit and to interesting places nearby, or take tourists on short or long-distance horse rides.

Himeville Nature Reserve is a useful starting point for a thorough exploration of all levels of the southern Berg. This very small sanctuary (104 ha) was created as a captive breeding centre for all three South African crane species. It is still an important conservation area that includes montane and mist-belt grassland. Together with the neighbouring Coleford Nature Reserve, it protects practically the only 'major' area of mist-belt grassland in the Drakensberg area.

Himeville Museum has a wide selection of settler paraphernalia, a small natural history section, and an up-to-date section on the San and their rock art. Some early Bhaca handicraft is also on display at the museum.

Winter morning in Himeville Nature Reserve.

Basotho ponies

'Horses! Give me more horses! They are our greatest and principal need,' demanded Jan van Riebeeck at the Fairest Cape in the 17th century. Van Riebeeck brought only a few horses with him from Europe to the southern tip of Africa, where he was surprised to discover the horse was unknown. More horses were accordingly introduced over the following centuries.

The Basotho pony evolved from the so-called 'Cape Hantam', a cross between the Arab and a pony-like mount brought to southern Africa from the Far East. When Khoi-khoi raiders on horseback harassed the people of Lesotho, they were at first awestruck by what appeared to them to be strange oxen without horns. Soon, however, the Basotho became a nation of horsemen by buying or rustling from their neighbours. Under pressure of the harsh surroundings a rather plain, shaggy little horse developed during the first half of the 19th century. With a long back and short legs, it stood 12–14 hands high, was sure-footed, tireless and resistant to the cold. Able to survive on a diet of poor grasses, it became indispensable to the new nation on the rugged high plateau. British soldiers later discovered its qualities and used the Basotho breed as polo ponies.

Basotho ponies were also used in the Anglo-Boer War of 1899–1901. Colonel Deneys Reitz captured some horses running wild near the border of Lesotho and led a column of 15 000 shaggy men on shaggy horses to invade the colony of Natal. Thousands of horses perished in the war. Some experts claim that this, together with subsequent attempts from the 1970s to cross it with imported English thoroughbreds, led to the decline of the Basotho pony. Already diminished in number, the tough little mountain horse's oriental blood was repressed by that of noble stallions, destroying its bloodline.

The mounts seen in Lesotho today are no longer truly Basotho ponies, although a group of enthusiastic South African horse lovers still try to keep the Basotho pony's revered qualities alive by propagating a breed they call the Nooitgedachter ('never-thought'). It may be the only living memorial to the sturdy pony that was once the lifeline to a forgotten world high in the mountains.

Black wildebeest at Himeville Nature Reserve in the early morning.

Wildlife
Mammals

At Himeville Nature Reserve you can get quite close to a herd of blesbok with their young. Although black wildebeest once used to inhabit these upland grasslands in great numbers, and they still flourish at Coleford Nature Reserve and Penworn Game Farm nearby, conservationists have not succeeded in reintroducing them into the montane grassland at higher altitude. Himeville has just four fairly unsociable individuals.

Birds

About 150 species have been listed. Many can be seen on the drive up to Sani Top. Two trout dams at Himeville Nature Reserve attract species such as Yellowbilled Duck, Redknobbed Coot, Moorhen, Whitebreasted Cormorant, Red and Golden Bishop. Raptors include the European Marsh Harrier, which has started to breed there, and Longcrested Eagle, while the Spotted Eagle Owl can be heard at night. Crowned Cranes can be seen during harvest time and European White Storks are still attracted in great numbers by tiny grassland locusts in summer.

Crowned Crane (*Balearica regulorum*).

Tourist attractions

Drives

Sani Pass and Sani Top: The drive up Sani Pass is a fascinating experience. As the altitude changes, so does the habitat – from virgin grassland and river rubble to forest margins and basaltic screes, resulting in a surprising variety of flowers and birds.

The journey begins in earnest as a geological excursion near the disused Good Hope Trading Store at a height of about 1 600 m. On the left and right are grassland slopes with fire-resistant protea stands. The road winds between boulders and Clarens sandstone cliffs where Jackal Buzzard and Black Eagle nest. Stop the car to listen for Barratt's Warbler, or look out for mountain reed-buck, eland and rhebok. Shortly after the border post, at a height of 1 800 m, the sandstone gives way to the basalts of the High Berg, evident in the Twelve Apostles that form the escarpment to the right. Before the road begins to zigzag steeply up the escarpment into the clouds, the vegetation changes to Drakensberg fynbos. Stop at a lay-by to admire the view before some 14 hair-pin bends require your full attention as you approach the gate with the sign, 'Sani Top 2 873 m'.

Tour guides take visitors to the typical rondavels of the tiny Sani Top settlement to see how the Basotho master life in this barren wilderness. The Mountain Chalet nearby offers meals, drinks and accommodation. A fairly easy outing is a day hike to Thabana Ntlenyana (see route 136 on page 118). Alternatively, hire one of the sturdy horses used by the locals, either by direct negotiation or with the help of the Mountain Chalet management.

Mokhotlong: Sani Pass connects to the tiny highland outpost of Mokhotlong in Lesotho, once known as the 'loneliest settlement in Africa'. Driving along the main route via Mokhotlong to Katse Dam is relatively easy. From Katse, tarred, scenic roads connect with Maseru or Ficksburg via Leribe.

Katse Dam: This two-day excursion is an easy drive from Sani Top via Mokhotlong. Katse Dam was the first to export hydroelectricity and water to South Africa and will be partly accessible for water sports. The 185 m concrete arch of the dam is the highest in Africa. The view over 45 km of flooded valleys is awesome but leaves an uneasy feeling about the future environmental impact of the huge Highlands Water Project.

Katse Lodge, overlooking the dam, provides accommodation and meals tel +266-312 896, fax +266-323 638. Camping is possible in the yard of the interpretation centre.

Looking over 45 km of flooded valley at Katse Dam.

Mountain biking

After testing by a number of mountain bikers, the Sani Pass has been divided into three sections of varying difficulty. The first starts at Himeville and ends at the South African border post (14 km or – via the Sani Lodge Backpackers/Sani Pass Hotel – 15 km). It is rated green, i.e. for beginners and children. The second section stretches from the border post to the base of the hairpin bends (5 km) and carries the red rating (i.e. for inter-mediate riders). The third stretch – up the steep hairpin bends to Sani Top (3 km) – is the shortest, but carries the black rating (i.e. for riders with high fitness and stamina levels).

Very fit bikers could proceed from Sani Top to the Black Mountains and try to tackle Thabana Ntlenyana, or proceed to Mokhotlong (52 km). Alternatively, they could return the same day to the foothills or stay overnight in the Mountain Chalet. The gravel road is quite rough in places and always carries a moderate amount of traffic.

Microlight flights

To take a short flight by microlight aircraft along the Drakensberg, contact Tyrone Wood, tel 033-701 1318/701 1091.

PRACTICAL TIPS

How to get to Sani Pass/Himeville
From north or south on the N3, take the off-ramp between Pietermaritzburg and Howick (near Midmar Dam) sign-posted Bulwer–Underberg (115 km) and proceed on the R617 to Underberg–Himeville.

Where to stay
Camping site at Himeville Nature Reserve, with hot/cold water. There are gas lights in the ablution block but no electricity. Firewood is available. Bookings through the officer-in-charge (tel 033-702 1036). You can also stay at the Himeville Arms Hotel, built in 1906 (tel 033-702 1305), one of several B&B establishments, or the Mountain Chalet at the top of Sani Pass (tel 033-702 1158).

Where to eat
Himeville Arms Hotel and Sani Top Chalet.

Local weather
The Sani Pass area is the coldest part of the KwaZulu-Natal Berg, with very cold winter nights. Heavy snowfalls are common in July and August, when skiing on Sani Top is possible. At higher altitudes, snowfalls can occur throughout the year. Rain can be expected mainly in summer, peaking from January to March, when mist is also common. Be prepared for rapid weather changes.

Facilities
Supermarkets in Himeville or Underberg.

Information
The non-commercial, computerized Sani Pass border post, controlled by the SA Police Services (tel/fax 033-702 1169) is open from 8:00 to 16:00. No access to Sani Pass is allowed to two-wheel drive vehicles from the South African side. A valid passport is required; a South African ID book suffices only to purchase a temporary travel document.

SANI PASS WALKS
(return distance, unless otherwise stated, different starting points)

EASY TO AVERAGE	INTERMEDIATE TO DIFFICULT	DIFFICULT TO EXTREME

133 HIMEVILLE NATURE RESERVE, ROUND TRIP: 2 km

A path leads around the Top and Bottom Dams. Move carefully and you should see a number of waterbirds and other species, as well as blesbok .

134 SANI PASS: 16 km (from S A Police Post)

This walk is not as severe as it looks, and provides a chance to see rare birds of the Berg. Park at the South African border post.

135 HODGSON'S TWIN PEAKS: 12 km (from Sani Top)

Not too difficult, this walk leads south to Hodgson's and gives superb views over Lesotho's Sehlaba-Thebe National Park and down into KwaZulu-Natal.

136 SANI PASS AND THABANA NTLENYANA: 30 km (from Sani Top)

Hike or drive up Sani, spend the night in the Mountain Chalet and tackle the 'Beautiful Little Mountain' the next day, either on foot or on horseback.

Cobham Mountain Reserve

This largely untouched and bucolic – some would say underdeveloped – reserve, dominated by Hodgson's twin peaks (3 244 m and 3 256 m), includes 52 000 ha of unspoilt wilderness. It snuggles, almost oblivious to the world, in the valleys of the Little Berg, with vast Themeda and Festuca grasslands, emerald green in summer. From the camping site you can sometimes see eland gather in large herds on the left bank of the Pholela River, with its countless pools. Cobham is famed as a wetland area and is, in fact, known as the 'Lake District' because of the numerous small lakes and tarns in the vicinity.

Highlights include exceptional rock art sites, river walks and the chance to hike to Southern Africa's highest mountain via Sani Pass, or drive up the historic pass in a 4x4 and hire a horse at Sani Top.

Hodgson's Peaks dominating the skyline at Cobham.

Wildlife

Mammals

Carnivores in the area include black-backed jackal, caracal, serval, large spotted genet, Cape clawless and spotted-necked otter, and grey and water mongoose. Bushbuck, eland, grey duiker, grey rhebok, klipspringer, oribi, common and mountain reedbuck, Natal red rock rabbit and scrub hare are also found.

Birds

Cobham Visitor's Guide's bird list includes 165 species. The short Ouhout Trail (see route 138, overleaf) is recommended for bird watching, especially in the early morning.

Reptiles

With luck, the Drakensberg crag lizard may be seen sunning itself somewhere along the Gxalingenwa River path. Look out for the short-legged, five-toed *Seps tetradactylus*, which looks a bit like a skaapsteeker but has tiny, hairlike legs. This lizard is a good example of the tendency towards progressive degeneration of the limbs that is found in several groups of lizards.

Flora

A great number of flowers, trees, shrubs and ferns grow in the reserve. Many can be found on a walk along the Pholela River or on the paths towards Sani Pass, but perhaps the easiest way to get to know some of the common Drakensberg plants is to take a walk along the Gxalingenwa Botanic River Trail (see route 139, overleaf).

Dragonflies

Well-vegetated Berg streams are the ideal habitat for dragonflies, as are the many small dams and tarns found around Cobham. These robust hunters are among the most beautiful flying insects, although the female is less colourful. Damselflies are sometimes confused with dragonflies but are less robust, less active and less colourful.

Of some 130 species of dragonfly distributed throughout South Africa more than 20 can be found above 1 500 m. Several are South African endemics and one, the Drakensberg Sylph, is so specialized that it survives only in the alpine belt. For millions of years it has survived the harsh winters on the summit of the Berg without any known changes.

The hilly ground lies opposite the Sani Pass Hotel golf course, outside the official conservation area, and is part of the Pholela Biosphere Reserve, an association of local farmers with an environmental conscience. The path leads through the narrow valley to a patch of typical montane forest regarded as one of the best in the southern Drakensberg. It involves at least four river crossings – easy in winter, although boulder hopping is required during the rainy season. Note the Tussock Grass, used by broom makers, at the second crossing. Straight ahead after the third crossing is well-established grassland with Red Grass (*Themeda triandra*) and iNcema Grass, used by Zulu women in their skilful grass-weaving, in the sedges near the river.

Tourist attractions

Walks and hikes

Cobham offers a number of interesting walks and hikes. The Giant's Cup National Hiking Way is probably one of the longest and best known of the KwaZulu-Natal Berg range. Giant's Cup was once the name of the twin mountains known today as Hodgson's Peaks in memory of a tragic incident when a young farmer was accidentally shot during a hot pursuit of San cattle rustlers in 1862.

San rock art

See routes 140, 143 and 144 below.

COBHAM MOUNTAIN RESERVE WALKS		
(return distance, starting at camp, unless otherwise stated)		
EASY TO AVERAGE	INTERMEDIATE TO DIFFICULT	DIFFICULT TO EXTREME

137 LAKE DISTRICT RAMBLE: 2+ km

Saunter about at leisure and discover the extensive network of paths around the camp. Sizeable herds of eland may be encountered in summer.

138 OUHOUT TRAIL: 2 km

Cross the swing bridge below the camping site and follow the Pholela River upstream. Cross the river again after 1 km and head back to camp through the indigenous Ouhout/Ntshishi bush and grassland.

139 GXALINGENWA RIVER AND FOREST, ROUND TRIP: 7 km

This botanic excursion, mainly following the Gxalingenwa River, begins opposite the Sani Pass Hotel golf course. The start is well sign-posted. The path passes interesting stands of local flora and ends in a patch of magnificent natural forest. A descriptive leaflet is available from the Cobham office.

140 ROCK ART: 12 km

This easy walk is a segment of the complete Heritage Trail (see route 144). A commercial guide takes you to some of the historic sites within easy reach of the camp.

141 PHOLELA RIVER TRAIL: 12 km

An easy route for the unhurried, with many beautiful pools. Choose your own distance. Return distance to the confluence of the Pholela and iNhlabeni Rivers is 12 km. The complete river walk leads through grassland and forest patches for about 15 km towards the upper reaches of the Pholela River. Generous views of Hodgson's Peaks and interesting geological formations along the river.

Along the Pholela trail.

COBHAM MOUNTAIN RESERVE WALKS (contd.)
(return distance, starting at camp, unless otherwise stated)

EASY TO AVERAGE	INTERMEDIATE TO DIFFICULT	DIFFICULT TO EXTREME

142 EMERALD STREAM: 16 km

The route runs through grassland along the left side of the Emerald Stream towards the Main Berg and winds along the cliffs above the Emerald Stream. After about 6 km it reaches a large plateau, offering unrestricted views in all directions. Look out for antelope and baboons along the route.

143 HERITAGE DAY HIKE: 16 km

This round trip leads to Mpongweni Shelter with its fabulous exhibition of San rock art. The final, short climb is rather steep.

144 HERITAGE TRAIL: 25 km

This circular route involves 3 days' trekking with qualified commercial guides. It takes in the wild scenic beauty, as well as the fauna and flora of the rugged wilderness before concentrating on the grand legacy of San rock art, Stone Age tool-shaping sites, remains of early Zulu occupation, and the first indications of the arrival of white settlers at Boundary Rock. A highlight is a visit to the celebrated Mpongweni Shelter, one of the early National Heritage Sites. Overnight in your own tent or in the caves.

145 HODGSON'S PEAKS: 38 km

Allow 2–3 days for this historical route along the Pholela River towards the escarpment. The final climb through Masubasuba Pass is arduous. Add another day or two to trek along the escarpment to Rhino from where you can clamber down the Mashai Pass. Save time by taking the Landrover trip from Himeville/Underberg to Sani Top.

146 GIANT'S CUP NATIONAL HIKING WAY: 59,3 km

This premier Drakensberg hiking trail leads for 5 days along the foothills from Sani Pass to Bushman's Nek. Only the first day passes through forest patches; the rest involves hiking through montane grassland with the escarpment almost always in sight. Suitable for reasonably fit adults and children. Overnight stops are in old farmhouses at Pholela and huts at Mzimkhulwana, Winterhoek, Swiman and Bushman's Nek. Basic facilities like bunk beds, mattresses, benches and tables, as well as cold-water taps and flush toilets are provided. Firewood and hot showers are available only at Pholela. You can book for only a section of the trail.

PRACTICAL TIPS

How to get to Cobham

From N3 in both directions, take the Bulwer–Underberg off-ramp onto the R617 to Underberg and then the right turn onto the R315 to Himeville. Turn left onto the D7 at the village entrance.

Where to stay

There is a rustic camping and caravan site with cold water only, and limited toilet facilities. The Pholela Hut, an old farmhouse, can be booked when not in use by hikers. Overnight hikers can use nine caves throughout the reserve, sleeping 2–12 persons.

Where to eat

You may prepare your own meals or drive to Himeville (14 km) or Underberg (19 km) for restaurants, hotels and fast-food outlets.

Facilities

The camp office shop sells basic groceries. All amenities are available at Himeville and at Underberg.

Information/bookings

Advance booking for camping and caves is mae through the camp office, tel/fax 033-702 0831.

The Giant's Cup Trail and Pholela Hut must be booked through Central Reservations, Box 13069, Cascades 3202 tel 033-845 1000, fax 033-845 1001.

Outlines of Garden Castle: a Scottish castle against an African sky.

Garden Castle Mountain Reserve

Garden Castle is named after the heavily eroded free-standing peak, Garden Castle (2 356 m), which can be seen on the way to the reserve. Captain Allen Gardiner, an ex-naval officer who travelled the Berg in 1835 as missionary and explorer, originally named this peak 'Giant's Castle'. He found its resemblance to Edinburgh Castle startling. A rock painting in one of the caves in the area depicts men and ox wagons, possibly his party. It may have been one of the last works of the San artists. Numerous San rock art sites are protected, and some can be visited in the company of experienced guides.

The principal peak inside the conservation area, which covers 35 000 ha, is the free-standing Rhino (3 051 m) although some other peaks nearby, including Mlambonja (3 309 m), Wilson's Peak (3 276 m), Mashai (3 313 m) and Walker's Peak (3 306 m), are even higher. Together, they account for the dramatic impact of the landscape of the area, gently counterpointed by clear streams, rivers and tarns.

This reserve, the southernmost in the KwaZulu-Natal Drakensberg, is part of the Mzimkhulu Wilderness Area, which is accessible from here, from Cobham or from Bushman's Nek further south. Its northern border lies just north of the road to Sani Top.

Wildlife
Mammals
Eland, mountain reedbuck and baboons are seen regularly in the reserve. Klipspringer may be encountered near Sleeping Beauty Cave.

Birds

A list available from the office records 87 bird species, including most Drakensberg specials such as Lammergeier, Black Eagle, Jackal Buzzard and Drakensberg Siskin.

Tourist attractions

Walks and hikes

The Mashai River path leads to most destinations and to several caves suitable for overnighting, including the three most popular: Monk, Sleeping Beauty and Engagement. Sleeping Beauty can take groups of up to 12 people, while Engagement Cave – perhaps romantically – accommodates only two. Garden Castle is also known for its major share of the Giant's Cup National Hiking Way. Three of the Giant's Cup's five hiking huts are on the reserve's territory. For the less energetic, short walks and day hikes are plentiful.

San rock art

Starting at 08:00 on Mondays, Wednesdays and Saturdays, guided walks are offered to groups of at least three people. Each walk takes about three hours. Book in advance at the KZN Wildlife office from 08:00 to 16:30 daily, or tel 033-701 1823. Please cancel bookings in good time.

Ruby *Brunsvigia* sp., a high-altitude plant.

PRACTICAL TIPS

How to get to Garden Castle

The Pietermaritzburg–Bulwer–Underberg route (R617) is recommended. A gravelled district road (D317) branches off to the right about 10 km past Underberg (35 km). It leads to the Drakensberg Gardens Hotel entrance and through the hotel grounds to the reserve.

Where to stay

A camping site and 12 caves are suitable for overnighting. Camping in the Wilderness Area is permitted (see 'Restrictions', page 173). Three hiking huts accommodate up to 30 people each and are equipped with beds and mattresses. Bring everything else with you. Casual visitors and hikers may book the huts, preference given to National Hiking Way hikers.

Where to eat

Bring your own food. Cold drinks and sweets are available at the office. Restaurants and fast-food outlets can be found in Underberg (35 km).

Facilities

There is a picnic area next to the car park but no fires are allowed. Super markets and other amenities at Underberg (35 km) or Himeville (40 km).

Bookings

Reserve huts through Central Reservations, Box 13069, Cascades 3202; tel 033-8451000, fax 033-8451001. All other bookings must be made through the officer-in-charge, tel 033-7011823.

GARDEN CASTLE MOUNTAIN RESERVE WALKS
(return distance, starting at Visitors Centre, unless otherwise stated)

EASY TO AVERAGE	INTERMEDIATE TO DIFFICULT	DIFFICULT TO EXTREME

147 THREE POOLS: 4,5 km

An easy short walk, ideal for hot days as it leads to clear pools ideal for swimming. Follow the 'Three Pools' signs from the parking lot. The path crosses the Mlambonja River and leads steeply up to the ridge. Descend and cross the stream at the bottom. After 1 km take the right turn at the fork to Three Pools and Champagne Pools about 400 m on.

148 PILLAR CAVE AND MLAMBONJA RIVER: 6 km

This fairly easy walk, signposted 'Pillar Cave and Mashai Pass', starts at the parking area and Blue Gum Forest and follows the Mlambonja River in a north-westerly direction, crossing the river several times. Enjoy beautiful river scenery and pools ideal for swimming.

149 SLEEPING BEAUTY CAVE: 8 km

This is a fair to moderate trip with some steeper parts. It is one of the more popular short walks in the reserve, with grand views of mountain and river, several river crossings, and patches of indigenous forest. Follow the signs from the office and cross the first river over the bridge. The valley narrows after 2 km and enters the sandstone portals of Swiman and the Monk. Rhino Peak is visible to the north. Pools along the path are suitable for swimming. The path gets steeper as it approaches Mlambonja and Wilson's Peak. Sleeping Beauty Cave follows on a steep slope above the river. The first section of the two-part walk is easy but, after the wooden ladder, the path gets much steeper and can be very slippery after rain. Engagement Cave is nearby in a side gully, about 700 m further upstream.

150 ENGAGEMENT CAVE, ROUND TRIP: 9 km

Follow the same path as for Sleeping Beauty Cave (see route 149). Pass the cave; follow the path on the left-hand side of the river then cross the river just above the cave. Follow the path going up a steep incline. At the top of a huge triangular rock the path splits, with the right fork leading to Engagement Cave about 100 m ahead.

151 HIDDEN VALLEY: 14 km

The hike up the Mzimude Valley, where the sandstone of the Little Berg is bizarrely eroded, is rewarding for anyone interested in geology. The return trip can be arranged as a day excursion leading partly along the National Hiking Way. The path begins behind the National Hiking Way's Swiman hut, passes Sunken Valley and continues to Bushman's Nek. The Hidden Valley path branches off to the right and offers a pleasant detour down to the suspension bridge. You will walk part of the way outside the reserve.

152 RHINO PEAK: 18 km

This challenging hike offers sweeping views from Lesotho to East Griqualand. An early start is advised. Start from the office and follow the main path in a north-westerly direction along the Mlambonja River, first on the right then on the left bank, past Pillar Cave. Above Pillar Cave, a 4 km slog up the pass begins, passing the Mashai Fangs on the left. The Mashai Shelter marks the top of the pass. From here the path gains another 150 m in altitude leading across the saddle between the escarpment and Rhino Peak. The knife-edged ridge should be avoided during bad weather conditions.

The road to Bushman's Nek.

Bushman's Nek

The Bushman's Nek part of the Garden Castle Reserve and Mzimkhulu Wilderness Area marks the southern end of the KwaZulu-Natal Drakensberg and the beginning or end of the 68 km long Giant's Cup National Hiking Way.

Here, the montane grassland is somewhat less verdant than further north, forest patches are rare, and the mountains – even the dominant peaks, such as Devil's Knuckle (3 028 m), Thomathu (2 734 m) and Thaba Ngwangwe (3 068 m) – look less menacing. Devil's Knuckle is the last of the mighty 3 000 m peaks before Ben MacDhui in the north-eastern Cape. From here southwards the escarpment becomes moderate, dropping almost abruptly to an average height of 2 400 m.

Wildlife

Mammals

Animals that may be spotted high up on the spurs and ledges include eland, reedbuck, grey rhebok, dassie and klipspringer. Oribi and the nocturnal porcupine are also present, but seldom encountered.

Birds

There is a good chance of seeing the rare Lammergeier and the imposing Black Eagle.

Rock dassie (*Procavia capensis*).

Tourist attractions
Walks and hikes

The border post and KZN Wildlife office at the bottom of Bushman's Nek Pass are the starting points for all walks and hikes through the adjacent wilderness and to six caves, all of which can be reached on day trips. Two caves with excellent San paintings can be visited with accredited guides booked at the Bushman's Nek Hotel.

It is relatively easy to walk or ride up Bushman's Nek Pass (2 400 m) and Jonathan's Gate to reach the rather inhospitable Lesotho plateau. From here, bridle paths lead

Crowned Cranes (*Balearica regulorum*) in Berg wetlands.

to the nearby Sehlaba-Thebe National Park (see opposite page). Horses are not easy to come by on the South African side, although horses, ponies and guides are available for short trips at the nearby Silverstreams Trading Store, built of Molteno sandstone in the early 1900s, where Basotho herdsmen and local farmers traded bales of wool for essential supplies.

BUSHMAN'S NEK WALKS		
(return distance, starting at police post)		
EASY TO AVERAGE	INTERMEDIATE TO DIFFICULT	DIFFICULT TO EXTREME

153 LANGALIBALELE CAVE: 5 km

This is a short but fairly steep hike.

154 HALFWAY CAVE: 5 km

An easy excursion, even for the not so fit.

155 TARN CAVE: 18 km

The cave, named for the number of tarns in the vicinity, is reached by following a relatively easy path up the Ngwangwane Valley towards Devil's Knuckles. Unfortunately, most of the tarns are on the Lesotho side, in Sehlaba-Thebe National Park.

156 THOMATHU CAVE: 7 km

The path winds its way along on the northern flank of the Thomathu Ridge and gets very steep.

157 LAMMERGEIER CAVE: 11 km

A 4x4 track leads westwards from the police post. It is easy to get lost if you do not know the area: as always, a good map is essential.

158 BUSHMAN'S CAVE AND NGWANGWANE PASS: 11 km

The path leads westwards along the Bushman's River. After passing Halfway Cave it reaches the steep pass through a small forest patch.

PRACTICAL TIPS

How to get to Bushman's Nek

Take the R617 from Underberg (35 km) to Swartkop and turn at the second turn-off to the right (well sign-posted) onto a gravel road leading directly to the park entrance and border post.

Where to stay

There are no overnight facilities in the reserve except wilderness camping or overnighting in caves. Silverstreams private camping site has been developed next to the entrance. It is well grassed though presently shadeless, and has electricity; tel 033-701 1249, fax 033-701 1227 e-mail: geyer@telkomsa.net

The revamped Bushman's Nek Hotel and Timeshare Resort, a few kilometres from the border post, offers self-catering chalets and hotel-type accommodation, all with views of the peaks tel 033-701 1460.

Where to eat

At the hotel or bring your own food.

Facilities

There is a picnic spot at the waterfall near the border post, and a small supermarket-cum-farm stall opposite the caravan park. Other amenities at Underberg (35 km).

Information

As the area is a bit out of the way and not much frequented by visitors it is advisable to sign the mountain register at the KZN Wildlife office, even for short walks. A valid passport or ID book is necessary when entering Lesotho. Bushman's Nek/Nkonkoana Border Post, controlled by SA Police Services, is open between 08:00 and 16:00; tel/fax 033-701 1212. No road, only a bridle path across the border for pedestrians and hikers.

Bookings

Book wilderness camping and caves through Garden Castle Reserve's officer-in-charge tel 033-701 1823.

Excursion to Sehlaba-Thebe National Park

The Mountain Kingdom in the Sky's only significant (6 500 ha) conservation area nestles in the south-east corner of Lesotho where the crystal clear Tsoelikana River, a tributary of the Senqu, has its source. 'The Shield', as this plateau of the Little Berg is called, is known for its rock arches, beautiful waterfalls and diverse sub-alpine flora.

To date, about 240 bird species have been recorded in the area, 14 of them listed in the Red Data Book. A highly threatened species is the Drakensberg Minnow, once thought to be extinct but rediscovered in the Tsoelikana River.

To get there: *Sehlaba-Thebe can be reached on foot or horseback via Bushman's Nek Pass, 10 km from the South African border post, or by driving up Ramatseliso's Gate or Qacha's Nek from Matatiele. A more arduous route is from Mokhotlong. All access roads are reasonable gravel roads, but the route from the entrance gate of the lodge and the park's rustic camping site is negotiable only by 4x4 vehicles.*

Accommodation: *The park has a lodge with all facilities, a basic five-bed hostel, and allows camping.*

Eating: *At the lodge, or bring your own food.*

Facilities: *Neither basic foodstuffs nor fuel is available.*

Information: *Lesotho Tourist Board, Box 1378, Maseru, Lesotho; tel +266-312 896, fax +266-323 638, e-mail: ltbhq@ltb.org.ls*

Bookings: *Sehlaba-Thebe National Park, Jonathan's Lodge, Box 92, Maseru 100; or phone the Lesotho Tourist Board (above).*

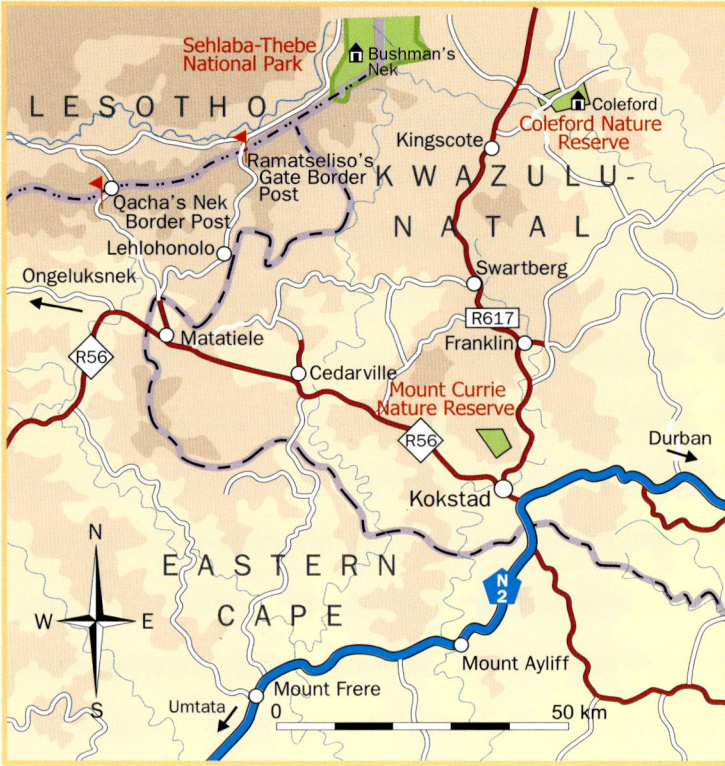

Map labels:

Sehlaba-Thebe National Park
Bushman's Nek
LESOTHO
Coleford
Coleford Nature Reserve
Kingscote
Ramatseliso's Gate Border Post
KWAZULU-NATAL
Qacha's Nek Border Post
Lehlohonolo
Swartberg
Ongeluksnek
R617
Matatiele
Franklin
R56
Cedarville
Mount Currie Nature Reserve
R56
Durban
Kokstad
N
W   E
S
EASTERN CAPE
N2
Mount Ayliff
Mount Frere
Umtata
0   50 km

KwaZulu-Natal to the Eastern Cape

The Griquas, led by Adam Kok, crossed the escarpment in 1862 during their trek from Griquastad to the 'No-man's-land' later known as East Griqualand. Now part of KwaZulu-Natal, this area forms the connecting link with the north-eastern Cape area of the Drakensberg and provides access to the Lesotho plateau via rugged mountain passes.

From the Bushman's Nek turnoff in the southern KwaZulu-Natal Drakensberg, a 55 km drive leads to Swartberg. To the west lies Matatiele, a town on the Eastern Cape border, founded by the Griquas after a trek of 2 000 people and 20 000 head of cattle led by the legendary Adam Kok III across the Drakensberg. To the south lie Franklin and Kokstad, which Kok founded in 1862, the centre of his short-lived republic on the fertile grassland below Mount Currie (2 224 m) – a place once known as Nomansland. Today, Kokstad is the centre of a flourishing cattle-farming region known as East Griqualand.

For the ongoing traveller, the tranquil border town of Matatiele, once reached, affords two choices: to proceed to the top of the Lesotho escarpment and nearby Sehlaba-Thebe National Park via Lehlohonolo-Ramatseliso's Gate; or to make a quick trip to Ongeluksnek past Roamer's Rest and an inconspicuous little mountain named 'Drakensberg'.

En route to Sehlaba-Thebe National Park.

Matatiele and environs

Named after an adjacent vlei, Madi i Yilaa (meaning 'the ducks have flown'), this tranquil border town was once a sanctuary for cattle rustlers, gun-runners, horse thieves and smugglers using the nearby Berg as a perfect hiding place. Extensive farmland now stretches around Matatiele, where horses figure more in polo than in the drama of theft.

There are two nature reserves in these southern reaches of the Drakensberg.

Matatiele Museum

Housed in a historic Molteno sandstone building, now a national monument, the museum concentrates on local cultural history. It includes a fine collection of San rock art, Early Middle and Late Stone Age implements, as well as pottery, beadwork and personal items of local people and early missionaries and farmers.
Opening hours: Mondays–Fridays, 09:00–12:00 and 14:00–16:00; tel 039-737 3135.

PRACTICAL TIPS

How to get to Matatiele
From the Bushman's Nek turnoff, take the tarred R617 to Swartberg (55 km), from where a 70 km gravelled road leads to Matatiele.
Where to stay
Matatiele Caravan Park, 14 West Street, Matatiele tel 039-737 3333.
Royal Hotel, tel 039-737 3100 fax 039-737 4088.

Wilfried Bauer Nature Reserve

Hiking and game watching are possible in this 200 ha reserve 5 km west of Matatiele, stocked with black wildebeest, plains zebra and springbok. Look for the so-called 'zebdonk' – a zebra-donkey cross breed – roaming the grasslands.

The zebdonk of the plains.

Mountain Lake Nature Reserve

Rising from 1 200–2 000 m, a 12 km drive from Matatiele leads to a 30 ha mountain lake surrounded by grassland, protea savannah, rocky gorges and wetland. The location is known by keen birders as one of KwaZulu-Natal's most reliable for high-altitude birds, including the rare Rudd's Lark, as well as African Rock Pipit, Mountain Pipit, Buffstreaked Chat, Gurney's Sugarbird, Cape Eagle Owl and Stanley's Bustard. The reserve is accessible by normal vehicle except in bad weather. A chalet with bunk beds can be rented from the local trout-fishing club (tel 039-737 3170).

matatiele and environs

131

Franklin and environs

The road to Franklin passes through extensive marshes to the east and north of the village. The marshy Franklin Vlei is known to birders as the place where the endangered Whitewinged Flufftail was rediscovered. Two other Flufftail species occur, while a third, the Buffspotted Flufftail, has been seen in nearby woodland. Wattled Crane and Southern Crowned Crane are also found in encouraging numbers. Bittern and Little Bittern, African Rail, African Crake, Ethiopian Snipe, as well as several heron and duck species can also be seen.

Kokstad and environs

East Griqualand covers about 4 070 km², including parts of the former Transkei and the district of Mzimkhulu. The centre of the region is Kokstad.

Kokstad Museum

The building housing the museum, once the town's library, is now a national monument and provides an insight into the history of the Griqua, as well as the role of the military in the area.

PRACTICAL TIPS

To get to Franklin
Franklin lies on the R617, 80 km from Underberg, 12 km south of Swartberg and about 30 km north of Kokstad.
Where to stay
The nearest overnight accommodation is at the Waterfront Guesthouse, 10 km from Franklin in the direction of Swartberg; tel 039-747 9002.

The Last Hope – a stone formation near Qacha's Nek.

Zebra (*Equus burchelli*) at Mount Currie Nature Reserve.

Mount Currie Nature Reserve

Take the Swartberg-Franklin Road. Turn 150 m outside Kokstad onto the gravelled D623 and proceed 4,5 km to the main gate of this 1 800 ha reserve of rolling grassland. The Crystal Springs Dam is stocked with large-mouth bass, bluegill and trout, but is also a haven for bird-watchers. A bird list with more than 220 recorded species is available from the office. Flufftails are quite common and Bearded Vultures are regularly seen soaring overhead. Blesbok, mountain reedbuck and grey rhebok are seen regularly and, with luck, grey duiker, bushbuck or oribi.

Blesbok (*Damaliscus dorcas phillipsi*).

PRACTICAL TIPS

Where to stay in the area

Ten campsites at Mount Currie Nature Reserve, with hot and cold water, some electric plug points and communal dishwashing and laundry facilities; tel 039-727 3844. Kokstad has a wide selection of B&Bs and hotels and several restaurants.

Information

The SA Police Services border post at Ramatseliso's Gate is open from 8:00–16:00; tel/fax 0551-41839. Qacha's Nek Gate opens from 08:00–22:00; tel/fax 0551-41839. Ongeluksnek opens from 08:00–16:00; tel/fax 0551-41839/3382.

north-eastern cape
drakensberg

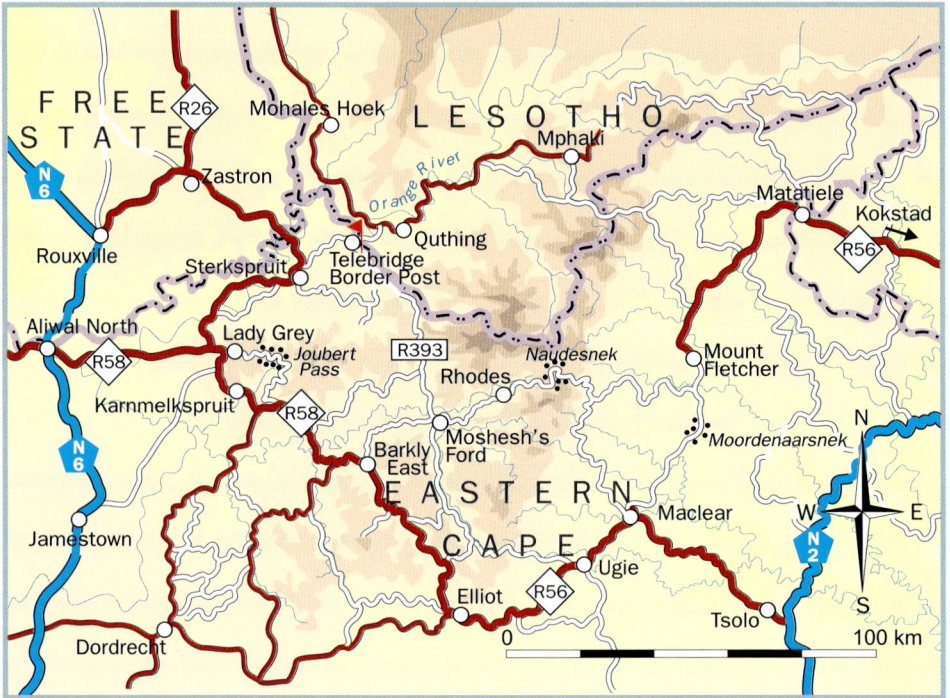

North-eastern Cape Drakensberg

The tail of the dragon – the north-eastern Cape Drakensberg –
winds around the southernmost part of Lesotho before
merging with the dry Karoo in the west. The environmental assets
of the region are not as well protected as in the KwaZulu-Natal
Berg, but with its grand scenery, this half-forgotten corner of the
country affords a sense of quiet solitude and has much to offer
naturalist and adventurous traveller.

The land along the north-eastern Cape Drakensberg contrasts sharply with the KwaZulu-Natal Berg and its wilderness areas. Devoid of official conservation areas, though it has some privately owned nature reserves, it consists largely of privately owned farmland marked by rusty barbed-wire fences. Resorts do not follow each other like pearls on a string, and some of the lower valleys are overgrazed or overrun by alien plants.

Nevertheless, the region's remoteness, simple infrastructure and pollution-free environment create a sense of quiet solitude. Here the highest peak of the escarpment is Ben MacDhui (3 001 m). Branching out towards the picturesque town of Lady Grey to the west are the Witteberge, with Balloch (2 648 m), Avoca (2 771 m), Snowdon (2 769 m) and Pelion (2 682 m) as the highest peaks.

The bleak Stormberg mountain range is a continuation of the Drakensberg in the south. The region has always been of special interest to geologists, who named the youngest of the four sequences of the Karoo system and the Stormberg series after the imposing Stormberg Mountain (2 127 m).

Although this corner of the country has much to offer the naturalist, a number of its far-flung valleys are accessible only via steep mountain passes that call for 4x4 transport. Many of its clear rivers and streams were once stocked with trout and are now home to an increasing population of 'wild trout' that has adapted perfectly to the ideal conditions.

Also called the Eastern Cape Highlands, the north-eastern Cape Drakensberg was probably the last San stronghold in the Drakensberg. Over 1 000 San rock art shelters have been rediscovered, some as old as 10 000 years. Some 20 rock shelters on private farms are open to the public. Although the area is becoming more popular for its well-developed hiking trails, these sites, fossilized animal and plant fragments, and the dinosaur footprints that have been discovered remain its biggest attractions.

Part of a thighbone and the upper jawbone of a dinosaur were found near Aliwal North in 1985. *Aliwalia rex* was about 12 m long and weighed 1,5 tons. Fossilized remains of an enormous herbivore, *Euskelosaurus*, are kept at Transwillige Primary School in Lady Grey, and fossilized evidence of the four-footed dinosaur, *Massospondylus*, can be seen at Prentjiesberg Nature Reserve, a Natural Heritage Site owned by North East Cape Forests (Mondi).

The region is known also for its large Blue Crane and Crowned Crane populations (see page 140). Birding is excellent and game animals still to be seen in farmland and grassland below the higher reaches of the 'Great Escarpment'.

Bizarre rock formations etch the sky at a stud farm near Elliot (below left). Many farms in the area contain rock art (below centre) and animal life less tame than this flock of sheep crossing Barkly Pass road (below right).

Mountain grasses and forest

The region below the 'Great Escarpment' between Barkly East and Molteno–Steynsburg is largely covered by mountain grassland that reaches westwards onto the upland of the Karoo. Known as Stormberg Plateau Sweetveld, this grassland grows from 1 400–2 150 m above sea level, changing at the Drakensberg foothills into moist upland grassveld that extends to the Amatola-Winterberg mountains.

Pockets of Afro-montane forest thrive in adjacent kloofs and valleys. The lowland Pondoland-Tongaland forests influence montane forest vegetation here, where the tree line seems to be much lower than in the KwaZulu-Natal Berg. Woody plants in the region above 1 500 m are largely represented by gnarled Ouhout trees.

The seasons

Annual rainfall in the area ranges from 650–1 000 mm in the foothills to just 450–600 mm at heights above 1 400 m. At the highest altitudes, it may reach 1 900 mm or more.

Summers are moderate, but the weather changes rapidly and thunder storms are frequent. In winter, spectacular snowfalls, especially on mountain peaks and slopes, draw an ever-increasing crowd of winter sports enthusiasts. Autumn, when exotic trees and grasses turn yellow and brown, is considered the best time for outdoor activities such as walking, hiking, horse riding and biking.

Rolling grasslands lead westwards to the higher mountains.

The African Potato Plant (*Hypoxis rooperii*) has healing roots containing anti oxidants said to clean the blood.

Grasses become shorter and denser in high rainfall areas and in the foothills. Red Grass, Tussock Fescue, Wire Grass, Spear Grass and Common Thatchgrass are among the dominant species. Patches of dry, grassy fynbos occur where Water Heath, Cliffortia and restio species grow in profusion. Rocky areas are quite bare compared with similar KwaZulu-Natal Berg areas, covered, at most, with sparse succulent vegetation.

Commercial forests, a relatively recent phenomenon in the region, are slowly nibbling away at the grassland below the high mountain region although, for the time being, heavy frosts and inaccessible terrain continue to protect the indigenous fauna and flora.

The local flora has adapted to the ravages of regular frost. Many plants of the KwaZulu-Natal Drakensberg thrive here, too, among them a number of endemics. Between December and February the foothills and high-lying areas are ablaze with flowering everlastings, gladioli, *Kniphofia* and *Rhodohypoxis* species, as well as Fire Lilies and bright red River Lilies, which are pollinated by the mountain pride butterfly (*Meneris tulbaghia*). Proteas and ericas represent Cape fynbos. In the evening, Ground Orchids attract moths with their sweet scent. Some of them produce an oily substance collected by solitary *Rediviva* bees.

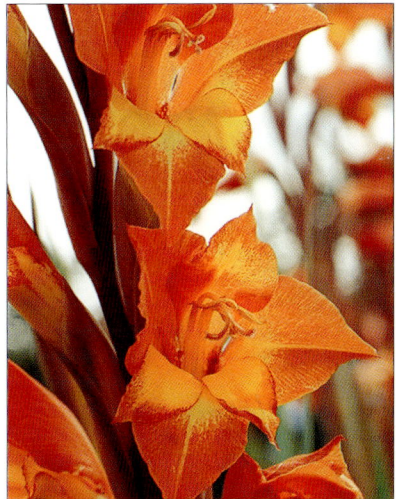

African Gladiolus (*Gladiolus dalenii*).

Cape Drakensberg wildlife

Mammals

Since the grasslands of the region are used for agriculture and stock grazing and none have been set aside for conservation purposes, remnants of the once-thriving mammal population are hard to find. Blesbok, grey rhebok, mountain reedbuck and others have been reintroduced to the Prentjiesberg Nature Reserve and still occur on some farms, but big game is not the reason why this region is visited.

Secretary Bird (*Sagittarius serpentarius*).

Birds

Birding is excellent, although bird diversity decreases towards the bleak, almost treeless higher regions. No comprehensive bird list of the region is available, but some 230 species have been listed in the Barkly East-Rhodes area alone, among them

Blue Crane
(*Anthropoides paradiseus*).

Crane trade

The region has one of the largest populations of Blue Crane and Crowned Crane in the country, as well as a small number of Wattled Cranes. Both Wattled and Blue Cranes are classified as 'critically endangered' in South Africa. Numbers of the country's national bird, the endemic Blue Crane, have declined by as much a 80% in some areas. The main threats for all three species stem from habitat destruction, electrocution by power lines, poisoning (accidental or wilful) and removal of chicks from the nests for pets or the illegal trade.

There is a lively trade in young birds in the region. About 100 Crowned Crane chicks were removed from breeding sites in the wild during the 2000/2001 breeding season, most of them apparently from the Ugie area, although Underberg in KwaZulu-Natal is also affected. It is alleged that up to R8 000 is offered for Blue Cranes and that farm labourers and school children are used to assist unscrupulous traders in obtaining these stately birds.

The South African Crane Working Group estimates that about 2 000 Blue Cranes are kept illegally in captivity as pets, their wings clipped. Conservation groups of the north-eastern Cape try to combat the threat to the crane population through 'crane awareness' campaigns.

Intensive wetland rehabilitation could, to a certain extent, improve breeding conditions for these highly specialized birds. Without it, future generations may no longer be able to observe the graceful birds in their natural surroundings.

40 species that do not occur in the KwaZulu-Natal Berg region. Grassland birds that are wide-spread and relatively easily found include the migrating European White Stork, Secretary Bird and the tiny Cisticola.

More rare are Yellowbreasted Pipit and Mountain Pipit, Black Stork, Booted Eagle and Black Harrier. Cape Vulture, Bearded Vulture, Black Eagle and Jackal Buzzard fly overhead to their nesting places in out-of-the-way cliffs in Lesotho and the nearby Karnmelkspruit Canyon.
• See lists of birds at the back of this book.

Towns and villages

The best way to get to know the region is to cross the scenic southern margin of the high interior plateau at a gentle pace, approaching from Matatiele in the north via Mount Fletcher and Moordenaarsnek to Maclear, Ugie and Elliot or Barkly East. Alternatively, you may travel from East London, three hours by car to the south.

Maclear and environs

Maclear is a good place from which to explore the area's natural and cultural history. Naudesnek, South Africa's highest and most photogenic mountain pass, is a relatively short drive away. Several Natural Heritage Sites can also be visited, generally by appointment only. The 26 m Tsitsa Waterfall nearby is worth a visit.

Maclear in the beauty of its natural setting.

PRACTICAL TIPS

Where to stay
Comfortable hotels, a well-equipped caravan park and many guesthouses and B&Bs are located in the town and on surrounding farms.
Information
Ugie-Maclear Tourist Association, PO Box 179, Ugie 5470
tel/fax 045-933 1335.

north-eastern cape

Ugie and environs

Ugie has become a centre of the North East Cape Forest industry (NECF), which is slowly making inroads into the original grasslands. Some outstanding natural features have been or will be set aside as nature reserves or Natural Heritage Sites.

PRACTICAL TIPS

Information/bookings
Ugie-Maclear Tourist
Association, P O Box 179,
Ugie 5470;
tel/fax 045-933 1335.
North East Cape Forests,
Private Bag Ugie 5470
tel 045-932 1177.

Prentjiesberg Nature Reserve

The reserve is best visited on a three-day hike starting at the forest station 6 km north-west of Ugie (see route 160, page 150). Major attractions of the 'picture mountain' include its views, protea savannah, indigenous forest and caves with San rock art. Blesbok, mountain reedbuck and dassie occur, as well as Bearded Vulture, Black Eagle, Crowned Eagle and Lanner Falcon.

A new species of fairy shrimp was recently discovered in the rock pools at the top.

Bastervoetpad

Despite its name, this is not a footpath but a scenic drive that is very rewarding in spring, summer and autumn for wildflower fans. Starting west of Ugie, the route connects to the R393 near the summit of Barkly Pass. Originally used for moving livestock, it became negotiable by motor vehicle in the 1960s. The road is currently in disrepair and a sturdy 4x4 vehicle is needed to negotiate it. The view from the summit of the pass, which can be reached after a short hike (see route 164, page 150), is rewarding.

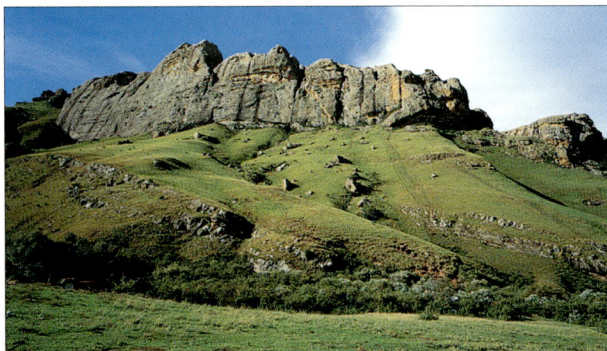

On the Bastervoetpad scenic drive.

Elliot

Elliot (called 'Ikowane' by the Xhosa people, after a mushroom that grows profusely in the area) nestles in the foothills of the Drakensberg. Worth a visit are the Twelve Apostles and Giant's Castle – threatening and weird-looking sandstone formations best viewed (or photographed) at dawn or dusk. The longest gallery of San paintings is found on the farm Dinorben on the way to Barkly East. The paintings appear to be deteriorating fast.

An empowerment project born out of the need to uplift impoverished township women and to help to preserve and promote the cultural heritage of the district has given rise to 'Beaders and Crafters' (located at Kruger St, Elliot 5460; tel 045-9311333, fax 045-9311361).

PRACTICAL TIPS

Where to stay
Hotels, guesthouses and B&Bs.
Two camping and caravan sites,
one in town, the other in more
natural surroundings at Thompson
Dam, with relatively rich birdlife;
tel 045-323 1025.

Information
Elliot Tourism Association,
PO Box 313, Elliot
tel 045-931 1333
fax 045-931 1361.

Bizarre rock formations, including the north-eastern Cape's own 'Giant's Castle'.

Barkly East and environs

The tarred Barkly Pass (2 000 m) is one of South Africa's most spectacular. The road climbs from Elliot at a maximum gradient of 1:12 to its highest point near the Mountain Shadows Hotel. It descends into a fertile valley before reaching Barkly East (1 814 m) after 40 km. An almost haunted landscape is dominated by bizarre sandstone formations sculpted by erosion. There are several hikes, painstakingly marked by the hotel's owner, for instance to the highest point (2 609 m) next to Bastervoetpad (see routes 164–166 below).

Barkly East lies on the slopes of the Witteberge, the 'Switzerland of South Africa', where snow-capped peaks reach heights of 2 600–3 000 m. An important sheep centre, the town was founded in 1874 and named after Sir Henry Barkly, governor of the Cape. Nearby are a number of large caves and rock shelters with relatively well-preserved San paintings. They occur mainly on farm land and are generally well looked after by the landowners. Several trails starting in and around the town allow sweeping exploration of the pristine mountains.

The Municipal Dam offers good bird watching. A bird list is available from the offices of the 110-year-old newspaper, *The Barkly East Reporter*, tel 045-971 0016.

> **PRACTICAL TIPS**
>
> **Where to stay**
> Old Mill Inn, tel 045-971 0277 fax 045-971 0972.
> Judy's Guesthouse, tel 045-971 0302 or cell 082-423 3662.
> B&Bs on farms.
> Mountain Shadows Hotel on Barkly Pass, tel 045-931 2233 fax 045-931 1139.
>
> **Information**
> Barkly East Municipality
> tel 045-971 0073
> fax 045-971 0350.

north-eastern cape

Towards the top of Barkly Pass.

Rhodes and environs

Rhodes, which was declared a national monument in 1997, was named Rossville until the villagers asked Cecil John Rhodes, then prime minister of the Cape, to boost the economy of the area. Rhodes sent them pine saplings, which have grown to create a splendidly shaded avenue.

The scenic Rhodes area, also known for its rock art.

Winter sports

Once a haven for those seeking isolation, the charming old-world settlement is famous for its cold climate and snow-capped peaks. It has become the epicentre of South Africa's alpine winter sports activities. The National Ski Championships are held annually on the slopes of nearby Ben MacDhui (3 001 m).

Mountain biking

A 60-km slow gravel road linking Rhodes to the town of Barkly East has become a starting point for 4x4 devotees – a bone of contention between them and those in search of solitude and quietness. Mountain biking takes over in October during the annual Rhodes mountain bike marathon. The 84,5 km course starts and ends in Rhodes and is very steep in places. Private parties using the trail at other times can arrange transport to the top of the steep mountain passes. Contact Rhodes Hotel. Horses and guides can be hired in the village.

Drive to Naudesnek

This is the highest drivable mountain pass (2 623 m) on the South African side of the Drakensberg. The narrow gravel road with a maximum gradient of 1:11 is usually in fair condition, but rock falls are possible in wet weather. Recommended speed is 30 km/h. Do not forget to have your tyres checked! All four seasons can be experienced in a day, so bring warm clothes and rain gear. The public phone booth near the top of the pass, a corrugated iron shack, is probably the highest in the country. Once of great help to stranded motorists, it has become somewhat obsolete since the advent of the cell phone.

Bird watching

Rhodes and environs are a bird watcher's paradise. Nowhere else can birds of the Drakensberg alpine and sub-alpine belt be observed with such ease from a car window. The bird list includes 225 species. A leisurely drive along the R396 between Mount Fletcher, Naudesnek, Rhodes and Moshesh's Ford (135 km) or a round trip including the famous Bastervoetpad and Barkly Pass are good choices for bird lovers. The gravel road winds through montane grassland dissected by gullies covered in fynbos, passing moist east-facing slopes and drier west-facing inclines. It crosses a number of fast-flowing streams where you can find Cape Bunting, Yellow Canary, Barratt's Warbler and Fairy Flycatcher, as well as kingfishers, sparrows, wagtails and waxbills. A tally of 50 or 60 species a day is easily attainable, among them Drakensberg Siskin, Mountain and African Rock Pipit, Orange-breasted Rockjumper, Striped Flufftail and Sickle-winged Chat.

If you extend your drive to Barkly Pass, look out for Crowned Crane, Black Eagle, Martial Eagle, Gymnogene, African Marsh Harrier and Lanner Falcon. The Forest Buzzard and Red-breasted Sparrowhawk favour patches of exotic timber plantations.

Martial Eagle (*Polemaetus bellicosus*).

north-eastern cape

Tiffindell Ski Resort

This is the only resort south of the Sahara where people can pretend they are skiing in a real winter wonderland – an impression kept alive by 'snow canons' imported from Austria.

Situated on a south-facing slope of the north-eastern Cape Drakensberg's highest mountain, Tiffindell Ski Resort can be reached from Rhodes (22 km away) by 4x4s or vehicles with high clearance. Alternatively, for a fee, in season, visitors can make use of the daily shuttle service from Rhodes.

Overnight guests are accommodated in wooden chalets surrounding a double-storey lodge in Swiss style. A full range of the equipment needed to get down the slopes on skis can be hired on the spot, and competent instructors are available. There is no 'best time' for skiing as conditions vary from day to day. (The lodge is open, however, only during certain months of the year.)

Information/bookings: Tiffindell Ski Resort, tel 045-974 9004 (e-mail: tiffresort@global.co.za) or 011-787 9090 (e-mail: tiffindell@global.co.za)

Lady Grey and environs

Set in a well-wooded valley in the rolling Witteberge, this picturesque village marks the start of the north-eastern Cape Drakensberg for visitors from the Cape.

Railway line

The town rocketed to fame when steam train enthusiasts from around the world discovered the 70 km railway line from Lady Grey to Barkly East. It passes through magnificent scenery at altitudes up to 2 000 m. The trains negotiate an awesome gradient by reversing not less than eight times. Construction of the line was started in 1902 from Lady Grey and took 23 years to complete because the bridge to cross Karnmelkspruit Gorge, which had been manufactured in the United Kingdom, was lost on the Atlantic Ocean. Instead, the engineers designed a zigzag system, also called a 'switchback', to traverse the gorge, thus immortalizing the otherwise insignificant railway line.

Vulture Sanctuary

About 10 km south of Lady Grey, to the right of the R58 to Barkly East, the farm Karnmelkspruit borders on the magnificent Karnmelkspruit Canyon. The stream has carved a deep gorge through the reddish sandstone, creating spectacular cliffs where 40–60 Cape Vultures breed between April and July. The nesting site is visible from the edge of the cliffs, but good binoculars are needed for a closer look. The owner of the farm will gladly give permission for a visit to the sanctuary but expects reasonable behaviour. Contact Ian & Elize Cloete, tel 051-603 0447 for permission and farm accommodation.

Joubert Pass

Further upstream, just east of Lady Grey, is the scenic Joubert Pass. In spite of the gradient of 1:6, it can be negotiated in a normal sedan car except when wet or damaged by heavy summer rains. A group of farmers, five Jouberts among them, built the pass in 1914 so that they could transport cheese from their homesteads over the Witteberge to Lady Grey.

For about 50 km the narrow gravel road meanders through the austere beauty of the north-eastern Cape montane grassland. Watch out for Greywing Francolin, Lammergeier, Cape Vulture and Jackal Buzzard. Stop now and then to listen to the silence, interrupted only by the murmur of the sparkling Karnmelkspruit, where 'wild trout' proliferate in the unpolluted water.

Joubert Pass starts at Lady Grey.

The reserve's natural diversity.

Lammergeier Nature Reserve

About 15 km before it links up again with the tarred R58 from Lady Grey to Barkly East, Karnmelkspruit Road crosses the privately owned Lammergeier Nature Reserve. This is probably the region's only serious attempt to preserve at least a part of the montane grassland in its natural state by 'sound application and practice of the principles of range and forage conservation and science' for which the owners were honoured in 1997 with the 'Conservation Farmer of the Year' award by the Grasslands Society of SA.

Part of their farm, Pelion Farm, straddling the upper reaches of the Karnmelkspruit, has been declared a Natural Heritage Site. Nature walks and wilderness trails, as well as one- to five-day trails (see routes 169–171) have been developed. A 4x4 track to the summit of Snowdon Peak has also been designed.

The 7 500 ha Lammergeier Reserve spreads from an altitude of about 1 700 m to the alpine height of Snowdon Peak. Conservation has increased plant diversity in the reserve, where the variety of wild flowers is currently being documented.

Mammals include mountain reedbuck, grey rhebok, Cape grysbok, scrub hare, red hare, porcupine, dassie, clawless otter, black-backed jackal, Cape fox, bat-eared fox, caracal, small spotted genet, yellow mongoose and zorilla (polecat). Birds include African Black Duck, African Marsh Harrier, Bearded Vulture (Lammergeier), Black Eagle, Black Sparrowhawk, Cape Vulture, Crowned Crane, Eastern Redfooted Kestrel, Gymnogene, Jackal Buzzard, Little Sparrowhawk, Orangethroated Longclaw, Red Bishop and Yellowbilled Duck.

Accommodation ranges from simple mountain huts to lodgings in an old farmhouse in the subalpine valley of the Karnmelkspruit. Information/bookings: tel/fax 051-603 1114 e-mail: margot@eci.co.za

north-eastern cape

In spring, the grasslands along Joubert Pass are peppered with wild flowers. Here, the cold wet climate favours an even greater diversity of bulbous plants than in the KwaZulu-Natal Drakensberg. Some wildflower species appear as early as July. Mountain Balloon Pea (*Sutherlandia montana*), flowers from July to January, preferring dry areas like boulder beds at altitudes of 1 500–3 000 m, where they can survive snow and frost. The Riverbell or Wild Fuchsia flowers from October to July in rocky streambeds at 1 200–2 200 m. The Trailing Mauve Daisy flowers between September and June in rocky grassland. The African Gladiolus, also known as Natal Lily, masses spectacularly in grassland and woodland, blooming in its various colours at different times, mainly from October to January and February to June.

PRACTICAL TIPS

Where to stay
Mountain View Country Inn
tel 051-604 0421
fax 051-603 0114.

Information
Lady Grey Information Centre/At Home Coffee Shop, tel 051-603 0176.

Quthing/Moyeni

After you cross the border into Lesotho at Telebridge, a tarred road leads to several interesting places around Quthing, a little town on the River Senque, where post office, banks, hospital and government offices are located. Quthing, the San word for 'colonial camp', is now being replaced by the name of the straggling village of Moyeni. It is the starting point for exploring several sets of dinosaur footprints at nearby Mount Moorosi. A large panel of San paintings can be viewed after driving 8 km from Lower Moyeni to the Qomoqomong General Dealer's Store, where you can hire a guide for the 20-minute walk to the rock paintings. A cave house where a missionary once lived can be visited at the Masitise Mission on the tarred Mohales Hoek Road.

Aliwal North

Aliwal North, 53 km west of Lady Grey, is the first town reached by the Gariep (Orange) River after it breaks through the southern Lesotho and Free State highlands. The river is so wide and calm here that the second longest bridge in South Africa had to be built to cross it. Aliwal North was once a destination for health-conscious tourists, but its two hot mineral springs have fallen out of favour and facilities need to be upgraded.

Buffelspruit Nature Reserve

The entrance to this 1 000 ha reserve lies just over 1 km from Aliwal North. A blend of grassland and karoo scrub provides habitat for eland, black wildebeest, blesbok, mountain reedbuck, red hartebeest, gemsbok (oryx), steenbok, Burchell's zebra, springbok and ostrich.

Burchell's zebra (*Equus burchelli*).

Burgersdorp

This 'town of citizens' is the oldest in the north-eastern Cape. It was involved in the early struggle for rights of the Dutch language and has a 'Taalmonument' dating back to 1893. Lying in a sheltered valley surrounded by the Stormberg Mountains, Burgersdorp enjoys a milder climate than other Karoo towns and has access to plenty of water from the Stormberg Spruit.

Berg Nature Reserve

A good way to experience the transition between montane grassland and karoo shrub is to visit the 425 ha Berg Nature Reserve at the De Bruin Dam a short distance east of town. Kudu, blesbok, black wildebeest and red hartebeest have been introduced, and mountain reedbuck, common duiker and steenbok still occur naturally. The semi-arid habitat attracts several lark species and the dam attracts waterbirds.

Towards the mountains – the road to Lady Grey, with a turnoff to Quthing.

north-eastern cape

Molteno

The town was founded in 1884 and named after Sir John Molteno, first prime minister of the Cape. It still has some fine Molteno sandstone buildings dating back to the late 19th century. Stone masons found Molteno sandstone easy to work with as it is quite soft and starts to erode when exposed to the elements.

The Old Mill

This is the oldest Molteno sandstone building in the town. It was originally planned as a water mill but converted to steam after the supply dam burst. The mill was restored to its former glory in 1991.

Molteno Museum

Established on the border between the Drakensberg foothills and the Great Karoo, Molteno is the ideal starting point for an examination of San rock art. Apart from a range of rock shelters in the vicinity, Stone Age implements and a wealth of semi-precious stones are on display in the Molteno Museum, which also claims to have the largest collection of rock paintings on display in the southern hemisphere.

4x4 routes

Various 4x4 routes have been established near the town, for instance those set up by Deon Cloete, owner of Cloeteggo Boereperd Stud.

Tourist attractions
Mountain bike trails

The terrain in this region is ideal for mountain biking. The trails are complemented by a wealth of walks and hikes at different levels of difficulty. Organized biking trails are offered by some private operators.

Collecting trail horses at Little Caledon River – an alternative to mountain biking in rugged terrain.

Walkerbouts (Rhodes): Trails are self-catering or fully catered. Transport provided from Rhodes to starting points.

Rhodes Trail: 1–2 days, 84,5 km. The 'Rhodes Mountain Trail Challenge' route is used, and the option offered of only certain sections (e.g. from Tiffindell Ski Resort down to Rhodes, 22 km).

Bokspruit Trail: 2–3 days, 98 km. On request, a vehicle will follow you on off-road sections. Information and bookings: Dave Walker, P O Box 15, Rhodes 9787; tel 045-974 9290, e-mail dave@wildtrout.co.za

NORTH-EASTERN CAPE DRAKENSBERG WALKS		
(return distance unless otherwise stated, starting at different points)		
EASY TO AVERAGE	INTERMEDIATE TO DIFFICULT	DIFFICULT TO EXTREME

160 CIRCULAR PRENTJIESBERG TRAIL: 50 km

Limited to 12 hikers daily. Return the same day or overnight in a cave. Set off from the Mondi Education Centre just outside Ugie and walk through woodland and mountainous terrain. Bookings: NE Cape Forest, Ugie, tel 045-933 1042.

161 CIRCULAR ECOWA TRAIL: 41 km

Starting from Elliot, this is said to be one of South Africa's toughest trails and is recommended for experienced hikers only. There is an overnight hut and dormitory available for a maximum of 15 people. Bookings: Elliot Municipality, tel 045-931 1011, fax 045-931 1361.

162 TSITSA WATERFALL: 30 km

An easy, short walk to this waterfall in the Maclear district. Bookings: tel 045-932 1025.

163 GILLIE MCCULLUM WATERFALL: 24 km

This waterfall in the Elliot area is said to be breathtaking but is hard to get to. Bookings: tel 045-313 1011.

164 BARKLY PASS FROM MOUNTAIN SHADOWS HOTEL: 3,4 km

Follow the yellow, red, blue and orange markers to the radio masts on the mountain summit. Enjoy panoramic views of Ben MacDhui to the north and Hangklip near Queenstown to the west. Bookings/Information: Mountain Shadows Hotel, tel 045-931 2233.

EASY TO AVERAGE	INTERMEDIATE TO DIFFICULT	DIFFICULT TO EXTREME

165 CAMEL ROCK FROM HOTEL, CIRCULAR ROUTE: 7,6 km

Descend in a southerly direction from the radio masts along the yellow route to Camel Rock, with good views over the escarpment and onto Barkly Pass Road. Bookings: Mountain Shadows Hotel, tel 045-313 2233.

166 CASTLE ROCK FROM HOTEL: 10,4 km

Follow orange route past Vulture's Roost. Continue down the slope in a south-westerly direction to Castle Rock (2 178 m). Excellent close-up views of bizarre sandstone formations and sweeping views in all directions. Bookings: Mountain Shadows Hotel, tel 045-313 2233.

167 VALLEY OF ART HIKE: 16 km

Five easily accessible rock art sites on the farm Lelieskloof between Burgersdorp and Jamestown are visited during the first day of this 2-day hike. The second day's hike leads through steeper terrain to another five San shelters. Accommodation is available at the farmhouse or bring your own equipment for a night in the wilderness at a rock shelter. Water available. Bookings: tel 051-653 1240.

168 PROTEA WALK: 8 km

This circular walk starts at Elliot and leads through protea savannah to the Guardian Peaks and Valies Cave. Bookings: Elliot Municipality, tel 045-931 1011.

169 NATURAL HERITAGE WALK: 5–10 km

Within the Lammergeier Nature Reserve, this easy walk usually starts at Upper Pelion Farmhouse. Its duration depends on how you feel. Bookings: tel/fax 051-603 1114.

170 BLACK EAGLE TRAIL: 11 km

The circular walk in the Lammergeier Nature Reserve leads down to Tempe and Karnmmelkspruit Valley, past Black Eagle and Hamerkop nests. It includes four or five stream crossings and spectacular views of Olympus Gorge. Bookings: tel/fax 051-603 1114.

171 CIRCULAR WITTEBERGE SKYWALK: 22 km

A wilderness walk at Lammergeier Nature Reserve for the very fit. The steep hike leads to the top of Snowdon Peak with magnificent views over the north-eastern Cape and Lesotho. No facilities; overnight in your own tent. Bookings: tel/fax 051-603 1114.

172 CIRCULAR BEN MACDHUI HIKING TRAIL: 51 km

This 3-day trail starts on a farm near Rhodes. Maximum of 24 hikers. Overnight in the farmhouse, mountain huts or Tiffendell Ski Resort in summer. The hike is generally not very steep, but part of the well-marked route to the peak leads through fairly rough terrain on the second day. Bookings: Gideon van Zyl, tel 045-971 0446.

north-eastern cape

north-eastern free state drakensberg

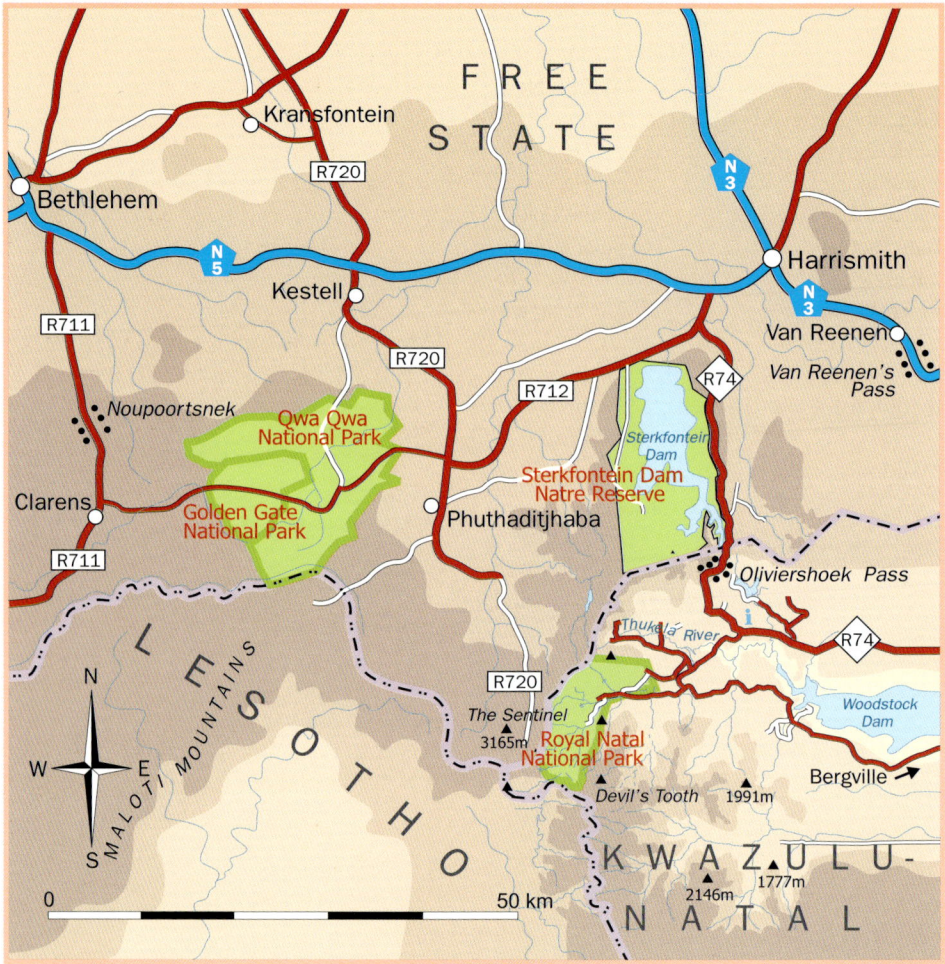

Map labels:
- Kransfontein
- FREE STATE
- R720
- Bethlehem
- N5
- Kestell
- N3
- Harrismith
- R711
- R720
- R712
- Van Reenen
- N3
- Van Reenen's Pass
- R74
- Noupoortsnek
- Qwa Qwa National Park
- Sterkfontein Dam
- Sterkfontein Dam Natre Reserve
- Clarens
- Golden Gate National Park
- Phuthaditjhaba
- R711
- Oliviershoek Pass
- LESOTHO
- MALOTI MOUNTAINS
- Thukela River
- R74
- Woodstock Dam
- R720
- The Sentinel 3165m
- Royal Natal National Park
- Devil's Tooth 1991m
- Bergville
- KWAZULU-NATAL
- 2146m
- 1777m
- 0   50 km

North-eastern Free State Drakensberg

Lesotho's Maloti Mountains form a natural extension of the high plateau spreading westwards from the Drakensberg escarpment. Two of South Africa's most scenic nature reserves, with spectacular mountain landscapes and magnificent sandstone formations, are located in these mountains in the north-eastern corner of the Free State, a haven for those who wish to get away from it all.

From the Royal Natal National Park in the northern reaches of the KwaZulu-Natal Berg, the Drakensberg winds northwards to Oliviershoek and Van Reenen's Pass. Easily accessible from the N5 between Harrismith and Bethlehem, the area is home to the Golden Gate Highlands and Qwa-Qwa National Parks. It is likely that the two parks will one day merge to create a coherent conservation area and tourist mecca.

The escarpment above the Amphitheatre in the Royal Natal National Park is a short drive away. Other destinations in the region are the Sterkfontein Dam Nature Reserve between Harrismith and Oliviershoek Pass, the Eastern Highlands (made accessible through the Highlands route running from Bethlehem to Zastron) and the short Voortrekker route to the Free State escarpment past Kerkenberg and Retief Klip, where colourful wildflowers abound in season.

Many interesting species are also to be found in the easily reached Drakensberg Botanical Gardens in Harrismith.

A patch of indigenous forest near the entrance to Golden Gate National Park.

Towns and villages

Clarens and environs

Named after the village near Montreux, Switzerland, where President Paul Kruger died, Clarens lies between the Rooiberge and the Maloti Mountains. Some San paintings are found in shelters on farms in the vicinity. There are numerous B&Bs and mountain resorts in and around the town. Several hiking trails are available.

Phuthaditjhaba and environs

Formerly Witsieshoek, the capital of the former Qwa-Qwa homeland, this smoky industrial and agricultural town sprawls in a spectacular mountain setting. It is the passage way to the Sentinel Car Park and the Witsieshoek Mountain Resort.

Sentinel and Witsieshoek

The area around Phuthaditjhaba, dominated by the huge basalt block of the Sentinel (3 165 m), becomes one of the coldest points of the country in winter, when snowfalls are frequent (see Route around the Berg on page 51). Montane and high-altitude grassland give way to sub-alpine vegetation. Some 140 bird species still survive in these hostile surroundings. Bird species include the Drakensberg Siskin, Orangebreasted Rockjumper, Bush Blackcap, Bald Ibis and Lanner Falcon. The Witsieshoek Mountain Resort maintains an interesting hide where Bearded Vulture, Cape Vulture,

The Sentinel parking lot ('the Witches' visible on the left).

Black Eagle and Jackal Buzzard come to feed, subject to the availability of carcasses supplied by conservation- conscious farmers of the area.

At an altitude of 2 286 m, the Witsieshoek Mountain Resort (tel 058-713 6361/2, fax 058-713 5274) huddles just below the alpine belt. Several hiking trails starting from the resort lead to well known landmarks of the Royal Natal National Park (see routes 176–182 on pages 166-167).

Harrismith and environs

From Harrismith, the northern KwaZulu-Natal Drakensberg is reached via a short scenic drive on the R74, passing the Sterkfontein Dam Nature Reserve before winding down Oliviershoek Pass. This route to KwaZulu-Natal is more interesting than the direct drive along the N3 to Ladysmith via Van Reenen's Pass. At the village of Van Reenen, the halfway house between Johannesburg and Durban, South Africa's smallest church holds just eight people.

Harrismith has several hotels, and a camping and caravan site. For information or bookings, contact Harrismith Marketing Bureau, Box 43, Harrismith 9800; tel 058-622 3525, fax 058-623 0923.

Drakensberg Botanical Gardens

The prominent Platberg (2 400 m) forms a fitting backdrop to the gardens laid out around two dams. About 20 per cent of typical Drakensberg montane grassveld flora is displayed, including the delicate Berg Barleria, the robust Kroonalwyn from Lesotho, the Fire Lily, *Eurypos* and Red-hot Poker. A 250 million-year-old fossilized tree has been given pride of place. The 114 ha garden, originally designed by experts from Kirstenbosch, should be an attraction for the whole region, but is currently in need of expert attention.

Oliviershoek Pass and the Voortrekker route

The Voortrekker route branches off from the alternative road from Harrismith via Oliviershoek Pass, opposite Sterkfontein Dam. For 10 km it leads along an old, out-of-use irrigation channel, which has blossomed over the years into a narrow strip of wetland. A wide range of wildflowers can be found in spring and summer between the channel and the gravel road that ends at the edge of the escarpment.

The border between the Free State and KwaZulu-Natal runs along the top of Oliviershoek Pass south of Harrismith. It was named after Adriaan Olivier who lived on the farm, Thukela Hoek, at the foot of the pass.

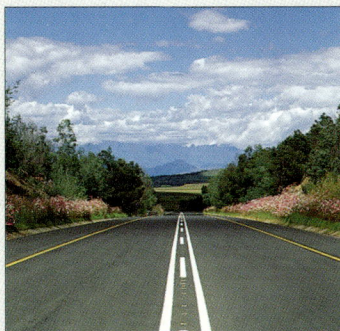

Top of Oliviershoek Pass.

In 1837, the Voortrekkers led by Piet Retief did not find this pass but descended the Drakensberg into the colony of Natal from a point not too far away – by removing the rear wheels from their wagons and using trees as levers and brakes. A monument has been built at the edge of the Little Berg's escarpment to commemorate them. Nearby is a bronze statue of the young woman who apparently hated the English so much that she returned barefooted over the mountains from Natal to the Transvaal.

Oliviershoek was supplanted as the main gateway between Natal and the Highveld when Van Reenen's Pass was constructed in the 1850s. In 1871, after the discovery of the Kimberley diamond fields, however, Oliviershoek Pass was improved to accommodate increasing traffic between Natal and Kimberley.

Viewpoints close to the top of Oliviershoek Pass provide magnificent vistas of the Drakensberg and of the storage dams of the Thukela-Vaal scheme.

PRACTICAL TIPS

Where to stay

Little Switzerland Resort near the summit of the pass offers excellent views; tel 036-438 6220, fax 036-438 6222.

Local weather

Oliviershoek Pass is sometimes shrouded in mist, especially in summer.

Information

Oliviershoek Pass Information Centre is situated at the top of the pass, tel 036-438 6130.

north-eastern free state

In the evening glow at Golden Gate.

Golden Gate National Park

Nestling in a corner of the north-eastern Free State, Golden Gate comprises 11 630 ha of spectacular scenery at a height of between 1 900 m and 2 800 m. The park has magnificent Clarens sandstone formations, allowing glimpses into a prehistoric past, and the tops of the highest peaks in the region are capped with Drakensberg basalt.

Cliffs glowing in the evening sun and trees turning golden in autumn make this one of South Africa's premier scenic national parks. Other highlights include game drives, colonies of rare birds, a vulture restaurant, walks along the river to caves or the summit of Wodehouse Peak (2 438 m) or Generaalskop (2 732 m), and excellent lodgings as well as sports facilities.

Clarens sandstone

Clarens sandstone, originally known as 'cave sandstone', is sedimentary rock that is prone to weathering at its base, resulting in the formation of many caves and overhangs used by the San people in the Little Berg. When exposed to the elements, it is at first a whitish colour but assumes beautiful yellow and red hues as it weathers. The San called the sandstone cliffs Qwa-qwa, which means 'whiter than white'. Another interpretation, perhaps more convincing, is that this word refers to the snow-capped mountains of the Maloti range.

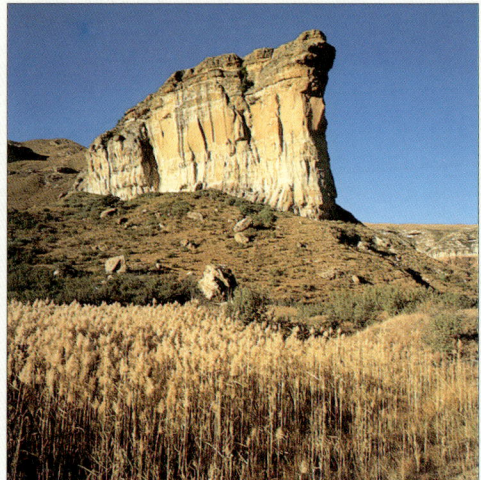

Brandwag Buttress in golden sandstone colours.

Wildlife

Mammals

Created primarily to preserve its magnificent scenery, the park also provides a home for various mammals, their numbers limited by the low carrying-capacity of sour grass. Once common in this region, eland, mountain reedbuck, blesbok, grey rhebok, springbok and Burchell's zebra have now been reintroduced. The park also claims to have the region's largest herd of black wildebeest.

Birds

More than 175 bird species occur in the park, including a breeding pair of Bearded Vultures (Lammergeier) and about 40 cliff-nesting Cape Vultures that sometimes visit the 'vulture restaurant', as do Black Eagle, Martial Eagle and Jackal Buzzard. A colony of 30 pairs of Bald Ibis has settled in the park. The Secretary Bird, Blue Crane and Redwing Francolin also occur on the grasslands. Greywing Francolin may be found higher up on the grassy slopes, where some endemic species survive, among them Orangebreasted Rockjumper, Stone Chat, Sentinel Rock Thrush and South African Rock Pipit. Malachite, Greater and Lesser Doublecollared Sunbirds visit the proteas and aloes while Fairy Flycatchers hide in thick bushes. Common Kestrel, Peregrine and Lanner Falcon regularly harass smaller birds.

Reptiles

A number of snake species live in the park but – as elsewhere in the Drakensberg – are seldom seen. The very rare Sungazer or Giant Girdled Lizard (listed in the *Red Data Book* as vulnerable) has been reintroduced in an attempt to save the species from extinction. It is a Free State endemic, surviving only in this part of the Berg.

Small grey mongoose (*Galerella pulverulenta*).

Cape Vulture (*Gyps coprotheres*).

Sungazer or Giant Girdled Lizard (*Coedylus giganteus*).

Flora

Although the vegetation consists mostly of grassland, some remarkable trees are present: Blue Guarri, Common Spike-thorn, Common Wild Currant, Fire-sticks, Karoo Bluebush, Mountain Cabbage Tree, Nana-berry, Ouhout, Parsley Tree, Real Yellow-wood, Sagewood, Tree Fuchsia and White Stinkwood.

Tourist attractions
Walks and hikes

Many short walks and day walks start at Glen Reenen, including Mushroom Rock and Echo Ravine (45 minutes), Brandwag Buttress and Boskloof (one hour) and a longer, more strenuous walk to Wodehouse Peak (four hours, return). A one-hour round trip to Holkrans starts from the Brandwag Rest Camp. Bookings are required only for the two-day Rhebok Hiking Trail (see route 173 on page 166).

More information about short walks is available at rest camp offices.

Brandwag Rest Camp.

4x4 training

Maloti Mountain Lodge's 'Continental Off-road Academy', Clarens, offers 4x4 training; tel 058-256 1422.

PRACTICAL TIPS

How to get to Golden Gate

From Harrismith take the R712, which leads to Golden Gate past Phuthaditjhaba, and through the Qwa-Qwa National Park. There are no entrance gates and one can drive through the park free of charge at any time of the day.

Where to stay

Glen Reenen Rest Camp offers an old farmhouse with three bedrooms, rondavels with loft, bathroom and kitchenette, and a well-sited caravan and camping site. Brandwag Rest Camp is more like a country lodge, with telephone and TV in all chalets. It has conference facilities, central heating and a catering service. Wilgenhof Hostel offers four dormitories for young people and tour groups. Alternatively, you can stay at the Maloti Mountain Lodge at Clarens, tel 058-256 1422.

Where to eat

Brandwag has a licenced restaurant, women's bar with pub lunches, coffee shop, take-aways.

Facilities

Information centre and laundromat at Brandwag, petrol and diesel at Glen Reenen. Garage, medical and other services at Clarens (20 km).

Information/bookings

Make reservations through SA National Parks, Box 787, Pretoria 0001 tel 012-343 1991, fax 012-343 0905 e-mail: reservations@parks-sa.co.za For additional information or to book for the hiking trail and caravan/camping sites, contact Golden Gate's tourist office directly, tel 058-255 0012.

Qwa-Qwa National Park

The 22 000 ha nature reserve has impressive sandstone formations, healthy wildlife populations, and a variety of birds and indigenous flora. Vleis, kloofs, small rivers and dams provide further variations and habitats. The park borders on Lesotho's Maloti Mountains and merges seamlessly into the adjacent Golden Gate Highlands National Park. The two parks are linked by the tarred R712, and there are several stopping places along this extremely scenic part of the Highlands Tourist Route. Qwa-Qwa National Park is managed as one unit together with Sterkfontein Dam Nature Reserve.

Maloti Mountains, the escarpment's north-eastern boundary.

Wildlife

Mammals

Herds of blesbok, black wildebeest, eland, red hartebeest and plains zebra liven up the grassland. Other animals include white rhino, mountain reedbuck and the widespread baboon.

Birds

About 210 species have been listed at Qwa-Qwa National Park and Sterkfontein Dam Reserve, including Bearded and Cape Vulture, Black Eagle, Crowned and Blue Crane, and Gymnogene. High altitude species such as the rare summer migrant Mountain Pipit, Yellowbreasted Pipit, Orangebreasted Rockjumper and Drakensberg Siskin are also present. Large reed beds at dams and vleis attract species such as Little Bittern, Corncrake and African Rail. Gurney's Sugar Bird and Malachite Sunbird may be encountered in the protea savannah. Whitebellied and Blue Korhaan prefer isolated habitat in the eastern part of the conservation area.

Gurney's Sugarbird (*Promerops gurneyi*).

Flora

The vegetation consists mainly of montane and mist-belt grassland. There is a rich variety of wild flowers in the higher-lying protea savannah and isolated pockets of the Silver Tree protea. Trees include Yellowwood, White Stinkwood, Cabbage Tree, Karee, Wild Olive and Ouhout.

Member of the Iris family.

Tourist attractions
Walks and hikes
A short walk with a sangoma (see route 174 on page 166) starts at the Cultural Village. There is also an overnight trail starting and ending at Avondsrus (see route 175 on page 166). Both must be booked in advance.

4x4 routes
Several easy to challenging 4x4 routes are laid out but are closed in summer. They can be negotiated unaccompanied or with a knowledgeable guide.

For riders, a unique cross of Arab horse and Norwegian Fjord.

The routes can be interlinked for a longer excursion. A winch, tow-rope and spade could be useful.

Night drives
Bird-watching or game-viewing night drives can be organized at reasonable prices.

Horse riding
Hourly horse rides for up to 10 people are available, as well as a two-day weekend horse trail from Eerstegeluk to Welgedacht.

Basotho Cultural Village
On Qwa-Qwa National Park land, about 8 km before the Golden Gate park begins, is the Basotho Cultural Village, displaying the culture, customs and traditions of the South Sotho people. Guided tours are conducted throughout the week, and there are demonstrations of traditional homestead decoration, the making of pots and basketware.

A colourful display of Sotho life at Qwa-Qwa.

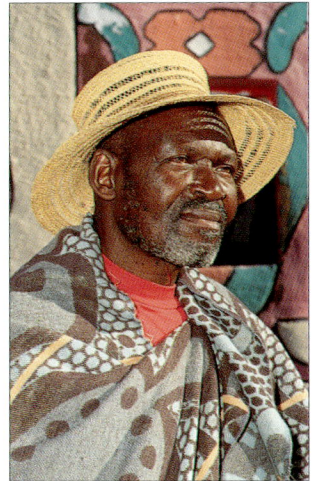

north-eastern free state

Sterkfontein Dam Nature Reserve

The 7 000-ha Sterkfontein Dam, South Africa's third largest, lies at a height of about 1 800 m in the valley of the Nuwejaarspruit (New Year Stream) in the far north-eastern corner of the Free State. It was commissioned in 1977 to store water pumped from the Thukela-Vaal Water Scheme. Since then, 18 000 ha of its limited catchment area have been declared a nature reserve. The stark mountain grassland and rugged krantzes at the edge of the Highveld lie waiting to be discovered by the true nature lover, especially the birding enthusiast.

Sterkfontein Dam at the edge of the escarpment.

Wildlife
Mammals
The reserve is stocked with mountain and common reedbuck, blesbok, eland, black wildebeest and red hartebeest, and also offers the chance to see oribi and grey rhebok. Temminck's hairy bat, Geoffroy's horseshoe bat and Schreiber's longfingered bat patrol rocky slopes and marshy areas.

Birds
In winter, Lammergeier, Cape Vulture, Black Eagle, Eastern Redfooted Kestrel, Jackal and Steppe Buzzard visit the vulture restaurant, which is becoming internationally famous for the quality of sightings and its accessibility. Other raptors include Martial Eagle, Secretary Bird and Gymnogene. The dam attracts South African Shelduck, African Fish Eagle, Osprey and Goliath Heron.

Fish
Sterkfontein Dam has large populations of indigenous Largemouth and Smallmouth Yellowfish, both highly regarded as prime game fish. Catfish, Orange River Mudfish and Carp also flourish.

How to get to Sterkfontein Reserve

From Harrismith take the Bethlehem–Bloemfontein road. Turn left onto the road to Phuthaditjhaba. After 9 km turn left again to Oliviershoek–Bergville. The entrance to the reserve is on the right, 7 km after the last turn-off. From Bergville, follow the R74 over Oliviershoek Pass. The entrance to the reserve is on your left shortly after you pass the bulky Kerkenberg with Retief Rock on the right.

Where to stay

Overnight facilities consist of self-catering chalets with views of lake and mountains; a farmhouse for groups; and a shore-side camping and caravan park with 360 sites (63 with power points), modern ablution and laundry facilities.

Where to eat

Bring your own food or visit restaurants and shopping centres in Harrismith (25 km).

Local weather

The area creates its own, very changeable, microclimate. Annual rainfall is 750–1 400 mm. Take precautions against sudden cold spells. Winters are cold, although the chalets are equipped with fireplaces.

Information/bookings

The Tourism Officer, Sterkfontein Dam Nature Reserve, Box 24, Harrismith 9880; tel 058-622 1093 fax 058-622 1772.

Flora

Patches of lush indigenous forest are found on the northern shores of the dam, but are accessible only from a nearby private nature reserve. The ravines contain Yellowwood, Wild Peach, Redwood, Myrtle and the hardy Koko Tree, once used for building ox wagons. Ferns, fungi, mosses and lichens flourish in the sheltered surroundings.

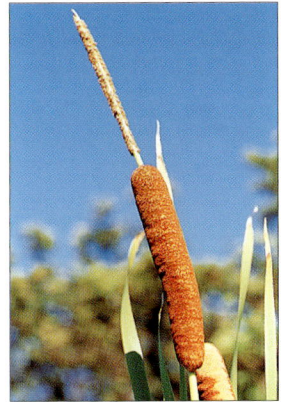

Bullrush (*Typha capensis*).

Tourist attractions
Walks and hikes

The hiking potential of the reserve has been developed to an extent. Some of the reserve's attractions can be experienced via short walks. Contact the tourism officer.

Other activities

Wind conditions are generally ideal for sailing and windsurfing. Boatsheds and access ramps for game fishing are available. A clubhouse with kitchen and bar can be rented.

The Thukela's waters are pumped over the escarpment into Sterkfontein Dam.

north-eastern free state

EASY TO AVERAGE	INTERMEDIATE TO DIFFICULT	DIFFICULT TO EXTREME

173 RHEBOK HIKING TRAIL (GOLDEN GATE): 30 km

The 2-day trail leads to Generaalskop (2 757 m), regarded as the highest point inside the Golden Gate National Park. Panoramic views of the Drakensberg and Maloti Mountains compensate for the rather strenuous hike. The trail hut sleeps 18. Cooking facilities, firewood and drinking water are available.

174 NGAKA (SANGOMA) TRAIL (QWA-QWA): 2 hr

The 2-hour walk, guided by the Ngaka, begins at the Basotho Cultural Village and includes the explanation of indigenous plants in traditional medicine and customs. Shelters with San rock art are also visited.

175 AVONDSRUS HIKING TRAIL (QWA-QWA), ROUND TRIP: 27 km

The trip starts at Avondsrus, with the option of 1–2 overnight stays at Spelonken hut. It leads mainly through grassland at an altitude of 1 700–2 000 m. The scenery is varied and includes ravines with indigenous trees. Many of the park's species, including the white rhino, may be encountered en route.

176 SENTINEL CAR PARK TO MOUNTAIN RESORT: 5 km

This easy walk provides good panoramas. Alpine belt plants will be found along the way.

177 MAHAI FALLS AND VALLEY: 3 hr

A relatively easy walk used by locals to do their shopping in the villages near Royal Natal National Park.

Mountain Cabbage Tree
(*Cussonia paniculata*).

178 GUDU FALLS: 3–4 hr

Start by following the path running parallel to the clearly sign-posted Metsi Matsho Trail, and proceed past the Gudu stream catchment area to Plowmanskop Ridge with excellent views over Royal Natal National Park. The path leads further down the valley to the edge of the falls, with a picturesque pool close by. Return the same way. The trip is recommended as a day outing.

179 BROOM HILL: 4 hr

Follow the well-defined path along the boundary fence leading down to Broome Hill from where views right across to Camel's Hump and little Switzerland can be enjoyed. Return on the same path.

180 FIKA PATSO TRAIL: 6–7 hr

Organized by the resort management. Involves some relatively steep climbs. Save time and effort by driving to the nearby Fika Patso resort to explore the dam and its environs.

EASY TO AVERAGE	INTERMEDIATE TO DIFFICULT	DIFFICULT TO EXTREME

181 AMPHITHEATRE ESCARPMENT, (FROM CAR PARK): 7 hr

Follow the path running right of the Witches, skirt the base of the Sentinel and head for the chain ladder, which is relatively easy to negotiate. Alternatively, choose the somewhat longer way through the gully. From the top of the ladder, a well-defined path leads towards the old Parks Board hut. Enjoy spectacular views of Thukela Falls, Devil's Tooth and the park at your feet. Consider spending the night in Crows Nest Cave near the Beacon so you can enjoy the sunrise over the falls the next morning. There should still be enough time to walk to Mont-aux-Sources Peak. **Beware of thieves and of cloud/mist that moves in very rapidly, reducing visibility to a few metres.**

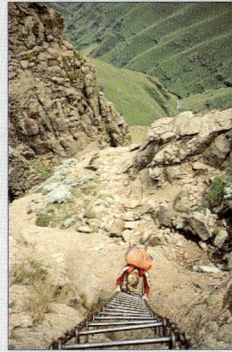

182 PROTEA VALLEY AND SUGAR LOAF: 8 hr

This is an extension of walk 179, including a steep descent from Broome Hill/Cold Hill into the valley. It makes the return trip longer and somewhat arduous. Enjoy fabulous views and a rich variety of wildflowers.

At the foot of the Sentinel.

* except for 173–175.
  Where exact distances are not available, the walking time in hours of a person of average fitness is given.

Thukela-Vaal Scheme: where water flows uphill

Water from the Thukela River Basin, collected in Kilburn Dam at the foot of Oliviershoek Pass, is pumped up more than 450 m over the escarpment into the Sterkfontein Dam, which has a storage capacity of 2 656 m and low annual evaporation of 1 300 mm. During peak periods the water is fed back into Kilburn Dam, falling about 500 m and passing through four power-generating turbines. From Sterkfontein Dam, it travels along the Nuwejaarspruit and the Wilge River into the Vaal Dam to augment the water supply of the Gauteng province. Part of the pumped water is used to generate electricity through one of the largest power stations of its kind ever built in Africa. Its generators serve mainly as a standby and can supply up to 100 megawatts to relieve shortages at peak hours.

Hailed in the mid-1970s as one of the most ambitious water utilization projects of its time, the scheme has since proved itself. Initial fears that it might place too much strain on KwaZulu-Natal's water resources or have a negative ecological impact have not materialised. In fact, the power of the Thukela has not yet been fully tapped: although it is six times shorter than the Orange River, it could generate about 10 times more power.

For information and exhibitions contact the Drakensberg Visitors' Centre, Box 93, Lagersrust 3354; fax 036-438 6015.

north-eastern free state

useful
information

information a–z

Walking the Berg, the Amphitheatre in view.

Berg speak: In the language of the Berg, free-standing peaks are separated from the main escarpment by so-called **cutbacks**. A sharp rise of the escarpment's edge is called an **attached peak**. **Spurs** are grassy slopes descending more or less at right angles from the main escarpment down to the top of the **Little Berg** (the minor mountains at the foot of the main KwaZulu-Natal escarpment). Basalt formations eroded to needle-sharp spires are called **pinnacles** and, sometimes, **fangs**. A **dome** is an elevation on the summit plateau close to the edge of the escarpment. The Little Berg is usually covered by sandstone **cliffs**, topped by basalt, which, in turn, is covered by grass-land. The **contour path** runs along the top of the Little Berg for almost the full length of the KwaZulu-Natal escarpment (commonly known as the '**Berg**').

Biodiversity: Some 10 per cent of all plant species in the world occur in South Africa. Of these, about half occur nowhere else on earth. Plants, in particular, have trouble keeping up with rapid climatic change, and small, isolated populations could become extinct as a result. Global warming and changes in seasonal rainfall are of concern to conservationists.

Bookings: Requests for bookings (of hutted camps, bush camps and lodges) can be sent to KZN Wildlife's Central Reservations Office up to nine months in advance but will be allocated only six months before occupation date (see 'Central Reservations Office', below, for address.) Reservation of camping sites and caves must be made directly with the camp manager/officer-in-charge (see 'Reservations and emergencies', below).

Camping: Choose a tent that is as sturdy and roomy as possible so that you can ride out the inevitable rain and thunderstorms in relative comfort. Some people cut their Berg holiday short after they have been heavily drenched. Use a small, lightweight tent on overnight hikes and when camping out in demarcated wilderness areas. (See 'Restrictions'. Also 'Reservations and emergencies', below.)

Caves: To enable visitors to get close to nature KZN Wildlife has made 60 caves available from the Cathedral Park area in the north to Garden Castle in the south. All bookings for sleeping in caves must be made directly with the officers-in-charge/camp managers of the respective conservation areas (see 'Reservations and emergencies', below). Only one party is allowed at a time. The maximum number of persons each cave accommodates is given here in brackets.

Mnweni Area: Busingati (12), Ifidi (4), Icidi (5), Jubilee (12), Grasscutter's (12), Mbundini (6), Rat Hole (4), Fang (4), Star (5), Shepherd's (8), Rwanqa (12), Pins (6), Ledger's (8), Mponjwana (10), Sunshine (8), Scaly (8), Waterfall (12).

Cathedral Peak: Barker's Chalet (5), Bell (5), Ndumeni One (4), Ndumeni Two (4), Outer Horn (10), Ribbon Falls (6), Schoongezicht (8), Sherman's (10), Twins (12), Xeni (12).

Injisuthi: Lower Injisuthi (8), Grindstone (12), Marble Baths (8).

Monk's Cowl: Anton's (12), Cowl (6), Hospitaalspruit (10), Nkosasana (4 summer/10 winter), Stable (12), Wonder Valley (12), Zulu (12).

Giant's Castle: Spare Rib (12), Tom's/Hillside (10).

Highmoor: Aasvoëlkrantz (8), Caracal (8).

Mkhomazi: Cypress (6), McKenzie's (12), Sinclair's (6).

Lotheni: Ash (4), Yellowwood (6), Hlathimbe (4).

Vergelegen (Cobham North): Bird's Nest (8), Bridge (6), Kaula (12), Mlahlangubo (12, camping only), Runaway (4) Sicocosebhaca (12), Small (4).

Cobham: Chameleon (10), Gorge (2), Gxalingenwa (12), Lakes (12), Nutcracker (6), Pholela (12), Sakeng (2), Siphongweni (12), Spectacle (10), Venice One (4), Venice Two (4), Weaver (10).

Garden Castle: Bushman's (12), Engagement (2), Fun (12), Goats (12), Halfway (4), Lammergeier (12), Mashai (2), Pillar (12), Sleeping Beauty (12), Tarn (12), Thomathu (12), Verkyker (12), Wilson's (12).

Cave etiquette: Ensure that you are at the cave you booked; do not impose on other people by simply turning up at any cave. Do not make open fires or use candles in caves. Gas cookers and lamps or torches are permitted. Do not alter entrances or cave floors or use grass for bedding. Never leave anything behind – not even your name – and leave the cave as clean as you would like to find it. Take everything back to camp. Remember that you are liable for heavy fines – or even a jail sentence – if you deface the priceless rock art. Answer the call of nature at least a five-minute walk away from the cave, preferably in grassland.

Cell phones: From the summit and the Little Berg, all you can see below you is usually in cell-phone range. Try to reach higher, open ground when in caves, valleys, gorges or forests. Many of the valleys of the north-eastern Cape Berg have no reception.

Central Reservations Office: Hutted camps, bush camps and lodges can be booked through Central Reservations, KZN Wildlife, Box 13069, Cascades 3202 tel 033-845 1000, fax 033-845 1001.

Children: Correct clothing is essential for a successful holiday in the mountains. Take enough changes of clothing – especially if you have children with you. Children's shoes should protect the ankles and have non-slip soles. Carry extra socks on every walk and hike. When children play around a mountain stream their socks and shoes will quickly get wet and can chafe the feet. Take plenty of sun block and protective lip balm. Bear in mind that children need protection against rain, sun and cold at all times. A lightweight space blanket could be useful on longer walks. Your rucksack should be big enough to carry all children's gear and have enough space for 'emergency rations' like nuts, dried fruit and muesli bars. Pack a pocket-knife and first-aid box, as well as field guides matching your interests. Sturdy walking sticks are always helpful, especially if you have to carry small children.

Dangers of the Berg: The epigraph at the Memorial Wall near the Visitors Centre at Royal Natal National Park gives fair warning to all who set out to challenge the Berg: *'Venture if you will, but remember that courage and strength are naught without prudence, and that a moment of negligence may destroy the happiness of a lifetime. Do nothing in haste, look well to each step and from the beginning think what may be the end.'* (The wall was donated by the Sutton family in memory of their daughter, Jenny, who died in the mountains she loved on 20 September 1987.)

Hiking maps: Good, official maps covering the KwaZulu-Natal Berg range are available from local KZN Wildlife offices or directly from Head Office, Box 13069, Cascades 3202, tel 033-845 1000, fax 033-845 1001.
No. 1 Royal Natal, Rugged Glen, Mnweni.
No. 2 Cathedral Peak, Monk's Cowl.
No. 3 Giant's Castle, Injisuthi, Monk's Cowl.
No. 4 Highmoor, Kamberg, Lotheni.
No. 5 Vergelegen, Sani Pass, Cobham.
No. 6 Garden Castle, Bushman's Nek.

Hiking parties: KZN Wildlife (formerly Nature Conservation Service) recommends that hiking parties consist of three or more people as single hikers are at higher risk. A search for a single person greatly complicates rescue efforts by the KZN Emergency Service and can be expensive. At present, part of your entrance fee goes towards funding this important service.

Hiking routes: The lists of walks in this book are intended to stimulate interest in the vast number of walks and hikes in the Drakensberg mountains. There are countless other paths to choose from and new routes to be explored in the wilderness areas. For such adventures, reliable contour maps are essential. The simple sketches available as handouts at most KwaZulu-Natal Wildlife reception desks are helpful only for casual strolls or short walks. Beginners may need expert advice about basic equipment and would benefit during their first hikes from the experience of seasoned hikers.
Like the sea, the Berg is unpredictable and merciless. Seek advice from a mountain or hiking club in your area that organizes carefully routed excursions. Ensure you have the essential expertise and equipment before you attempt to 'go it alone'.

Information: KZN Wildlife, tel 033-845 1000, fax 033-845 1001.

Mountain biking: Simple training on a good mountain bike strengthens the legs and provides a good cardiovascular work-out, particularly if you train for an hour or two at least three times a week. Real mountain biking, however, can be a very tough sport, requiring intensive, multi-faceted training, and can be dangerous, especially when the terrain is extremely bumpy or wet. Mountain biking in the Drakensberg is still in its infancy but planners and environmentalists are increasingly aware of its potential.

Health matters

Abrasions, grazes: Disinfect and dry out immediately but do not dress the sore. Blisters should also be disinfected and left to dry out.

Health hazards: The Drakensberg region is free of malaria and bilharzia. Ticks and their larvae are abundant on grass stems in summer, especially at lower altitude and at the peak of the rainy season. Avoid walking in tall grass. The use of a tick repellant is recommended.

Liquids: Drink plenty of water, especially on warm days and on long hikes. Disorientation and fainting are signs of dehydration.

Mountain hikes and your body: A high fitness level, exact tour planning and the right equip-ment are prerequisites for an enjoyable holiday in the higher Berg. A healthy body can adapt to changing climatic conditions at all heights but heart, respiration and circulation must be able to cope with a heavy workload. Even very fit people should allow for an acclimatization period of two to five days if long hikes above 2 000 m are planned. Anyone with a history of high blood pressure, lung disease, irregular heart beat or myocardial insufficiency should avoid strenuous exercise in the high mountain regions.

Mountain hiking involves almost all parts of the body. Ankle joints are under heavy strain when climbing, while knee joints and ligaments are under stress when descending. To reduce strain, keep strides short while walking uphill and longer when going downhill.

Remember that more accidents happen dur-ing descent than when climbing. You are well advised, also, to avoid eating too much before or during long hikes, as prolonged digestion deprives the muscles of needed oxygen.

Snake bite: Encounters with poisonous snakes are not common, but in the unlikely event of an attack by one of the three poisonous species of the Berg – puff adder, berg adder, rinkhals – remain calm. Send someone for help while keeping the victim immobile and relaxed. Note: Snakes generally avoid contact with people and would rather flee than fight. Watch where you are going. When confronted, freeze until the snake withdraws. Retreat – slowly – only if you cannot bear the tension!

Sprains: An ankle sprain is the injury most like-ly to occur during walks and hikes. If you are near a stream hold the ankle in cold water for about 10 minutes to bring relief. A crepe band-age and walking stick will ease the walk home. Comfortable, lightweight walking shoes help to minimise the risk of sprains.

Sun shield: Protection from the sun is vital. Use barrier creams with a very high Sun Protection Factor (SPF). Ultraviolet radiation in the moun-tains is extremely high (visible as a bluish tinge on your photographs if you do not use a UV or skylight filter). Don a hat or cap and do not forget other protective clothing when walking in the Berg as the weather is unpredictable.

Mountain boots: Boots should be waterproof, ankle-high, with leather uppers and very thick soles. They should be big enough that your toes do not touch the front of the boot when you walk downhill. Good hiking socks help to avoid bruises and blisters.

Mountain climate: Low temperatures and low atmospheric pressure, as well as increasing solar radiation and rainfall, influence the climate at higher altitudes all-year round. Mountain climate is thus characterized by extreme variations. The need for careful preparation before visiting the higher Berg regions cannot be over-emphasized.

Mountain clubs:
KZN Wildlife liaises with the following clubs on a regular basis:
• Durban Rambler's Hiking Club, tel 031-764 4721.
• Mountain Backpackers Club, tel 031-266 3970.
• Mountain Club of South Africa, KwaZulu-Natal Section, Box 70550, Overpoort 4067; cell 082-990 5877. Website: http://mcsa.org.za

Mountain register: Plot your route carefully and enter the correct details in the mountain register when you sign in. Never forget to sign off as soon as you return – the oversight could be expensive! Signing the mountain register – your lifeline – is essential, especially before starting a long or difficult hike. Registers are displayed prominently at all KZN Wildlife starting points. Never hike alone in the Berg! Even parties of two are strongly discouraged; only three or more people are secure in all situations. An injured lone hiker cannot return to base or expect a rescue operation to start until after his/her expected return date as entered in the register.

Passports: A valid travel document is required for border crossings into Lesotho. Carry one even if you intend to walk the escarpment only on the South African side. For a visit to Sani Top, however, a valid ID-book clearly stating South African citizenship is sufficient.

Reservations and emergencies:
Reservations of camping sites and caves are made directly with the camp manager or the officer-in-charge (as listed below). Emergency services offered include mountain rescue.
• Cathedral Peak Mountain Reserve, tel/fax 036-488 1880.
• Cobham Mountain Reserve, tel/fax 033-702 0831.
• Garden Castle Mountain Reserve/Bushman's Nek, tel 033-7011823, fax 033-701 1823.
• Giant's Castle Mountain Reserve, tel 036-353 3718.
• Highmoor Mountain Reserve, tel/fax 033-263 7240.
• Injisuthi Mountain Reserve, tel/fax 036-488 1050.
• Lotheni Mountain Reserve, tel/fax 033-702 0540.
• Mkhomazi Wilderness Area, tel 033-263 6444.
• Monk's Cowl Mountain Reserve, tel/fax 036-468 1103.
• Vergelegen Mountain Reserve, tel 033-702 0712.
• Wagendrift Public Resort, tel 036-352 5520.

Restrictions: Hikers may use their tents to sleep in wilderness areas and reserves except for intensive-use zones and the Royal Natal National Park; the area within 3 km of major camp developments; or within 1 km of a mountain hut. Intensive-use zones are demarcated on official hiking maps. No party may exceed 12 persons. Do not camp near streams as you could get washed away in a sudden storm. Fires are prohibited. Leave nothing behind, not even footprints, if possible. Take your litter, including all cigarette ends, back to the nearest dustbin. When nature calls, walk at least five minutes away from streams, paths and forests. Do not use any soap or shampoo in the clear mountain streams.

Warden's tips: Some hard-earned words of advice from those who know are scattered across these pages. Watch out for snakes, loose rocks, sunburn and changing weather conditions.

Your heritage: This book aims to assist people who want to get to know the Drakensberg better. After all, this is not only a World Heritage Site but a wonder of nature, a treasure house right on our doorstep. Your help in preserving it will be appreciated by all who follow you.

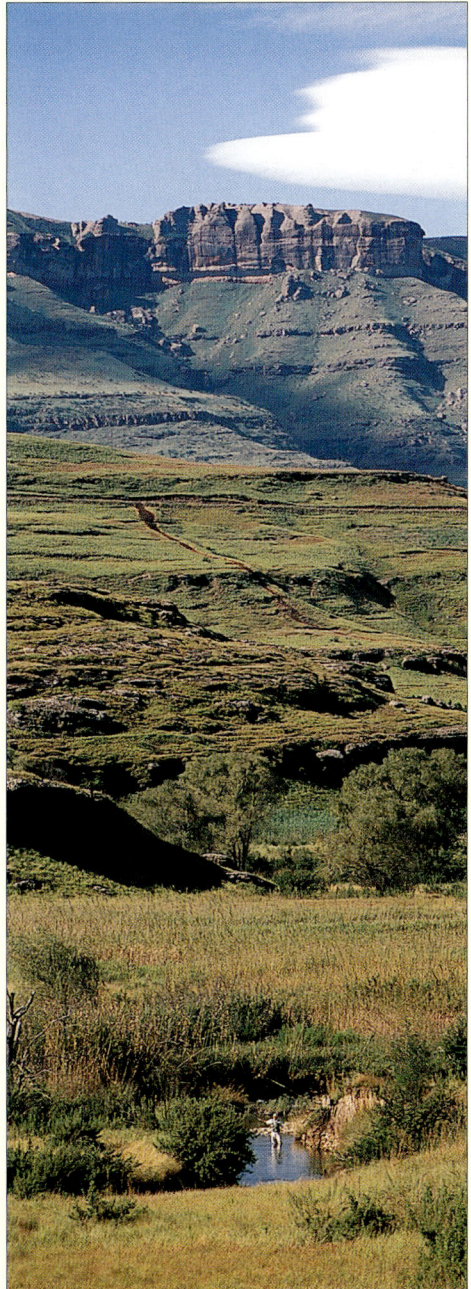

At the foot of Bastervoetpad, north-eastern Cape.

wildlife

Of the 64 mammal species that occur in the KwaZulu-Natal Berg, 11 are endemic: forest shrew, greater musk shrew, Sclater's golden mole, Hottentot golden mole, black wildebeest, blesbok, grey rhebuck, Cape mole rat, Sloggett's rat, white-tailed rat, and Natal red hare.

There are 32 endemic birds among the 300 recorded bird species, 48 reptile species (25 of them snakes, 23 lizards) and 26 different species of frog.

MAMMALS

INSECTIVORA

Forest shrew	*Myosorex varius*
Greater musk shrew	*Crocidura flavescens*
Hottentot golden mole	*Amblysomus hottentotus*
Lesser grey-brown musk shrew	*Crocidura silacea*
Makwassie musk shrew	*Crocidura maquassiensis*
Reddish-grey musk shrew	*Crocidura cyanea*
Rough-haired golden mole	*Chrysospalax villosus*
Sclater's golden mole	*Chlorotalpha sclateri*

CHIROPTERA

Cape serotine bat	*Eptesicus capensis*
Geoffroy's horseshoe bat	*Rhinolophus clivosus*
Lesser yellow house bat	*Scotophilus borbonicus*
Mauritian tomb bat	*Taphozous mauritianus*

PRIMATES

Chacma baboon	*Papio ursinus*
Vervet monkey	*Cercopithecus aethiops*

CARNIVORA

Aardwolf	*Proteles cristatus*
African wild cat	*Felis lybica*
Black-backed jackal	*Canis mesomelas*
Caracal	*Felis caracal*
Clawless otter	*Aonyx capensis*
Large grey mongoose	*Herpestes ichneumon*
Large-spotted genet	*Genetta tigrina*
Leopard	*Panthera pardus*
Serval	*Felis serval*
Small grey mongoose	*Galerella pulverulenta*
Small-spotted genet	*Genetta genetta*
Spotted-necked otter	*Lutra maculicollis*
Striped polecat (zorilla)	*Ictonyx striatus*

Chacma baboon (*Papio ursinus*).

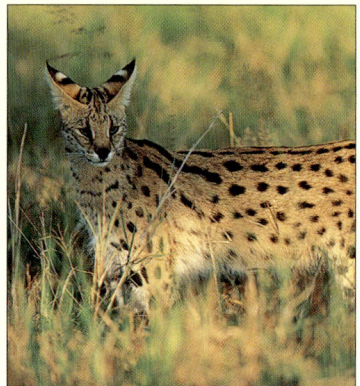

Serval (*Felis serval*).

Striped weasel (African weasel) ...... *Poecilogale albinucha*
Water mongoose .... *Atilax paludinosus*
White-tailed mongoose .... *Ichneumia albicauda*

HYRACOIDEA
Rock dassie .... *Procavia capensis*

PERISSODACTYLA
Burchell's zebra .... *Equus burchelli*

TUBULIDENTATA
Aardvark .... *Orycteropus afer*

ARTIODACTYLA
Black wildebeest .... *Connochaetes gnou*
Blesbok .... *Damaliscus dorcas phillipsi*
Bushbuck .... *Tragelaphus scriptus*
Common duiker, grey duiker .... *Sylvicapra grimmia*
Eland .... *Taurotragus oryx*
Grey rhebuck .... *Pelea capreolus*
Klipspringer .... *Oreotragus oreotragus*
Mountain reedbuck .... *Redunca fulvorufula*
Oribi .... *Ourebia ourebi*
Red hartebeest .... *Alcelaphus buselaphus*
Reedbuck .... *Redunca arundinum*

RODENTIA
Brant's climbing mouse .... *Dendromus mesomelas*
Cape mole rat .... *Georychus capensis*
Chestnut climbing mouse .... *Dendromus mystacalis*
Common mole rat .... *Cryptomys hottentotus*
Fat mouse .... *Steatomys pratensis*
Grey climbing mouse .... *Dendromus melanotis*
Kreb's fat mouse .... *Steatomys krebsii*
Laminate vlei rat .... *Otomys laminatus*
Mozambique woodland mouse ...... *Grammomys cometes*
Multimammate mouse .... *Mastomys natalensis*
Porcupine .... *Hystrix africaeaustralis*
Pygmy mouse .... *Mus minutoides*
Sloggett's rat (ice rat) .... *Otomys sloggetti*
Striped mouse .... *Rhabdomys pumilio*
Vlei rat .... *Otomys irroratus*
Water rat .... *Dasymys incomtus*
White-tailed rat .... *Mystromys albicaudatus*
Woodland dormouse .... *Graphiurus murinus*
Woodland mouse .... *Grammomys dolichurus*

LAGOMORPHA
Scrub hare .... *Lepus saxatilis*
Natal red hare .... *Pronolagus crassicaudatus*

Rock dassie (*Procavia capensis*).

Klipspringer (*Oreotragus oreotragus*).

Scrub hare (*Lepus saxatilis*).

mammals

Snakes

Of the 25 snake species occurring in the Berg only the rinkhals and puff adder have caused fatalities in southern Africa. There are 10 others that are mildly to moderately venomous but are seldom seen and have never resulted in death. Generally, snakebites are exceptional in the Berg and help is usually close at hand.

'A snake attack is most unlikely at high altitudes. At lower altitudes, the puff adder, berg adder and rinkhals are the only three whose bite could prove serious.'
(KZN Wildlife)

Rinkhals: Endemic to southern Africa. Common in montane grassland at lower altitudes, it is a close relative of the true cobras, but less dangerous, as its venom is diluted for spitting. It is the only Berg snake with the typical cobra threatening stance, rearing up, spreading its broad hood, then accurately spraying its potent venom up to 3 m at an intruder's face. Failing this, it usually shams death. Stay away, because its next action will be to bite. The venom affects the nervous system, especially breathing. Its common Afrikaans name refers to one to two pale cross-bands on the throat. Although nocturnal, it may be active on overcast days, hunting mainly rodents and toads. Viviparous.

Puff adder: Stocky and thick, it can be up to 1,1 m long. It has a large flat triangular head and a brown to light brown body (more brightly coloured in the Eastern Cape and KwaZulu-Natal). Common, but seldom seen as it is very well camouflaged, it emerges at dusk to ambush rodents and birds. Appears sluggish and will not move if encountered by humans while basking on rock or footpaths. It warns with loud hisses and strikes rapidly, deeply injecting its venom with its long fangs, usually on the victim's legs. The venom is cytotoxic (affects the soft tissues). Viviparous.

Puff adder (*Bitis arietans arietans*).

Berg adder: Endemic. Isolated populations occur in montane grassland up to 3 000 m in the Drakensberg region from the Eastern Cape to the Northern Province. Regional colours vary. It is well camouflaged like the puff adder, but less potent because of its small size (maximum 50 cm). Fond of basking in grass tussocks on rocky ledges. Be careful when clambering up grassy slopes, as it might attack hands or wrists. No fatalities are known but minor symptoms of the cytotoxic venom (e.g. drooping eyelids, loss of smell/taste) may occur for one or two days. Viviparous.

REPTILES

GEKKONIDAE

Lesotho flat gecko	*Afroedura karroica halli*
Moreau's tropical house gecko	*Hemidactylus mabouia*
Mountain flat gecko	*Afroedura nivaria*

VARANIDAE

Nile monitor	*Varanus niloticus niloticus*
Rock monitor	*Varanus albigularis*

Natal Midlands dwarf chamaeleon
(*Bradypodion thamnobates*).

CHAMAELEONIDAE

Drakensberg dwarf chamaeleon	*Bradypodion dracomontanum*
Natal Midlands dwarf chamaeleon	*Bradypodion thamnobates*

AGAMIDAE

Distant's ground agama	*Agama aculeata distanti*
Southern rock agama	*Agama atra*

LACERTIDAE

Burchell's sand lizard	*Pedioplanis burchelli*
Cottrell's mountain lizard	*Tropidosaura cottrelli*
Delalande's sandveld lizard	*Nucras lalandii*
Essex's mountain lizard	*Tropidosaura essexi*
Natal mountain lizard	*Tropidosaura montana natalensis*

SCINCIDAE

Cape skink	*Mabuya capensis*
Speckled skink	*Mabuya striata punctatissima*
Variable skink	*Mabuya varia varia*

Nile Monitor (*Varanus niloticus niloticus*)

CORDYLIDAE

Breyer's long-tailed seps	*Tetradactylus breyeri*
Drakensberg crag lizard	*Pseudocordylus melanotus subviridis*
Eastern Cape short-legged seps	*Tetradactylus seps laevicauda*
Lang's crag lizard	*Pseudocordylus langi*
Spiny crag lizard	*Pseudocordylus spinosus*
Sungazer or giant girdle-tailed lizard	*Cordylus giganteus* Transvaal
grass lizard	*Chamaesaura aenea*
Yellow-throated plated lizard	*Gerrhosaurus flavigularis*

TYPHLOPIDAE

Bibron's blind snake	*Typhlops bibronii*

Bibrons blind snake (*Typhlops bibronii*).

LEPTOTYPHLOPIDAE

Peters's thread snake . . . . *Leptotyphlops scutifrons scutifrons*

BOIDAE

African rock python . . . . *Python sebae natalensis*

COLUBRIDAE

Brown house snake . . . . *Lamprophis fuliginosus*
Cape wolf snake . . . . *Lycophidion capense capense*
Common brown water-snake . . . . *Lycodonomorphus rufulus*
Common egg-eater . . . . *Dasypeltis scabra*
Cream-spotted mountain snake . . . . *Montaspis gilvomaculata*
Cross-marked grass snake . . . . *Psammophis crucifer*
Herald snake . . . . *Crotaphopeltis hotamboeia*
Many-spotted snake . . . . *Amplorhinus multimaculatus*
Mole snake . . . . *Pseudaspis cana*
Northern black water-snake . . . . *Lycodonomorphus laevissimus fitzsimonsi*
Olive house snake . . . . *Lamprophis inornatus*
Short-snouted grass snake . . . . *Psammophis sibilans brevirostris*
Southern brown egg-eater . . . . *Dasypeltis inornata*
Southern slug-eater . . . . *Duberria lutrix lutrix*
Spotted harlequin snake . . . . *Homoroselaps lacteus*
Spotted house snake . . . . *Lamprophis guttatus*
Spotted skaapsteker . . . . *Psammophylax rhombeatus rhombeatus*
Western Natal green-snake . . . . *Philothamnus natalensis occidentalis*
Yellow-bellied house snake . . . . *Lamprophis fuscus*

ELAPIDAE

Rinkhals . . . . *Hemachatus haemachatus*

VIPERIDAE

Berg adder . . . . *Bitis atropos*
Puff adder . . . . *Bitis arietans arietans*
Rhombic night adder . . . . *Causus rhombeatus*

Brown house snake (*Lamprophis fuliginosus*).

Cross-marked grass snake (*Psammophis crucifer*).

Rinkhals (*Hemachatus haemachatus*).

FROGS AND TOADS

Name		Breeding habitat and habits
Water rana	*Rana vertebralis*	Quiet pools, streams or ponds at about 3 000 m in alpine grassland of the whole range.
Drakensberg stream frog	*Strongylopus hymenopus*	Shallow pools and shallow fast-flowing water or grassy slopes near water at 2 000–3 000 m. Royal Natal to Sani Pass.
Bronze caco	*Cacosternum nanum*	Small pools in well-grassed land below 2 400 m.
Bubbling kassina	*Kassina senegalensis*	Standing water in grassland, wetland and marshes up to 1 700 m. Eggs laid on submerged grass and reeds. Nocturnal. Royal Natal to Champagne Castle.
Clicking stream frog	*Strongylopus grayii*	Damp shady spots at 1 500–3 000 m. Masses of eggs sometimes found. One of the most widespread frogs.
Common caco	*Cacosternum boettgeri*	Small pools in well-grassed land up to 3 000 m. Active day and night during breeding season.
Common river frog	*Rana angolensis*	Vleis and slow-flowing streams, or on steep slopes, in forests and grassland.
Drakensberg toad	*Bufo gariepensis nubicolus*	Wet vegetation in water-logged depressions in most summit areas. Whole High Berg range.
Natal chirping frog	*Arthroleptella hewitti*	In wet mud under vegetation or rocks up to 2 750 m, and often on forest floors or moss next to waterfalls. Northern to central Berg.
Natal sand frog	*Tomopterna natalensis*	Along streams and pool edges. Common in foothills below 1 400 m, Royal Natal to Champagne Castle.
Plain stream frog	*Strongylopus wageri*	Quiet pools at 2 000 m and below in forested areas. Whole range.
Rattling kassina/ Weale's running frog	*Semnodactilus wealii,* *(formerly Kassina wealii)*	Standing water. Males climb grasses or sedge to call. Mainly restricted to foothills, Royal Natal to Lotheni.
Raucous toad	*Bufo rangeri*	Submerged vegetation in shallow water below 2 000 m. Royal Natal to Sani Pass.
Snoring puddle frog	*Phrynobatrachus natalensis*	Quiet pools at 1 400–2 200 m. Up to top of Little Berg.

Name		Breeding habitat and habits
Striped stream frog	*Strongylopus fasciatus*	Wet grassy areas in valleys below 1 800 m. Whole range.
Penther's rain frog	*Breviceps adspersus pentheri*	Level to sloping grassland at 1 500–2 300 m. Males glued to the much larger females during mating. Cathedral Peak to Giant's Castle.
Spotted rain frog	*Breviceps maculatus*	Open to wooded grassland 2 000–2 700 m. Between Giant's Castle and Drakensberg Gardens Hotel.
Guttural toad	*Bufo gutturalis*	Submerged vegetation in shallow water in open grassland to woodlands up to 1 550 m. Mainly Cathedral Peak area.
Natal ghost frog	*Heleophryne natalensis*	Probably deep in crevices at 1 500–2 300 m. Champagne Castle to Sani Pass, Cobham.
Giant bullfrog	*Pyxicephalus adspersus*	Shallows of temporary rain-filled depressions. Favours grassland. where it remains underground for months or even years.
Dusky-throated river frog............	*Rana fuscigula*	Ponds, streams and rivers in open grassland and woodland, from the southern Berg foothills to about 1 500 m. Eggs laid on bottom of quiet streams and pools.
Common river frog.....	*Rana angolensis*	Along ponds, streams and rivers up to 2 200 m in open grassland to forest margins. Several thousand eggs laid in shallow water. Whole range.
Lesotho river frog......	*Rana dracomontana*	About 100–200 eggs laid in shallow calm water. Top of Sani Pass and elsewhere at high altitude.
Spotted stream frog....	*Strongylopus gravii grayii*	Damp shaded vegetation a little distance from water in a variety of habitats up to 3 000 m. Mont-aux-Sources to Sani Pass.
Striped grass frog......	*Ptychadena porosissima*	Amongst vegetation in shallow water in open grassy, marshy and rocky areas up to 1 700 m. Cathedral Peak to Lotheni.
Natal puddle frog......	*Phrynobatrachus natalensis*	Amongst aquatic vegetation during rain or near water in wide variety of habitats up to 1 500 m. Northern to central Berg.
Boettger's dainty frog...	*Cacosternum boettgeri*	Grassy swamps and pools up to 3 000 m. Eggs laid in shallow water attached to submerged grass or twigs. Royal Natal to Champagne Castle.
Boulenger's bronze dainty frog	*Cacosternum nanum-nanum*	Grassy stream banks. Similar to Boettger's Dainty Frog. Lotheni and elsewhere at lower altitude.
Long-toed tree frog	*Peptopelis xenodactylus*	Foothill marshes up to 1 900 m. Very rare. Central to southern Berg.

BUTTERFLIES

NYMPHALIDAE

African monarch	*Danaus chrysippus aegyptius*
Battling glider	*Cymothoe alcimeda trimeni*
Bowker's widow	*Serradinga bowkeri bowkeri*
Bush beauty	*Paralethe dendrophilus indosa*
Common bush brown.	*Bicyclus safitza safitza*
Common diadem	*Hypolimnas misippus*
Drakensberg brown.	*Pseudonympha poetula*
Dusky acraea.	*Hyalites esebria esebria*
Eastern hillside brown.	*Stygionympha scotina scotina*
Eyed pansy	*Precis orithya madagascariensis*
False silver-bottom brown .	*Pseudonympha magoides*
Forest-king charaxes	*Charaxes xiphares penningtoni*
Gaika brown	*Pseudonympha gaika*
Garden acraea.	*Acraea horta*
Gaudy commodore.	*Precis octavia sesamus*
Loteni brown.	*Neita lotenia*
Machacha brown	*Pseudonympha machacha*
Marsh acraea.	*Hyalites rahira rahira*
Mountain pride	*Aeropetes tulbaghia*
Neita brown	*Neita neita*
Orange acraea.	*Hyalites anacreon*
Painted lady	*Vanessa cardui*
Paludis brown	*Pseudonympha paludis*
Pennington's brown	*Pseudonympha penningtoni*
Pirate.	*Catacroptera cloanthe cloanthe*
Pringle's widow	*Torynesis pringlei*
Rainforest brown.	*Cassionympha cassius*
Vari's brown.	*Pseudonympha varii*
Wandering donkey acraea. .	*Acraea neobule neobule*
Wichgraf's brown	*Stygionympha wichgrafi williami*
Yellow pansy	*Precis hierta cebrene*

Brown-veined white (*Belenois aurota*).

Gaudy commodore (*Precis octavia sesamus*).

Christmas swallowtail (*Palilio demodocus*).

LYCAENIDAE

Almeida copper . . . . *Aloeides almeida*
Amakosa rocksitter . . . . *Durbania amakosa
natalensis*
Amakosa rocksitter . . . . *Durbania amakosa ayresi*
Basuto skolly . . . . *Thestor basutus basutus*
Bowker's blue . . . . *Tarucus bowkeri bowkeri*
Brilliant blue . . . . *Lepidochrysops asteris*
Bush bronze . . . . *Cacyreus lingeus*
Common black-eye . . . . *Leptomyrina gorgias
gorgias*
Common fig-tree blue . . . . . *Myrina silenus ficedula*
Common meadow blue . . . . *Cupidopsis cissus*
Cupreous blue . . . . *Eicochrysops messapus
mahallokoaena*
Dotted blue . . . . *Tarucus sybaris sybaris*
Drakensberg daisy copper . . *Chrysoritis oreas*
Eastern opal . . . . *Chrysoritis orientalis*
Estcourt blue . . . . *Lepidochrysops pephredo*
Gaika blue . . . . *Zizula hylax*
Grizzled blue . . . . *Orachrysops subravus*
Henning's copper . . . . *Aloeides henningi*
Lucerne blue . . . . *Lampides boeticus*
Machacha opal . . . . *Chrysoritis pelion*
Marsh blue . . . . *Harpendyreus noquasa*
Mooi River opal . . . . *Chrysoritis lycegenes*
Mozambique bar . . . . *Spindasis mozambica*
Natal spotted blue . . . . *Azanus natalensis*
Nosy blue . . . . *Orachrysops nasutus remus*
Orangebanded
protea butterfly . . . . *Capys alphaeus extentus*
Oreas copper . . . . *Aloeides oreas*
Pennington's copper . . . . . . *Aloeides penningtoni*
Pennington's
protea butterfly . . . . *Capys penningtoni*
Rayed blue . . . . *Actizera lucida*
Restless blue . . . . *Orachrysops lacrimosa*
Riley's copper . . . . *Aloeides rileyi*
Sooty blue . . . . *Zizeeria knysna*
Tailed meadow blue . . . . . . *Cupidopsis jobates jobates*
Trimen's copper . . . . *Aloeides trimeni trimeni*

Variable blue . . . . *Lepidochrysops variabilis*
Velvet-spotted blue . . . . *Azanus ubaldus*
Water bronze . . . . *Cacyreus palemon palemon*
Yellow Zulu . . . . *Alaena amazoula amazoula*

PIERIDAE

African migrant . . . . *Catopsilia florella*
Broad-bordered
grass yellow . . . . *Eurema brigitta
brigitta*
Brown-veined white . . . . . . *Belenois aurota*
Lucerne butterfly . . . . *Colias electo electo*
Meadow white . . . . *Pontia helice helice*

PAPILIONIDAE

Christmas swallowtail . . . . . *Papilio demodocus
demodocus*
Emperor swallowtail . . . . . . *Papilio ophidicephalus
phalusco*
Green-banded swallowtail . *Papilio nireus lyaeus*
White-banded swallowtail . . *Papilio echerioides
echerioides*

HESPERIDAE

Bamboo sylph . . . . *Metisella syrinx*
Barber's ranger . . . . *Kedestes barberae
barberae*
Common hottentot skipper . *Gegenes niso nis*
Common sandman . . . . *Spialia diomus ferax*
Dark hottentot skipper . . . . *Gegenes pumilio gambica*
Dark ranger . . . . *Kedestes niveostriga*
Fulvous ranger . . . . *Kedestes mohozutza*
Gold-spotted sylph . . . . *Metisella metis paris*
Grassveld sandman . . . . *Spialia agylla agylla*
Grassveld sylph . . . . *Metisella malgacha
malgacha*
Large flat . . . . *Celaenorrhinus
mokeezi mokeezi*
Mountain sylph . . . . *Metisella aegipan aegipan*
Shaka's ranger . . . . *Kedestes chaca*
Star sandman . . . . *Spialia asterodia*

BIRDS

Numbers refer to Roberts' reference

PODICEPIDIFORMES
008   Dabchick . . . . *Tachybaptus ruficollis*

PELECANIFORMES
055   Whitebreasted Cormorant . *Phalacrocorax carbo*
058   Reed Cormorant . . . . *Phalacrocorax africanus*
060   Darter . . . . *Anhinga melanogaster*

CICONIIFORMES
062   Grey Heron . . . . *Ardea cinerea*
063   Blackheaded Heron . . . . . *Ardea melanocephala*
065   Purple Heron . . . . *Ardea purpurea*
066   Great White Egret . . . . . . *Egretta alba*
067   Little Egret . . . . *Egretta garzetta*
068   Yellowbilled Egret . . . . *Egretta intermedia*
071   Cattle Egret . . . . *Bubulcus ibis*
076   Blackcrowned Night
         Heron . . . . *Nycticorax nycticorax*
079   Dwarf Bittern . . . . *Ixobrychus sturmii*
081   Hamerkop . . . . *Scopus umbretta*
083   White Stork . . . . *Ciconia ciconia*
084   Black Stork . . . . *Ciconia nigra*
085   Abdim's Stork . . . . *Ciconia abdimii*
089   Marabou Stork . . . . *Leptoptilos crumeniferus*
090   Yellowbilled Stork . . . . . . *Mycteria ibis*
091   Sacred Ibis . . . . *Threskiornis aethiopicus*
092   Bald Ibis . . . . *Geronticus calvus*
094   Hadeda Ibis . . . . *Bostrychia hagedash*
095   African Spoonbill . . . . *Platalea alba*

ANSERIFORMES
099   Whitefaced Duck . . . . *Dendrocygna viduata*
101   Whitebacked Duck . . . . . . *Thalassornis leuconotus*
102   Egyptian Goose . . . . *Alopochen aegyptiacus*
103   South African Shelduck . . . *Tadorna cana*
104   Yellowbilled Duck . . . . *Anas undulata*
105   African Black Duck . . . . . . *Anas sparsa*
106   Cape Teal . . . . *Anas capensis*
107   Hottentot Teal . . . . *Anas hottentota*
108   Redbilled Teal . . . . *Anas erythrorhyncha*
112   Cape Shoveller . . . . *Anas smithii*
113   Southern Pochard . . . . *Netta erythrophthalma*
116   Spurwinged Goose . . . . . . *Plectropterus gambensis*
117   Maccoa Duck . . . . *Oxyura maccoa*

Whitebreasted Cormorant (*Phalacrocorax carbo*).

Egyptian Goose (*Alopochen aegyptiacus*).

Redbilled Teal (*Anas erythrorhyncha*).

FALCONIFORMES

118	Secretary Bird	*Sagittarius serpentarius*
119	Bearded Vulture	*Gypaetus barbatus*
122	Cape Vulture	*Gyps coprotheres*
126a	Black Kite	*Milvus migrans*
126b	Yellow-billed Kite	*Milvus aegyptius*
127	Blackshouldered Kite	*Elanus caeruleus*
128	Cuckoo Hawk	*Aviceda cuculoides*
131	Black Eagle	*Aquila verreauxii*
136	Booted Eagle	*Hieraaetus pennatus*
139	Longcrested Eagle	*Lophaetus occipitalis*
140	Martial Eagle	*Polemaetus bellicosus*
141	Crowned Eagle	*Stephanoaetus coronatus*
146	Bateleur	*Terathopius ecaudatus*
148	African Fish Eagle	*Haliaeetus vocifer*
149	Steppe Buzzard	*Buteo buteo*
150	Forest Buzzard	*Buteo trizonatus*
152	Jackal Buzzard	*Buteo rufofuscus*
155	Redbreasted Sparrowhawk	*Accipiter rufiventris*
157	Little Sparrowhawk	*Accipiter minullus*
158	Black Sparrowhawk	*Accipiter melanoleucus*
160	African Goshawk	*Accipiter tachiro*
161	Gabar Goshawk	*Micronisus gabar*
162	Pale Chanting Goshawk . .	*Melierax canorus*
165	African Marsh Harrier	*Circus ranivorus*
166	Montagu's Harrier	*Circus pygargus*
167	Pallid Harrier	*Circus macrourus*
168	Black Harrier	*Circus maurus*
169	Gymnogene	*Polyboroides typus*
170	Osprey	*Pandion haliaetus*
171	Peregrine Falcon	*Falco peregrinus*
172	Lanner Falcon	*Falco biarmicus*
180	Eastern Redfooted Kestrel	*Falco amurensis*
181	Common Kestrel	*Falco tinnunculus*
182	Greater Kestrel	*Falco rupicoloides*
183	Lesser Kestrel	*Falco naumanni*

GALLIFORMES

190	Greywing Francolin	*Francolinus africanus*
191	Shelley's Francolin	*Francolinus shelleyi*
192	Redwing Francolin	*Francolinus levaillantii*
196	Natal Francolin	*Francolinus natalensis*
198	Rednecked Francolin	*Francolinus afer*
199	Swainson's Francolin	*Francolinus swainsonii*
200	Common Quail	*Coturnix coturnix*
203	Helmeted Guineafowl	*Numida meleagris*

GRUIFORMES

205	Kurrichane Buttonquail . . .	*Turnix sylvatica*
206	Blackrumped Buttonquail .	*Turnix hottentotta*
207	Wattled Crane	*Bugeranus carunculatus*
208	Blue Crane	*Anthropoides paradiseus*
209	Crowned Crane	*Balearica regulorum*
210	African Rail	*Rallus caerulescens*
211	Corncrake	*Crex crex*
213	Black Crake	*Amaurornis flavirostris*
217	Redchested Flufftail	*Sarothrura rufa*
218	Buffspotted Flufftail	*Sarothrura elegans*
221	Striped Flufftail	*Sarothrura affinis*
226	Moorhen	*Gallinula chloropus*
228	Redknobbed Coot	*Fulica cristata*
230	Kori Bustard	*Ardeotis kori*
231	Stanley's Bustard	*Neotis denhami*
232	Ludwig's Bustard	*Neotis ludwigii*
234	Blue Korhaan	*Eupodotis caerulescens*
245	Ringed Plover	*Charadrius hiaticula*

CHARADRIIFORMES

249	Threebanded Plover	*Charadrius tricollaris*
255	Crowned Plover	*Vanellus coronatus*
257	Blackwinged Plover	*Vanellus melanopterus*
258	Blacksmith Plover	*Vanellus armatus*
260	Wattled Plover	*Vanellus senegallus*
264	Common Sandpiper	*Actitis hypoleucos*
266	Wood Sandpiper	*Tringa glareola*
269	Marsh Sandpiper	*Tringa stagnatilis*
270	Greenshank	*Tringa nebularia*
272	Curlew Sandpiper	*Calidris ferruginea*
284	Ruff	*Philomachus pugnax*
286	Ethiopian Snipe	*Gallinago nigripennis*
290	Whimbrel	*Numenius phaeopus*
297	Spotted Dikkop	*Burhinus capensis*
299	Burchell's Courser	*Cursorius rufus*
338	Whiskered Tern	*Chlidonias hybridus*

COLUMBIFORMES

348	Feral Pigeon	*Columba livia*
349	Rock Pigeon	*Columba guinea*
350	Rameron Pigeon	*Columba arquatrix*
352	Redeyed Dove	*Streptopelia semitorquata*
354	Cape Turtle Dove	*Streptopelia capicola*
355	Laughing Dove	*Streptopelia senegalensis*
356	Namaqua Dove	*Oena capensis*
360	Cinnamon Dove	*Aplopelia larvata*

PSITTACIFORMES
362   Cape Parrot . . . . *Poicephalus robustus*

CUCULIFORMES
374   European Cuckoo . . . . *Cuculus canorus*
375   African Cuckoo . . . . *Cuculus gularis*
377   Redchested Cuckoo . . . . . *Cuculus solitarius*
378   Black Cuckoo . . . . *Cuculus clamosus*
380   Great Spotted Cuckoo . . . *Clamator glandarius*
382   Jacobin Cuckoo . . . . *Clamator jacobinus*
384   Emerald Cuckoo . . . . *Chrysococcyx cupreus*
385   Klaas's Cuckoo . . . . *Chrysococcyx klaas*
386   Diederik Cuckoo . . . . *Chrysococcyx caprius*

STRIGIFORMES
392   Barn Owl . . . . *Tyto alba*
393   Grass Owl . . . . *Tyto capensis*
394   Wood Owl . . . . *Strix woodfordii*
395   Marsh Owl . . . . *Asio capensis*
400   Cape Eagle Owl . . . . *Bubo capensis*
401   Spotted Eagle Owl . . . . . . *Bubo africanus*
404   European Nightjar . . . . *Caprimulgus europaeus*

CAPRIMULGIFORMES
405   Fierynecked Nightjar . . . . . *Caprimulgus pectoralis*
408   Freckled Nightjar . . . . *Caprimulgus tristigma*
410   Pennant-winged Nightjar . *Macrodipteryx vexillaria*

APODIFORMES
411   European Swift . . . . *Apus apus*
412   Black Swift . . . . *Apus barbatus*
415   Whiterumped Swift . . . . . . *Apus caffer*
416   Horus Swift . . . . *Apus horus*
417   Little Swift . . . . *Apus affinis*
418   Alpine Swift . . . . *Apus melba*
421   Palm Swift . . . . *Cypsiurus parvus*

COLIIFORMES
424   Speckled Mousebird . . . . . *Colius striatus*
426   Redfaced Mousebird . . . . *Urocolius indicus*

TROGONIFORMES
427   Narina Trogon . . . . *Apaloderma narina*

ALCEDINIFORMES
428   Pied Kingfisher . . . . *Ceryle rudis*
429   Giant Kingfisher . . . . *Megaceryle maxima*

Threebanded Plover (*Charadrius tricollaris*).

Swainson's Francolin (*Francolinus swainsonii*).

Redeyed Dove (*Streptopelia semitorquata*).

430	Halfcollared Kingfisher	...	*Alcedo semitorquata*
431	Malachite Kingfisher	.....	*Alcedo cristata*
432	Pygmy Kingfisher	....	*Ispidina picta*
435	Brownhooded		
	Kingfisher	....	*Halcyon albiventris*
438	European Bee-eater	.....	*Merops apiaster*
439	Olive Bee-eater	....	*Merops superciliosus*

CORACIIFORMES

446	European Roller	....	*Coracias garrulus*
447	Lilacbreasted Roller	......	*Coracias caudata*
451	Hoopoe	....	*Upupa epops*
452	Redbilled Woodhoopoe	..	*Phoeniculus purpureus*
454	Scimitarbilled		
	Woodhoopoe	....	*Rhinopomastus cyanomelas*
463	Ground Hornbill	....	*Bucorvus leadbeateri*

PICIFORMES

464	Blackcollared Barbet	.....	*Lybius torquatus*
465	Pied Barbet	....	*Tricholaema leucomelas*
474	Greater Honeyguide	.....	*Indicator indicator*
476	Lesser Honeyguide	......	*Indicator minor*
478	Sharpbilled Honeyguide	..	*Prodotiscus regulus*
480	Ground Woodpecker	....	*Geocolaptes olivaceus*
483	Goldentailed		
	Woodpecker	....	*Campethera abingoni*
486	Cardinal Woodpecker	....	*Dendropicos fuscescens*
488	Olive Woodpecker	......	*Mesopicos griseocephalus*
489	Redthroated Wryneck	....	*Jynx ruficollis*

PASSERIFORMES

494	Rufousnaped Lark	......	*Mirafra africana*
495	Clapper Lark	....	*Mirafra apiata*
500	Longbilled Lark	....	*Mirafra curvirostris*
507	Redcapped Lark	....	*Calandrella cinerea*
512	Thickbilled Lark	....	*Galerida magnirostris*
515	Chestnutbacked		
	Finchlark	....	*Eremopterix leucotis*
518	European Swallow	......	*Hirundo rustica*
520	Whitethroated Swallow	...	*Hirundo albigularis*
523	Pearlbreasted Swallow	...	*Hirundo dimidiata*
526	Greater Striped Swallow	..	*Hirundo cucullata*
527	Lesser Striped Swallow	...	*Hirundo abyssinica*
528	South African Cliff		
	Swallow	....	*Hirundo spilodera*
529	Rock Martin	....	*Hirundo fuligula*
530	House Martin	....	*Delichon urbica*
532	Sand Martin	....	*Riparia riparia*

533	Brownthroated Martin	...	*Riparia paludicola*
534	Banded Martin	....	*Riparia cincta*
536	Black Sawwing Swallow	..	*Psalidoprocne holomelas*
538	Black Cuckooshrike	......	*Campephaga flava*
540	Grey Cuckooshrike	......	*Coracina caesia*
541	Forktailed Drongo	....	*Dicrurus adsimilis*
545	Blackheaded Oriole	.....	*Oriolus larvatus*
547	Black Crow	....	*Corvus capensis*
548	Pied Crow	....	*Corvus albus*
550	Whitenecked Raven	.....	*Corvus albicollis*
551	Southern Grey Tit	....	*Parus afer*
554	Southern Black Tit	....	*Parus niger*
560	Arrowmarked Babbler	...	*Turdoides jardineii*
565	Bush Blackcap	....	*Lioptilus nigricapillus*
567	Redeyed Bulbul	....	*Pycnonotus nigricans*
568	Blackeyed Bulbul	......	*Pycnonotus barbatus*
572	Sombre Bulbul	....	*Andropadus importunus*
576	Kurrichane Thrush	....	*Turdus libonyana*
577	Olive Thrush	....	*Turdus olivaceus*
579	Orange Thrush	....	*Zoothera gurneyi*
580	Groundscraper Thrush	..	*Turdus litsitsirupa*
581	Cape Rock Thrush	......	*Monticola rupestris*
582	Sentinel Rock Thrush	....	*Monticola explorator*
586	Mountain Chat	....	*Oenanthe monticola*
587	Capped Wheatear	....	*Oenanthe pileata*
588	Buffstreaked Chat	......	*Oenanthe bifasciata*
589	Familiar Chat	....	*Cercomela familiaris*
590	Tractrac Chat	....	*Cercomela tractrac*
591	Sicklewinged Chat	....	*Cercomela sinuata*
592	Karoo Chat	....	*Cercomela schlegelii*
593	Mocking Chat	....	*Thamnolaea meiventris*
595	Anteating Chat	....	*Myrmecocichla formicivora*
596	Stonechat	....	*Saxicola torquata*
598	Chorister Robin	....	*Cossypha dichroa*
600	Natal Robin	....	*Cossypha natalensis*
601	Cape Robin	....	*Cossypha caffra*
606	Starred Robin	....	*Pogonocichla stellata*
612	Orangebreasted		
	Rockjumper	....	*Chaetops aurantius*
614	Karoo Robin	....	*Erythropygia corphaeus*
615	Kalahari Robin	....	*Erythrpygia paena*
622	Layard's Titbabbler	......	*Parisoma layardi*
625	Icterine Warbler	....	*Hippolais icterina*
628	Great Reed Warbler	.....	*Acrocephalus arundinaceus*
631	African Marsh Warbler	...	*Acrocephalus baeticatus*

Blackeyed Bulbul (*Pycnonotus barbatus*).

Cardinal Woodpecker (*Dendropicos fuscescens*).

Kurrichane Thrush (*Turdus libonyana*).

Redwinged Starling (*Onychognathus morio*).

Masked Weaver (*Pioceus velatus*).

flora

With 2 153 plant species on record, the floral diversity of the Drakensberg is exceptional. Some 119 plant and animal species are listed in the Red Data Book as 'Endangered'.

Lichens

Of the 1 200–2 000 lichen species in South Africa many occur in the Drakensberg region, growing particularly well on sunny north-facing rocks and trees. They have not yet been documented in great detail. The best known is probably *Dermatiscum thunbergii*, a lichen that occurs only in southern Africa, where it is used to produce bright yellow dye.

Lichens are made up of groups of composite organisms, usually an algal and a fungal species assisting each other to survive in a symbiotic association. The algal cells provide food for the fungus by secreting carbohydrates, while the fungus supplies the necessary structure and moisture to protect the algae from drying out in the harsh environment.

Lichens are pioneer plants, which means that they are vital in nature for oxygen and carbon dioxide cycles, as well as for soil formation. Very sensitive indicators of environmental pollution, they provide food for certain animals and are used in medicines, perfumes and traditional beer. They were used in the preservation of mummies, and it is thought that some desert species, easily blown away by wind, might have been the 'manna' mentioned in the Bible.

Mosses

These small evergreen plants carry no sap in their vessels (non-vascular). Lacking true roots, they reproduce by spores. Mosses are found on soil, rocks and trees, in bogs and shallow streams. They occupy a variety of habitats in

Common alpine belt lichen.

the Drakensberg, where they are well documented. Among the better known are: 'Old Man's Beard', common on trees and shrubs in montane and sub-alpine belts; Pendent Forest Moss; Bristly Swan-neck Moss; and Red Alpine Thread Moss.

Ferns

About 70 species of ferns have been documented in the Drakensberg region. They grow almost everywhere, but prefer damp, shady places. Best known are the stately Common Tree Fern, and the Scented Fern, one of Africa's most common ferns, which smells of benzoin. The toxic crystalline solid is used in medications, perfumes and incense.

The Bracken Fern is often seen in grasslands and along forest margins in montane and sub-alpine belts up to 2 500 m. Many new individuals grow from creeping underground rhizomes, up to 5 m long, assisting in the invasion of grasslands.

Other common ferns are Mother Fern, Carrot Fern and Fine Maidenhair Fern, while Drakensberg Shield Fern and Lance Fern can be found attached to rocks and forest trees. They are epiphytic (i.e. they grow on but do not feed on other plants).

Ferns are flowerless and are among the oldest plants on earth. The earliest fossils date back at least 400–350 million years when they were the dominant plants. They are still flourishing, with about 10 000 species world-wide, ranging in size from a few centimetres to more than 20 m.

Many ferns have medicinal uses. Parts of the Tree Fern are used to counteract witchcraft and to ensure easy childbirth. Bracken Fern roots are used to eliminate worms and treat menstrual irregularities, chronic veld sores and stomach aches. It has been established, however, that Bracken Fern carries toxic and carcinogenic (cancer-causing) substances to which humans could be exposed by drinking milk from cows grazing bracken-infested pastures.

Cycads

The Drakensberg Cycad, *Encephalartos Ghellinckii*, grows in the sub-alpine fynbos area and is particularly partial to the Clarens sandstone cliffs of the Little Berg and boulders in the grassland. Common in the central Drakensberg, especially around Cathedral Peak and Injisuthi, it withstands fire and ice, but grows very slowly, needing hundreds of years to reach its maximum height of about 4 m. Baboons regard the fleshy coverings of the ovules as a delicacy, but discard the poisonous inner kernels, thus assisting in dissemination. The 'living fossil' has survived for millions of years virtually unchanged and is the only cycad species of the KwaZulu-Natal Berg region.

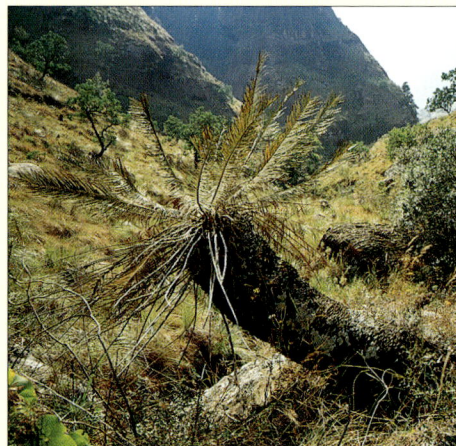

Drakensberg Cycad (*Encephalartos ghellinckii*) in the Cataract Valley.

Common shrubs and trees

Paperbark Thorn: *Medium to large tree with an umbrella-like crown and peeling grey-yellow bark. Widespread south of the Zambezi, but absent from southern KwaZulu-Natal and the High Berg. The woody pods are eaten by cattle and game but the leaves are believed to poison stock.*

Pompon Tree: *Relatively common shrub/ small tree in KwaZulu-Natal's northern Berg. Flowers from November to February. Often found in community with Wild Willow, Cape Holly, Tree Fuchsia and Common Tree Fern on stream banks and at the edge of pools in the montane belt.*

Ouhout (old wood) or Mtchitchi: *Very common shrub/small tree. Valuable food for eland in winter.*

Weeping Willow: *A native of Asia, it now stretches in an unbroken line from the Nile River down to KwaZulu-Natal. The roots are used to treat headache and fever, and the bark to treat burns and urinary complaints. Its sticks are rubbed together to kindle fire.*

Silver Sugarbush (*Protea roupelliae*).

Proteas

According to the statistics of the Protea Atlas Project, five protea species occur in the Drakensberg region: Common Sugarbush, Drakensberg Sugarbush, Silver Sugarbush, Dwarf Grassveld Sugarbush and Water Lily Sugarbush. A sixth species, the enigmatic Cloud Sugarbush, is found only in the Royal Natal National Park. A hybrid between *Protea caffra* and *P. dracomontana* occurs almost everywhere in the Berg from north to south.

Aloes

Strikingly beautiful, aloes used to be classified with the lily family but are now placed with their close relatives, Red-hot Pokers and Bulbines, in a family of their own, the *Asphodelaceae*. Of the 125 South African species, about 10 per cent are found in the KwaZulu-Natal and north-eastern Cape Drakensberg, and half of these have found an important place in Zulu traditional medicine.

For example, sap from the leaves of a number of species is widely used as an oral contraceptive. Modern biological and pharmacological tests have proved the value of the chemical and biological properties of aloes.

The aloe-like *Kniphofia* are easy to distinguish as they have non-succulent leaves and their inflorescences are usually unbranched and

Well-known Drakensberg aloes

Bitter Aloe (Aloe ferox): *Known in its northern form as* A. candelabrum. *Widely distributed, tree-like, growing on rocky hillsides and used in many medicinal and cosmetic products. Huge population found in Lotheni Mountain Reserve. Flowers May–August.*

Kroonalwyn (A. polyphylla): *Endangered high-altitude species restricted to steep basaltic mountain slopes above 2 000 m (mainly in Lesotho). Usually grows in a single, spiralling rosette. Often buried by snow in winter. Flowers September–October.*

Meadow Aloe (A. pratensis): *Fairly common in rocky places from sea level to high altitude around Cathedral Peak and Champagne Castle. Flowers June–October.*

Mountain Aloe (A. marlothii): *Widely distributed. Grows to 6 m or more. Able to withstand heavy frosts. Similar to Bitter Aloe but noted for colour variations from yellow and orange-gold to a striking red in KwaZulu-Natal's Utrecht district. Flowers May–September.*

Krantz Aloe (A. arborescens): *One of the most widespread species, on rocky hillsides and cliffs up to 2 000 m and in forests, especially in the foothills of the north-eastern Cape Drakensberg. Flowers May–July.*

Other species include: A.striatula, A. broomii, A. maculata *(Common Soap Aloe)*, A. aristata, A. boylei, A. cooperi *and* A. ecklonis.

tightly packed. Most *Kniphofia* prefer much wetter habitats than aloes.

Grasses

Red Grass (*Themeda triandra*) is very common on slopes up to 2 800 m. Spear Grass (*Heteropogon*) seeds stick to socks and skin, while Basket Grass (*Oplismenus hirtellus*) is often seen in the form of handicrafts along the roadside.

Wildflowers

Herbaceous, non-woody, herbs and forbs survive by means of underground storage organs like bulbs, tubers and rhizomes. Dependent on early rains, they begin to flourish as early as June or July. Iris, lily and daisy families are notably well represented amongst the 50-odd plant families to be found in the Drakensberg region.

Many spring flowers are used as fuel, food or medicine by local people. Natal Blood Flower bulbs are ground up with other vegetable matter to cure stomach complaints. Mountain Lilies are used as a tonic, blood purifier and treatment for colds. Early settlers swore by its anti-cancerous properties, hence the name Bergkankerbossie.

Poultices are made for nursing mothers' breasts from the leaves of White-Spotted Arum and the tubers are eaten as a vegetable. Zulu diviners use *Begonia sutherlandii* to establish whether a kraal is threatened by an enemy, while infusions of the roots of *Anemone fanninii* are used as a purgative and cure for gall-sickness.

The roots of Wild Verbena (called by the Zulu *iCimamlilo* or 'that which puts out the fire') are used for stomach pain, and infusions of Wild Iris roots promise help against dysentery.

Riverbell (*Phygelius aequalis*).

Gooseneck Drumstick Flower (*Glumicalyx goseloides*).

Streptocarpus

The genus is a member of the African Violet family, often growing on another plant without being parasitic (epiphytic). Of the 135 species in Africa – all with the same number of chromosomes – about 50 occur in South Africa, more than half between the KwaZulu-Natal Drakensberg and the Indian Ocean, where they grow naturally in the shelter of lightly shaded montane forests or under rock overhangs and outcrops with plenty light but no direct sunlight.

Wild Hibiscus species (*Malvaceae*).

Common Drakensberg wildflowers

Name (family in brackets)	Where to find it	When it flowers
Fire/Red Hairy Heath . . *Erica cerinthoides* (Heath)	Montane belt, above Clarens sandstone cliffs.	July–Dec
Mountain Lily . . . . *Sutherlandia montana* (Pea)	Occurs occasionally on sandy boulder-bed rivers from 1 500–3000 m	July–Dec
(Black-eyed Susan) . . . . *Barleria monticola*	Forms societies in moist parts of montane and sub-alpine belts. Very evident after fire.	Aug–Dec
Cat's Whiskers . . . . *Becium grandiflorum* (Mint)	Montane grassland, after fire.	Aug–Nov
Mountain Acalypha . . . . *Acalypha schinzii* (Euphorbia)	Frequent, forming large societies in montane and sub-alpine grassland.	Aug–Dec
Wild Verbena . . . . *Pentanisia prunelloides* (Gardenia)	Fairly frequent in grassland in montane and sub-alpine belt.	Aug–Jan
(Buttercup) . . . . *Anemone fanninii*	Common in montane and sub-alpine moist areas.	Sep–Dec
Blue-squill . . . . *Scilla natalensis* (Lily)	Common on cliffs, waterfalls and steep stream banks, in montane and sub-alpine area.	Sep–Dec
(Pea) . . . . *Eriosema kraussianum*	Occurs in clumps in (burnt) grassland of montane and sub-alpine belt.	Sep–Nov
Natal Blood Flower . . . . *Scadoxus puniceus* (Amaryllis)	Occasionally found in leaf mould on boulders in forests.	Sep–Nov
(Buttercup) . . . . *Ranunculus baurii*	Common on stream banks, wet cliffs, adjacent to waterfalls, in bogs and moist places on the summit.	Sep–Jan
Wild Crocus . . . . *Cyrtanthus breviflorus* (Amaryllis)	Common in moist places, grassland and rock outcrops from the base to the summit of the Berg.	Sept–Jan
Wild Pomegranate . . . . . *Burchellia bubalina* (Gardenia)	Occasionally found in Berg forest.	Sep–Dec
Yellow Dobo Lily . . . . . *Cyrtanthus flanaganii* (Amaryllis)	Occasionally in damp places, at base of cliffs.	Sep–Dec
Berg Tea . . . . *Helichrysum miconifolium* (Daisy)	Grassland of montane and sub-alpine belt.	Oct–Feb
Elegant Watsonia . . . . . *Watsonia lepida* (Iris)	Usually solitary in montane and sub-alpine grassland.	Oct–Jan

Name	Where to find it	When it flowers
(Geranium) . . . . *Geranium pulchrum*	Common in vleis and on stream banks in Little Berg.	Oct–Jan
Grey-leaved Aster . . . . . *Aster perfoliatus* (Daisy)	Fairly common on outcrops and in grassland at 1 400–3 000 m.	Oct–July
(Lily) . . . . *Ledebouria cooperi*	Fairly frequent in grassland of Little Berg.	Oct–Dec
(Lily) . . . . *Ledebouria ovatifola*	Solitary. Widespread in grassland and wood-land.	Oct–Dec
(Hypoxis) . . . . *Rhodohypoxis baurii*	In foothills below 2 000 m, often forming attractive carpets. Hybridises easily.	Oct–Jan
Watsonia. . . . . *Watsonia densiflora* (Iris)	Montane and sub-alpine grassland.	Oct–Jan
Wild Forget-me-not . . . *Myosotis sylvatica* (Wild Forget-me-not)	Frequent on stream banks at 1 500–2 900 m.	Oct–Dec
(Campanula). . . . . *Craterocapsa congesta*	Found on the summit. Mat-forming.	Nov–Feb
(Iris) . . . . *Dietes iridioides*	Locally common in Berg forest.	Nov–Mar
Drakensberg Harebell . . *Dierama dracomon-tanum* (Iris)	In clumps in moist sub-alpine grassland.	Nov–Feb
(Amaryllis) . . . . *Haemanthus humilis*	Mainly In rock crevices from edge of Little Berg to about 2 600 m.	Nov–Dec,
Honey Flower . . . . *Gladiolus longicollis* (Iris)	On the summit in the Little Berg,	Nov–Feb
Oblique-leaved Sorrel. . *Oxalis obliquifolia* (Oxalis)	Forms small colonies almost everywhere at up to 2 500 m.	Nov–Feb
(African Violet) . . . . *Streptocarpus gardenii*	On moist, mossy boulders in Berg forest, or as epiphyte.	Nov–Apr
White-spotted Arum . . . *Zantedeschia. albomaculata* (Arum)	Frequent in moist and wet areas.	Nov–Dec
(Begonia) . . . . *Begonia sutherlandii*	Forms societies on banks, cliffs and boulders in moist Berg forest.	Dec–May
Long-tailed Trewwa. . . . *Satyrium longicauda* (Orchid)	Grassland of Little Berg.	Dec–Mar

Name		Where to find it	When it flowers
Pineapple Flower . . . . . (Lily)	*Eucomis autumnalis*	In damp places, grassland and outcrops of Little Berg.	Dec–Mar
Royal Berg Lily . . . . (Lily)	*Galtonia regalis*	Common in moist crevices on vertical cliff faces and ledges, 1 700–3 000 m (name derived from Royal Natal National Park).	Dec–Feb
Spiny Berg Thistle. . . . . (Daisy)	*Berkheya multijuga*	Common in groups on stream banks and moist rock faces.	Dec–Feb
Agapanthus. . . . . (Lily)	*Agapanthus campanulatus*	In stream gullies, near waterfalls and moist places on cliffs 1 800–2 300 m.	Jan–Feb
Christmas Flower . . . . . (Snapdragon)	*Cycnium racemosum*	In montane and sub-alpine grassland.	Jan–Mar
(Lily)	*Kniphofia linearifolia*	In groups in moist or wet places up to 2 300 m.	Jan–Mar
Lion's Ear . . . . (Mint also L. Ocymifolia/variations)?	*Leonotis leonurus*	Common in tall grassland, forest and forest margin.	Jan–Mar
Nodding Wild Iris . . . . . (Iris)	*Moraea inclinata*	Forms societies in grassland on Little Berg.	Jan–Feb
African Gladiolus/. . . . . Natal Lily (Iris)	*Gladiolus daleniinatalensis*	Widespread in grassland and woodland up to 2 500 m.	Jan–Feb
Agapanthus . . . . (Lily)	*Agapanthus campanulatus*	Common in clumps in stream gullies near waterfalls, moist places on cliffs 1 800– 2 300 m.	Jan–Feb
Red-hot Poker (Lily) . . . *caulescens*	*Kniphofia ichopensis*	Grows, often in very large groups, in seepage areas, bogs, streambanks, 1 8 00–3 000 m.	Jan–Mar
Scarlet River Lily . . . . . . (Lily)	*Schizostylis coccinea*	On banks of rivers up to about 1 800 m. Not common.	Jan–Mar
(Iris)	*Gladiolus crassifolius*	Montane and sub-alpine grassland.	Feb–Mar
Suicide Gladiolus . . . . . (Iris)	*Gladiolus flanaganii*	Occasionally on moist, sometimes inaccessible cliff faces.	Feb–Mar
Alpine Everlasting . . . . . (Daisy)	*Helichrysum trilineatum*	80+ species grow mainly in short grassland above 1 800 m. Dominant in alpine heath.	All year

INDEX

Italics indicate illustrations.